Preservation Politics

Preservation Politics

Dance Revived, Reconstructed, Remade

**Proceedings of the Conference at
the University of Surrey Roehampton
November 8-9, 1997**

Editor: Stephanie Jordan

**DANCE
BOOKS**

Published in 2000 by Dance Books Ltd, 15 Cecil Court, London WC2N 4EZ

Copyright © Dance Books Ltd

ISBN: 1 85273 079 X
Design: Sanjoy Roy
Editorial: Lisa Wilson & Liz Morrell

Printed in Great Britain by
H. Charlesworth & Co., Huddersfield

Contents

Preface

Strong signals from both the profession and dance scholars prompted 'Preservation Politics', the first major European conference to examine our relationship to past dances and dance styles. And dance is now clearly wanting more of a past. Recently the reconstruction of lost work has burgeoned into a major enterprise. Many contemporary choreographers are developing a keen interest in preserving their own heritage and choreographers' estates wrestle with problems of maintaining the identity and authenticity of earlier work. We have seen the opening-up of lively debates that promote dynamic negotiation between contemporary practice and heritage, particularly in the other performing arts, but also among those working out of non-western dance traditions. Reconstruction is increasingly seen as a political manoeuvre to establish a power base for cultural identity as well as for the art itself. The radical reworking of heritage to make it new is a compelling theme for many of today's choreographers.

I could think of no better way to open *Preservation Politics* than with the following quotation from Richard Taruskin:

> A performer cannot please or move the ancient dead and owes them no such effort. There is no way that we can harm Bach or Mozart any more [read Petipa or Balanchine or Martha Graham], nor any way that we can earn their gratitude. Our obligations are to the living... turning ideas into objects, and putting objects in place of people is the essential modernist fallacy... It fosters the further fallacy of forgetting that performances... are not things but acts. (Taruskin, 1995: 24)

Is Taruskin disrespectful towards the notion of heritage perhaps? Good! And I was delighted that some of this conference turned out to be positively disrespectful towards the past – although I am driven by the belief that, as dance continues to find its present, it has a lot to learn from negotiating with its past. What evolved was a deliciously open attitude to heritage, to textual change with the revival or reconstruction of dances and the examination of personal prejudices and political standpoints.

It was also good to welcome, as we did at Roehampton's 1994 Ashton conference, such a range of participants – choreographers, scholars, dancers, rehearsal directors, critics and notators – which led naturally to a range of presentations; lecture-demonstrations, papers, interviews and panel discussions. The conference began on the first day with a presentation by our keynote speakers Millicent Hodson and Kenneth Archer, discussing their reconstructions of a series of seminal works, including Nijinksy's *The Rite of Spring* and Jean Börlin's *Skating Rink*. It concluded full circle with a Royal Ballet presentation led by Deborah MacMillan, with Monica Mason coaching her own solo from Kenneth MacMillan's *The Rite of Spring*. Another conference highlight was the cross-arts panel, which introduced perspectives from Shakespeare edition, opera and theatre; advanced thinking from other art forms posing a challenge to the dance community. About 200 people joined us for the conference, many from far afield, for example, America, Australia, Canada, Denmark, Germany, Japan, Scotland, Spain, South Africa and Wales.

Certainly, I am delighted to have the opportunity to document the conference in book form. Most of the papers presented as such have been edited for this volume. Other material from lecture-demonstrations, the interview with Matthew Bourne and the cross-arts panel, have been documented by our scribe Henrietta Bannerman.

It is a pleasure now to thank our collaborating organisations and sponsors who made this conference possible: The Society for Dance Research, the Society of Dance History Scholars, John S. Cohen Foundation, Miss V.L. Clore's 1976 Charitable Trust, the Linbury Trust, the Radcliffe Trust, and the Roehampton Institute, London. I am also very grateful for the generosity of my conference committee: Angela Kane, Lesley Main, Ann Nugent, Jane Pritchard and Jonathan Thrift; to our technical manager, Philippa Wickham; to Robert Jude for video recording a number of the performance events (the tapes to be housed in the Roehampton Learning Resources Centre); to Henrietta Bannerman, our scribe; and to Ann Holloway, our brilliant conference administrator who continued to assist towards the publication of this book. So many other staff and students helped with the conference. My thanks to them all. Finally, thanks to David Leonard, our publisher, and Liz Morrell, our editor at Dance Books, with whom it is a pleasure to work.

Stephanie Jordan
Conference Chair
January 1998

References

Taruskin, R. (1995), *Text and Act: Essays on Music and Performance*, New York and Oxford: OUP, p. 24

Confronting Oblivion: Keynote Address and Lecture Demonstration on Reconstructing Ballets

Kenneth Archer and Millicent Hodson

I Confronting Oblivion: Keynote Address

Part one: Statement of guiding principles

We will discuss five basic guidelines that help us resolve problems we face with each reconstruction. These guiding principles concern the following; preservation of masterworks, determination of authenticity, clarification of authorship, identification of the original ballet and our intervention as scholars and artists.

1. Preservation of masterworks

The first principle concerns our wish to preserve only masterworks: Do we believe the ballet in question was one of outstanding quality in both dance and design? Also, does the work have historical relevance and contemporary resonance? If we are to undertake all the effort and expense such projects entail and to ask ballet companies to do the same, we have to be convinced the work will prove to have been a lost jewel of the twentieth-century repertoire. Whatever the textbooks say, whatever the prevailing opinion, we take responsibility for this judgment.

In all but one instance during our decade of work together, we have chosen the ballets we wish to reconstruct. The exception occurred after we did *Le Sacre du printemps* with the Joffrey Ballet in 1987. Robert Joffrey then asked us to reconstruct *Cotillon*, a project he had long considered. We agreed to do *Cotillon* because it corresponded to the masterworks principle we had established.

2. Determination of authenticity

The second principle concerns the determination of authenticity: Is there sufficient evidence to ensure the reconstruction will be a reasonable facsimile of the original? How do we measure the degree of authenticity of the finished reconstruction?

Before we commit ourselves to work on a project, we do an evaluation of the types and amounts of information that we know survive or we think we can discover. We have to be convinced that the ultimate result will be based on at least 50% hardcore evidence both for dance and for design.

The press and public always ask at the time of the premiere, 'What percentage of the original does the reconstruction represent?' For *Le Sacre du printemps*, our first reconstructed ballet, Joffrey answered for us. He gauged 85%. His response was based on the density of information we showed him in each area; choreography and performance style, costumes and decor, music and lighting. Density is the measure, and, if we agree *Le Sacre du printemps* was 85%, then we estimate *Cotillon* was about 95%, *Till Eulenspiegel* and *La Chatte* 75% and *Skating Rink* and *Jeux* 65%.

3. Clarification of authorship

The third principle is clarification of authorship: Who in the original ballet was responsible for what? How did the collaborators work together?

In a ballet we choose to reconstruct, it is important to evaluate the contributions of individual creators, to consider attribution of credit and to ascertain any discrepancies between what each one actually did and how they were acknowledged. By addressing the problem of credit at the outset, we rediscover the process by which the work was created in the first place. Knowledge of this process governs the many decisions that we have to make, the minutiae of steps and gestures, the cut of garments, the colours on backdrops. Understanding the creative process of the original ballet generates not only details in each area but also the collaborators' working points of view. Awareness of their interaction also helps us to conjure up the ambience that permeated the original. A critic wrote recently that in *Le Sacre du printemps* we had managed to recapture an era and not just a work. This evocation of atmosphere has to be our goal.

4. Identification of the original ballet

The fourth principle concerns identification of the original ballet: What version of the original are we aiming to reconstruct? Is it the version of the first night, the first cast, the first season, or what the ballet eventually became before it was lost?

It would seem self evident that the premiere performance would be the original version that should be reconstructed. However that is not

Performance photograph by Suzanne Schwiertz of Luiz Bongiovani Martins pull-ing a knife on Kinsun Chan and Mariette Redel, the lovers tempting fate. The gangs have collided in a huge pile up across the front of the stage, freezing in silhouette to watch the conflict like a movie. As Canudo indicated in the scenario: 'Fate has entered the fray. The man brandished his knife, fierce as a cinema villain. But his gesture was useless. As useless as his claim to this lovely, distant female flesh.'

always possible or even desirable. If a work survived in repertoire for a period of years, it may be best to reconstruct the last known version, particularly if the choreographer was in charge of it until the end. Or, if a work became renowned after a change from the original cast, then the renowned version with its different soloists could be the best choice.

Of course we are bound by what is possible. As regards choreography, if a dancer survives who knows a complete role as it was performed after some years in repertoire, and if that dancer is the only survivor, then perforce this version would be the most authentic available and would be the best to reconstruct. That does not mean that we ignore other evi-dence. On the contrary, our object is to build up a matrix of proof about each role as it was performed in each version and to check the memories of any surviving dancer against this matrix.

As regards costumes and decor, it might seem there would be less variation over time. But this is not the case. Things may change quite radically as design elements are lost, replaced, altered or repaired. Therefore it is also important to build up a comprehensive visual history of each ballet as we reconstruct it.

5. Intervention as artists and scholars

The fifth principle concerns our intervention as artists and scholars. At certain stages in a reconstruction, scholarship must take priority over aesthetic judgment, but the opposite is also true; the moment comes when the work must live on stage, and when we must favour the artistry of the whole production over a singular detail of documentation.

Basically each reconstruction progresses from scholarly efforts to artistic tasks. The first stage is the research, and in this period we attempt to be as scientific as possible. We follow every lead in the same way as archaeologists do, to be sure that we have complete documentation before we try to draw conclusions or attempt any synthesis. At this early stage we consciously practise the kind of objectivity that is the intention of scientists. We allow options and possibilities to accrue.

The second stage is the synthesis of what we have gathered and learned. That means the facts are now framed by the larger context of all we have discovered. For example, what we know about the original creative process can now directly affect our interpretation of facts. At this point we prepare the design dossiers and choreographic score, which are both records of the research and handbooks for execution.

The third stage is our work with ballet companies. We use the design dossiers to guide costume and decor ateliers and the choreographic score as the basis for our studio rehearsals.

Just as ballets do not make themselves, they do not reconstruct themselves – we must intervene. As reconstructors, we place ourselves in the middle of a historical process. From the time we start the dossiers and choreographic score until the time the ballet is premiered, we function as artists as much as scholars. We must construct the lost parts and incorporate them with what we have been able to retrieve of the original. We take responsibility for the intervention and never claim that the reconstruction is identical to the original work. A 100% likeness would be impossible to achieve, even if all the collaborators survived, because they themselves would now perceive their work differently.

We try to reconstruct the *experience* of lost masterworks for the public, giving them the chance to judge the reconstructed ballets for themselves. The final stage of our work on each reconstruction is to write, lecture and exhibit our research documents and our reconstruction drawings. It is our conviction that we must *confront oblivion*, salvaging what we can of these masterworks – intervening as we must within the boundaries we set – rather than capitulate to the vagaries of fate.

The methodology of our creations is not so different from the reconstructions in so far as our first step is research, often in art history, biography or literature. But, of course, the original conception is ours and there is no creative process to follow as a model. In the second step of making design dossiers and choreographic scores, the work would appear on the surface to be quite similar, as we synthesise the research. However the enormous difference is that we have no specific responsibility to prior standards, points of view or extant material. And, naturally, in the final step of production, we are not bound in a new ballet by any *a priori* conventions or documentation. We can abandon facts from our research as we choose. The main difference in these two types of work is intention. To reconstruct a ballet we set up a whole structure of documentary limitations, and our challenge is to work within them.

Part two: Principles illustrated by reconstructions on video

We shall discuss material from ten of our reconstructions – six of which have been staged and four of which are in the process of being staged. Our purpose is to illustrate the five principles we have just outlined by specific reference to our work on these reconstructions. We have allocated two ballets to each principle. We will introduce each pair of reconstructions, indicating how the principle is applied in each case and what especially to observe.

1. Preservation of masterworks

For six decades Ballets Russes literature had dismissed *Till Eulenspiegel* as a failure following the rumour that Diaghilev promulgated in Europe at the time of its premiere in New York. However the American press in 1916 told the opposite story. On the basis of the reviews and the stunning visual evidence that survived, we believed *Till Eulenspiegel* was a masterwork as well as a popular success.

In the 'Triumph of Till' through to the 'Apotheosis', Nijinsky transforms the Strauss prankster into a revolutionary hero and, through the vivid contrast of costumes and body language, he delineates the conflict of the haves and have nots.

It was third time lucky for Stravinsky's score that began as the opera *Rossignol*, with choreography by Boris Romanov and designs by Alexander Benois. The work was then revised as a ballet suite, with choreography by Leonide Massine and designs by Henri Matisse. But only when Balanchine created new choreography for the Matisse costumes and decor did all the elements gel as a masterwork.

Our choreographic score documents corps work from the 'Festivities at the Palace of the Emperor' early in the ballet, which we derived from press accounts and interviews with surviving dancers Alexandra Danilova and Lara Ladre. The restriction of Matisse's Chinese robes liberated Balanchine, encouraging him to strip down his classicism and use parallel positions, tight group formations, eccentric acrobatics and a variety of shuffling steps which he later used for pointe work.

2. Determination of authenticity

The density of information for *Le Sacre du printemps* is well illustrated by the scene called 'Spring Rounds' about half way through Act 1. Stravinsky's notes on his score are complex, but even he said the choreographic counterpoint was too complicated to explain. It is at this moment in the ballet that the complexity of Roerich's palette is also revealed with the introduction of the pastel mauve amidst the primary colours, matching the lyricism of the music. A wealth of verbal, visual and musical proof made this scene a particularly exciting exercise in reconstruction.

For the reconstruction of *Cotillon*, we had the testimony of three generations of dancers who performed a ballet that was continuously in repertoire for 15 years on three continents. Also amid the vast photographic documentation, there were two films of *Cotillon* fragments. Some of these fragments were shot by an Australian eye specialist, Ringland Anderson, who was fascinated with cinematography and happened to be a fan of De Basil's Ballets Russes. His shooting position, from the wings, is unusual but fortunate, as the other film fragments, done by a New York journalist, had been taken from the front.

3. Clarification of authorship

The music for *Jeux* was commissioned from Debussy after Nijinsky had developed the scenario, but the composer kept separate from the production. Bakst, however, was deeply involved from the outset. He was with Nijinsky at the Bloomsbury party where the sight of the painter Duncan Grant playing lawn tennis inspired the ballet. Virginia Woolf and

Reconstruction drawing by Millicent Hodson. At the climax of the ballet, when the Madman has won the pyrrhic prize of the Woman' s unconscious body, it is clear that a role reversal has occurred. The refined Madman has become more like an Apache, taking his spoils by force, and the rejected Man has become the sensitive poet figure.

her sister, Vanessa Bell, were reputedly there, and both choreographer and designer were intrigued by this circle of London artists. Duncan, Virginia and Vanessa became the model for the ballet's love triangle. Even though Bakst was central to the aesthetic of *Jeux*, he did not achieve the futuristic tennis wear that Nijinsky requested, but which Diaghilev recouped just before the premiere, so Bakst's role was more important for his atmospheric decor, and for guiding Nijinsky through the post-impressionist ideas of Bloomsbury, than for providing costumes. The final scenes

'The Tripling' and 'The Interruption' are suffused with the ethos of Bloomsbury just before World War I.

Our research on *Skating Rink* confirmed that the painter Léger was at the centre of this ballet, with its panorama of the Parisian working class at play. The characters derive from visits De Maré and Börlin made to roller-skating rinks and Apache dance halls under Léger's tutelage. He showed them the artisans that populated his paintings – men in caps and factory girls – whose world was invaded by toffs in top hats. The poem that was the ballet's scenario profiled the social conflicts at the rink, as The Madman with his elegant clothes and virtuoso skating attracts The Young Woman from her proletarian boyfriend in patched jacket and cloth cap. Canudo's poem, based on the Chaplin film *The Rink*, opened up the expressionist possibilities of the skating rink as a field of emotional experience. The great achievement of Börlin was his receptivity. He contained all the Léger characters within the emotional frame of the love triangle and within the terse vocabulary of skating in Cubist style. Note how the Cubist costumes appear to be two-dimensional as the skaters round the bend of the cyclorama – women in wide skirts and men in wide jackets. The following scenes, 'The Falls' and 'The Madman's Dance', reveal Börlin's synthesis.

4. Identification of the original ballet

Börlin's *Dervishes*, which seems to be the first all-male ballet of the twentieth century, began as his own solo. Once De Maré had formed the Ballet Suédois, Börlin expanded the work adding four other male soloists as Dervishes and a small corps of men as Soldiers. Documentation suggests that the ballet was sometimes performed with just the five Dervishes. Essentially, therefore, we are dealing with three versions. What we are currently reconstructing is the full ballet with corps, which formed part of the premiere programme of the company in 1920. However we have traced everything we could on the Dervish solo. Just as Nijinsky had developed the ensemble work for *Le Sacre du printemps* out of the Chosen One's solo he had already made on his sister, we understood that Börlin used the material of his solo as the basis not only for his variation in the larger ballet but also for the other Dervishes. The brief film that survives of Börlin dancing shows the costume, which he designed, in motion and establishes his glossary of movement.

With *La Chatte*, we had to distinguish between versions to reconstruct the title role of the cat. Spessivtseva, who danced the premiere in Monte Carlo, feigned an injury for the Paris premiere, as she found Balanchine's new classicism completely alien with its extreme extensions, off-centre balances and twenties' mannerisms. Alice Nikitina learned the role the afternoon of the Paris premiere from her partner Serge Lifar. Nikitina's up-to-the-minute bob with spit curls was perfect for the look of the role, but she struggled with its technical demands. Balanchine was delighted two years later when Alicia Markova returned to the Ballets Russes. She had proved a sensation as the Nightingale in *Le Chant du Rossignol* and welcomed the challenge of the Cat. As Dame Alicia said about the role, 'Spessitseva would not do it and Nikitina could not do it.' Because Markova danced the role last, under Balanchine's supervision, we gave precedence to her recollections. However, this case was further complicated by the fact that there was an original before the original. Balanchine had wanted to cast Danilova, but Diaghilev refused. Nonetheless, the role was created on her in their tiny flat before the rehearsals with Spessitseva. So Danilova's ideas were part of our matrix, and we took our rehearsal videos from Montreal to show her in New York. We wrote down all her comments and advice for the dancers, especially the Cat, and used them in rehearsal on our return.

5. Intervention as artists and scholars

We did the basic research for *Man and his Desire* from 1992 to 1994 and then had to leave the project to stage other productions. It is only in recent months that we have started to assemble the dossiers and choreographic score. So, as regards our intervention, we are now at the point where our scholarly efforts are augmented by artistic tasks. As with *Skating Rink*, Börlin was extremely open to his collaborators and found ways to turn the limits they set into creative opportunities. The poet Claudel and the composer Milhaud wrote this ballet for Nijinsky when they all met in Rio de Janeiro in 1917. Nijinsky never choreographed or danced it, but Börlin did in 1921 as a homage to the Russian idol who inspired his work even more than Mikhail Fokine, Börlin's mentor in Sweden. This ballet contata, combining French avant-garde music with a samba band, is performed on four terraced platforms, evoking the mysteries of a tropical night. The choreography had to be constructed as horizontal processions with intense encounters in very narrow space. Börlin elaborated the kind of two-dimensional movement Nijinsky had pioneered but gave it the successive volume of the decor's receding terraces.

In this ballet *Within the Quota* by Börlin, which we set recently in Stockholm, every performer is a soloist. Murphy, the ballet's scenarist and designer, was an American painter whose passion was popular culture (Hollywood films, black music, dance fads, state of the art gadgets, etc.) much of which turned up in his monumental still-life canvases, precursors to Alexander Calder and Roy Lichtenstein. Murphy proposed as composer his Yale friend, Cole Porter, who also lived in Paris. Their ballet was a parade of silent cinema types in front of a gigantic newspaper page. The nature of the subject meant that where there were missing pieces in the choreography or costuming, we could go straight to the popular sources that inspired Murphy, Porter and Börlin in turn.

The lead character, played by Börlin, was the direct descendent of Charlie Chaplin in *The Immigrant*. Börlin arrives in New York and makes it 'within the quota' of Swedish immigrants admitted. He meets archetypal figures based on Gloria Swanson, Clara Bow the It Girl, Mary Pickford, Tom Mix the cowboy and a soft shoe dancer no doubt derived from Ulysses 'Slow Kid' Thompson, but is always interrupted by a puritanical figure. Börlin showcased his top dancers in this work and expected them to project the stars that they and their public knew so well. As we rebuilt the choreography on the dancers of the Royal Swedish Ballet, we drew upon the movements and gestures of these cinema celebrities and showed the dancers clips from the old films.

Reconstruction details

Le Sacre du printemps. Scenario: Nicholas Roerich and Igor Stravinsky; music: Stravinsky; decor and costumes: Roerich; choreography: Vaslav Nijinsky. Premiere: Paris, 29 May 1913, Sergei Diaghilev's Ballets Russes (Chosen One: Maria Piltz). Reconstruction premiere: Los Angeles, 30 September 1987, Joffrey Ballet (Chosen One: Beatriz Rodriguez).

Cotillon. Scenario: Boris Kochno; music: Emmanuel Chabrier, orchestrated by Chabrier, Felix Mottl and Vittorio Rieti; decor and costumes: Christian Bérard; choreography: George Balanchine. Premiere: Monte Carlo, 17 January 1932, Colonel Vassili De Basil's Ballets Russes (Young Girl: Tamara Toumanova; Young Man: George Balanchine). Reconstruction premiere: New York, 26 October 1988, Joffrey Ballet (Young Girl: Tina Le Blanc; Young Man: Edward Stierle).

La Chatte. Scenario: Boris Kochno; music: Henri Sauguet; decor and costumes: Naum Gabo with Antoine Pevsner; choreography: George Balanchine. Premiere: Monte Carlo, 30 April 1927, Sergei Diaghilev's Ballets Russes (The Cat: Olga Spessivtseva; Young Man: Serge Lifar). Reconstruction premiere: Montreal, 3 May 1991, Les Grands Ballets Canadiens (The Cat: Anik Bissonette; Young Man: Kenneth Larsen).

Till Eulenspiegel. Scenario: Richard Strauss and Vaslav Nijinsky; music Strauss; decor and costumes: Robert Edmond Jones; choreography Nijinsky. Premiere: New York, 23 October 1916, Sergei Diaghilev's Ballets Russes (Till: Nijinsky; Apple Woman: Lydia Sokolova; First Chatelaine: Flora Revalles). Reconstruction premiere: Paris, 9 February 1994, Paris Opera Ballet (Till: Patrick Dupond; Apple Woman: Marie-Claude Pietragalla; First Chatelaine: Elizabeth Platel).

Skating Rink. Scenario: Riciotto Canudo; music: Arthur Honegger; decor and costumes: Fernand Léger; choreography: Jean Börlin. Premiere: Paris, 20 January 1922, Rolf De Maré's Ballets Suédois (Madman: Börlin; The Woman: Jolanda Figoni; The Man: Kaj Smith). Reconstruction premiere: Zürich, 6 January 1996, Zürich Ballet (Madman: Kinsun Chan; The Woman: Mariette Redel; The Man: Luiz Bongiovani Martins).

Jeux. Scenario: Vaslav Nijinsky; music Claude Debussy; decor and costumes: Léon Bakst; choreography: Nijinsky. Premiere: Paris, 15 May 1913, Sergei Diaghilev's Ballets Russes (Young Man: Nijinsky; Young Women: Tamara Karsavina and Ludmilla Schollar). Reconstruction premiere: Verona, 9 May 1996, Arena di Verona Ballet of Carla Fracci and Beppe Menegatti (Young Man: Alessandro Molin; Young Women: Fracci and Beatriz Rodriguez).

Within the Quota. Scenario: Gerald Murphy; music: Cole Porter, orchestrated by Charles Koechlin; decor and costumes: Murphy; choreography, Jean Börlin. Premiere: Paris, 25 October 1923; Rolf De Maré's Ballets Suédois (Immigrant: Börlin; Heiress: Klara Kjellblad; Puritan: Toivo Niskanen; Coloured Gentleman: Kaj Smith; Jazz Baby: Ebon Strandin; Cowboy: Paul Eltorp; Sweetheart: Edith Bonsdorff). Reconstruction premiere: Stockholm, 5 June 1998, Royal Swedish Ballet (Immigrant: Carl Inger; Heiress: Anna Valev; Puritan: Ivaylo Valev; Gentleman: Brendan Collins; Jazz Baby: Madeline Onne; Cowboy: Johannes Ohman; Sweetheart: Liz Thomas; Cameraman: Weit Carlsson).

Dervishes. Scenario: Jean Börlin; music: Alexander Glazunov; decor: Georges Mouveau; costumes: Börlin; choreography: Börlin (Lead Dervish: Börlin). Premiere: Paris, 25 October 1920, Rolf De Maré's Ballets

Suédois. Reconstruction premiere: Stockholm, 5 June 1998, Royal Swedish Ballet (Lead Dervish: Hans Nilsson).

Man and his Desire. Scenario: Paul Claudel; music: Darius Milhaud; decor and costumes: Andrée Parr; choreography: Jean Börlin. Premiere: Paris, 6 June 1921, Rolf De Maré's Ballets Suédois (Man: Börlin; Woman: Margareta Johanson; Other Woman: Thorborg Stjerner; Pan Pipes: Kaj Smith; First Golden Note: Carina Ari). Reconstruction premiere: to be announced.

Le Chant du Rossignol. Scenario: Hans Christian Andersen; music: Igor Stravinsky; decor and costumes: Henri Matisse; choreography: George Balanchine. Premiere: Paris, 17 June 1925, Sergei Diaghilev's Ballets Russes (The Nightingale: Alicia Markova; Death: Lydia Sokolova). In progress.

II Lecture Demonstration, *Le Sacre du printemps* (Nijinsky, 1913) and *Skating Rink* (Börlin, 1922)

Transcribed by Henrietta Bannerman

Hodson and Archer were introduced by Ann Nugent who commented that this was the first time that their work had been seen in Britain. Their lecture demonstration was a unique opportunity to see how they coached and rehearsed the dancers during the process of reconstruction and Hodson commented later during the demonstration that this was the best way of absorbing the 'architectural layers of the movement.'

Archer explained how important it is in the reconstruction of lost works that the dancers themselves are involved in the total creative process and how helpful it is when they are interested in studying the dossiers and choreographic scores of the dance to be recovered. The dancers taking part in the demonstration, Kinsun Chan and Mariette Redel from the Zürich Ballet and Luiz Fernando Bongiovani Martins fiom the Scapino Ballet, Rotterdam, were not only highly-trained and experienced professional dancers but also practising visual artists.

Starting with the two male dancers as Young People at the opening of the ballet, Hodson demonstrated the complexity of the counting and explained that these dancers establish the idea of counterpoint for the whole ballet, 'someone said to us when we did this for the first time for the Joffrey that there was enough material in the first 60 seconds for the whole ballet, and, in a sense, this is true.'

Hodson explained that the first phrase of movement is counted in eights even though the music is written in 2/4 and that 'the first measure of eight has no accents.' After the first unaccented or straight phrase of eight, the second phrase of eight has accents on 2 and 4, the third is accented on 2 and 5 and the fourth on 1 and 6. This system forms the architectural unit of the whole first scene.

Stravinsky commented that, in this section of the ballet, the men were 'bobbing' and that they stressed the tonic accents which would be the 1 and 5 of the eight count phrase. Rambert confirmed this but added that the *port de bras* took place on the shifting accentsof each phrase of eight – the straight 8 with no accent then 2,4;2,5;1,6. Thus the dancers have the problem of having to maintain separate rhythms in two different parts of the body simultaneously. There are normally five men within the group, each doing different arm movements and Hodson demonstrated how the old woman, who 'knows the secrets of the earth,' joins the group and performs yet another variation of arm movements. This combination of shifting accents and varying *port de bras* provides a jagged texture fiom the beginning of the ballet. Hodson also explained that the emphasis on the foot stamps on the count of 1 at the start of the work creates an effect of 'shock' for the audience.

When demonstrating the material for the Maidens in Red from Scene 1, Hodson showed a typical posture from Nijinsky's choreography which has been preserved in drawings and recorded by both Stravinsky and Rambert. Here the head is dropped to one side and the body is drawn towards it. In this posture, the body moves from side to side and the phrase finishes with five pairs of maidens standing with feet together, knees slightly bent and arms crossed over the chest. They look at each other but the head extends 'way, way forwards' from a stretched neck. This particular position of the head emphasised the headdress that the maidens wore with its tight band and heavy coils over the ears. Hodson explained that Rambert had remembered Nijinsky's use of the stretched neck like a fifth limb in his choreography. The maidens beat the straight 8 with no accent then 2, 4; 2, 5; 1, 6 rhythm with their feet, stepping on the flat foot on the odd counts and on the ball of the foot on the even counts. Stravinsky referred to this as the 'trampling' step and it recurred in the ballet rather like a *bourrée*.

When the dancers performed the material to the recorded music,

Hodson herself, as she often does in a rehearsal, worked with the dancers. At times she danced with them as the old woman or as a maiden and at others she watched them or counted for them. She explained that the grouping at the end of Scene 1 had been clearly documented by Rambert as shown in *Quicksilver* (1972) but that this is the only extract from Rambert's notes to have been published in her lifetime. Hodson also referred to her own publication: *Nijinsky's Crime Against Grace* (1996).

Archer explained that in Scene 3 from *The Rite of Spring*, Nijinsky had taken a different approach to Stravinsky's rhythms. Stravinsky's music is lyrical and sustained here and creates an atmosphere of tranquillity. Instead of 'accumulating rhythms in the body and exchanging them amongst groups' and rather than sub-dividing the musical measures, Nijinsky allows 'everyone to breathe deeply'. The groups take turns delineating the rhythms 'that vary from measure to measure in a passage of five-part accompaniment that develops towards the first experience of unison in the ballet.' Hodson explained that this scene had been very well documented by Rambert and that there were many drawings of it by Valentine Gross. However her problem had been to create links between the various positions and steps that had been noted and recorded and she referred to the 'intervention' which had been discussed during the morning's keynote address. The delicate balance between scholarship and aesthetic judgement was a problem that always had to be addressed and the nature of the reconstructor's 'intervention' was a major element in the process of recovering a lost work.

Hodson recounted that there was a particular section which Rambert discussed with her but which at the time she had not been able to understand as she did not have access to Rambert's full score. Rambert had described a movement where the men 'face off like a challenge to each other' and that she had finally understood certain corresponding drawings by Gross when, after Rambert's death in 1982, Jane Pritchard, archivist of the Rambert Dance Company, recovered the whole score for *Le Sacre du printemps*.

The demonstration of *Skating Rink* (1922) comprised material from the beginning, middle and end of the ballet and revealed how Börlin's vocabulary was drawn from the Italian poet Canudo's scenario, Léger's characters and Honegger's score. Canudo's scenario revealed that, in Part 1 of the ballet, a number of couples are already circling the rink when a young woman enters followed by her boyfriend. Hodson and Archer found a copy of a scenario on which Börlin had written time-frames and this told them how he had divided the scenes from the point of view of time. The basic postures and gestures of the dancers were documented in photographs and in choreographic sketches by Börlin. Stick figures had been drawn on the orchestral score, either by Börlin or by the conductor[1], to indicate the exact measure on which the various dancers made their entrances. Canudo's scenario 'gave us much of the sequence of actions, the images, emotions and philosophical implications.' Canudo wrote that the skaters had no faces and Léger drew the skaters' figures in the costume designs without lips. 'Visual and verbal evidence', commented Archer, 'told us that the special make-up portrayed the grey faces of urban life, some with geometrically exaggerated eyes.' Canudo referred to each skater as a 'double-sided form of sliding flesh' and this description may have inspired Léger's two-dimensional, cubist costumes and encouraged Börlin to make movement with angular planes.

Skating Rink was a completely different kind of project for Hodson and Archer in terms of the material available from which they could draw their sources of information. Hodson stressed the importance of Canudo's[2] scenario, which was based on a poem called *The Skating Rink* – inspired by a Charlie Chaplin film. In reconstructing the characters from the ballet, the dancers worked closely with Hodson and Archer in interpreting and reproducing the available photographs. The dancers appeared for this part of the demonstration wearing the shoes and headgear appropriate for their characters. Hodson commented, 'we agreed amongst ourselves that if we took the documentation and believed it, the connections with the characters would develop very naturally.' They followed the text in French and English and this provided the emotional tension which helped to create the flow between the steps and movements. The latter were recovered from the photographs and drawings by Börlin. Hodson also mentioned the usefulness of caricatures that appeared in the American press and how these drawings seemed to spawn a school of expressionist drawings in the United States.[3]

The Woman is from the lower classes, a poor girl from an unfashionable part of Paris. The Man, referred to in the demonstration as an Apache, loves the woman more than she loves him. Martins, who danced the part of the Apache man, made a particular study of the postures and grotesque facial expressions of his character. Hodson explained that this character was influenced by the bully figure in Chaplin's black and white picture *The Rink* (1916). The actor, Eric Campbell, often played this kind of role in Chaplin films and it was his facial gestures that Börlin had reflected for the character of The Man in *Skating Rink*.

When the dancers showed the entrance for The Man and The Woman, Hodson commented that most of the ballet is counted in 3s. The movement emphasised skating postures and actions and it was important to maintain the simulation of skating in the movement while steps, such as jumps, had to be made as though being executed on roller skates. The movement also conveyed the strains and tensions between the male and female characters. Hodson described the character of The Madman as a suave, Fred Astaire type who skated as nobody else could in that part of Paris. It was quite natural that the woman should be attracted to him but, warned Hodson, there was 'something else behind his finesse and that is what the ballet is all about - the revelation of the manipulative side of his personality.' Chan explained that the predominantly black and white costume reflected the madman's 'black and white' personality and referred to this character as a 'Dr. Jekyll and Mr. Hyde' type who went from one extreme to another with no shades of grey in his nature. Hodson described the effect of the colourful decor behind the trio. The uppermost areas represent the decorative interior of Parisian skating rinks and the lower area is a strong orange or yellow with white discs into which light was thrown. Léger had particularly wanted these discs to be white as they created the shadow effect of the dancing figures (as intended by Börlin). The black and white figure of The Madman dancing in front of this colourful decor was particularly effective in evoking silent films.

The audience did not see the trio from *Skating Rink* as it is performed on stage. The video showing the trio and the other dancers that take part in the work was projected onto the white cyclorama and as the fully-costumed live performers moved in front of the projector, their enlarged shadows were superimposed on the images shown on the backcloth. Hodson remarked that this extra effect enhanced the 'aesthetic of the piece' since it related, as discussed earlier, to the shadows cast on Léger's white discs in the theatre production.

Questions from the audience included one that referred back to the morning's address.

The documentation and evidence from which to reconstruct *Skating Rink* was about the same as for *Till Eulenspiegel* (1916). There was one extant costume from *Skating Rink* and none from *Till Eulenspiegel* but Hodson and Archer had access to all Robert Edmund Jones's designs in colour as they did Léger's designs for *Skating Rink*. Various photographs,

Photograph of original stage model, stage left, from *Skating Rink* with trio in front of corps. The lower half of the Cubist decor is visible, showing forms that evoked the structural struts and girders of the rink. Except for the white disc behind the corps, where light was projected to catch shadows of skaters, the lower backdrop is solid orange or yellow as a ground for the myriad patterns of the costumes and choreography.

sketches and copious critical descriptions comprised the evidence for both ballets, plus the testimony of two survivors from the ballets, thus providing sufficient information to allow them to make acceptably authentic reproductions of these works.

Hodson gave an account of how they retrieved the choreography and were able to reproduce Nijinsky's dramatic mime style on the dancers from the Paris Opera Ballet. She described how they had located unpublished photographs of the work in the Library of Congress in Washington and snapshots of some of the dancers wearing their costumes in character from the only surviving dancer at the time of the reconstruction, Valentina Kachuba. Such visual sources made it possible to know which characters performed particular gestures. This same dancer described how the rich people performed movements in turn-out, the merchant class used parallel positions of the legs and feet and the poor turned the legs and feet inwards. The Apple Woman, for example, was not from the merchant class as she did not have a shop but sold her apples at a stall, so she used parallel and turned-in positions. Hodson deduced from historical writings on the work and verbal accounts of the movement that Nijinsky had used a dramatic approach to the choreography for *Till Eulenspiegel*. She felt that the dance may have been less suitable for a classical company than for a modern dance or mime company. Nevertheless from the dancer Vera Nemchinova, whom Hodson interviewed a decade before the *Till Eulenspiegel* reconstruction, she had learnt that there were certain components such as big jumps, musical syncopations and virtuoso technical elements that could only be achieved by ballet-trained dancers.

Each reconstruction that Hodson and Archer undertake demands considerable investment of time, energy and resources. Before embarking on a project, they have to take several elements into account. Not only do they need an acceptable amount of hard-core evidence on which to base their research, they also had to be convinced that the work to be revived contained enough dancing. In the case of Milhaud's ballet *Création du monde* (1923), for example, despite the fact that several companies had asked them to do it, Hodson felt that she could not expect classically-trained dancers to invest their time and energy in 'walking around in boxes' unless they had other extremely technical works on the same programme. Some decisions as to whether a ballet should be revived or not, she remarked, were based not on the amount of information available, but on human issues.

Companies commission reconstructions of lost works because artistic directors, such as Robert Joffrey, have a special regard for certain works, for example *Le Sacre du printemps* and *Cotillon* (1932), and the periods in which they were made. In the case of Hodson and Archer's work for Les Grands Ballets Canadiens in 1991, they were given the opportunity to choose any work from the late Diaghilev period and they had no hesitation in deciding on Balanchine's *La Chatte* (1927).

As to whether or not the revived works had been or were in the process of being notated, Hodson emphasised the importance of notating the reconstructed dances, although this was often a matter of available resources. She explained that a production of *Le Sacre du printemps* had been recorded in Benesh notation in South America. She also made the point that the notators often encountered the same problems that she did and in the case of a ballet such as *Cotillon* there were so many witnesses and dancers' recollections that conflicting information abounded. Here it was a question of aesthetic 'intervention' in creating what Hodson referred to as the choreographic matrix. She emphasised, as she had done throughout her keynote address and the lecture demonstration, that the work done by Archer and herself is art and, therefore, subjective - that they act as a 'conduit' of all the available documentation, information and evidence. She claimed however that their research includes working with the dancers and taking into account the way they absorb the sense of history and of lost choreographic styles.

As for the dancers in *Skating Rink*, all three agreed that the simulation of the skating movements had been difficult to develop, especially as they were trained as classical ballet dancers. Martins pointed out that the centre of gravity had to be much lower for these movements as the weighted quality is vital, and this was the opposite rule to the one followed in his daily ballet training. He remarked, too, that it had been difficult to bend the knees as much as is required for the style of *Skating Rink*. The three dancers felt that it had taken them over two years to develop the skills needed, and Redel commented that wearing high heels and 'pretending to be skating' is very difficult. Martins explained that his facial expression with its turned-down mouth was the last element that he acquired and that after the first general rehearsal of the work, he had experienced some facial pain from the effort of maintaining the expression. The dancers spoke of their commitment to the work, with Martins commenting on how the story-line of passion and jealousy was relevant to current everyday life.

Hodson reiterated how important it is that the works that she and Archer reconstruct have a contemporary relevance. 'It is not enough to have the Léger costumes, the Honegger score and something of Börlin,' she remarked, and went on to stress the need to communicate the characters' personalities and their situation so that the audience today care and feel involved with them. She recognises that there are other people working in the field of dance reconstruction and that the approach used by herself and Archer is only 'one way' of reviving dances. However, their relationship with the people with whom they work reflects the 'richness of the original collaboration' and this kind of collaboration with the dancers enables them to project the work to the public.

Notes

1. The conductor of the Ballets Suédois was the French composer Désiré Émile Inghelbrecht.
2. The Italian poet Riciotto Canudo lived in Paris and had founded the periodical *Montjoie* in 1913 of which he was also the editor. *Montjoie* published the first interview with Stravinsky concerning *Le Sacre du printemps*, where Stravinsky had described the ballet as ritualistic. By 1920 Stravinsky had refuted this remark and, using the language of the time, referred to the work as an objective construction.
3. Hodson and Archer are preparing an article on the popularisation of European avant-garde art movements with the American public through the Ballets Suédois tour in the USA of 1923.

References

Hodson, M. (1996), *Nijinsky's Crime Against Grace: Reconstruction Score of the Original Choreography for Le Sacre du printemps*, Stuyvesant, New York: Pendragon Press

Quicksilver: The Autobiography of Marie Rambert, (1972), London: Macmillan, p. 67

Reconstructing the Disturbing New Spaces of Modernity

The Ballet *Skating Rink*

Ramsay Burt

In the context of this conference it is only appropriate that I begin by saying how grateful I am to Kenneth Archer and Millicent Hodson and to the Zürich Opera House for allowing me to observe the final stages of the reconstruction of the ballet *Skating Rink*, and attend its premiere in Zürich in January 1996. When I saw the call for papers for this conference it seemed obvious therefore that I should offer a paper on *Skating Rink*.

While recognising that there were some interesting philosophical problems surrounding the status and nature of reconstruction as such, these seemed to me in no way to invalidate the contribution to contemporary scholarship made by this reconstruction of *Skating Rink*. I am convinced that what Millicent Hodson does with dancers is research, just as academic writing about dance history is research; the problem of how to construct history is common both to scholarly writing and theatrical rehearsal. Susan Manning, in her recent book about Mary Wigman, tacitly acknowledges this commonality when she calls her written descriptions of Wigman's dances 'reconstructions' (Manning, 1993). My initial intention was therefore to write a paper which pointed out what knowledge had been gained as a result of this reconstruction of *Skating Rink*. To a certain extent this is still my aim. What I think is of value is the evidence which Archer and Hodson have uncovered of a specifically avant-garde rather than modernist sensibility in the work of the Ballets Suédois.

However I have been provoked to reconsider and adjust my understanding of reconstruction as preservation after reading the introduction to Peggy Phelan's recent book *Mourning Sex*. In this Phelan expresses the opinion that:

> some of the most radical and troubling art of our cultural moment
> has inspired some of the most conservative (and even reactionary)

critical commentary. The desire to preserve and represent the performance event is a desire we should resist. For what one otherwise
preserves is an illustrated corpse. (Phelan, 1997: 3)

If Phelan is arguing against all attempts to create a history of performance, then I cannot agree with her. But, by making the case for a
reconsideration of how to write about live performances without killing
them off in the process, she identifies shortcomings in the way performances are turned into academic discourse which need to be
addressed. She argues that in order to find new ways of making histories
we need to interrogate something that is too often taken for granted: our
desire to preserve. In psychoanalytic terms, as Phelan points out, desire
is part of a process through which the psychic subject disavows a sense
of original loss. As writing about performance is always writing about
something that is lost, we should be alert to the possibility that where
writers explicitly lament losses, there are underlying causes. This paper
therefore seeks to address the question of what losses are being disavowed
and what needs are answered by our desire in these postmodern times to
see a reconstruction of *Skating Rink*.

For Marcia Siegel in 1972, at a time when hardly any research had
been done into the history of modern dance, there seemed a genuine
need to save dance heritage from oblivion through descriptive writing.
She protested, 'Why this failure to examine or even identify styles of
modern dance, to preserve anything but its most anecdotal history, [or]
to capture it by whatever admittedly inadequate means available? (...)
I'm not willing to consign forty years of creative achievement to oblivion
without a protest' (Siegel, 1972: 177). Diana Theodores in her recent
book on what she calls 'the New York School of Criticism', points out
that running through the writings of Siegel, Jowitt, Croce and Goldner is
a concern to 'preserve, clarify, define and distinguish between movement
qualities and movement styles' (1996: 87). Theodores points out that this
can occasionally verge on a preciousness about the purity of American
dance, and sometimes leads to protests about its erosion and impoverish-
ment (ibid.: 86). Such accusations are levelled from time to time by many
critics at those artists and companies who are fortunate (or perhaps
unfortunate) enough to be charged with the responsibility of preserving a
historical repertoire of work. These individuals have to face the problem
of how to keep dances alive and not turn them into illustrated corpses,
despite the fact that styles of dancing, performing and presenting per-

formance inevitably change with time. To perpetuate a particular dance or ballet by freezing the style in which it was originally performed is in my view to run the danger of turning it into an illustrated corpse. But there are nevertheless cases where the disappearance of a particular style of performing is a diminution of the overall range of possibilities. For example, speakers at a previous conference here in Roehampton expressed concern about whether the Royal Ballet were doing sufficient to keep alive the style necessary for Frederick Ashton's ballets.

Skating Rink did not last long enough to face the challenge of changes in dance technique and performance styles. A difficult question therefore arises: by reviving the choreographic and performing styles of the Ballets Suédois, or at least finding approximations of these within contemporary terms, does *Skating Rink* survive as any more than an illustrated corpse? I am going to argue that the answer to this question should be yes, based upon the new understanding the reconstruction gives us of the meaning of these styles in the context of postmodernity.

What often makes style such a contentious issue is the fact that, while (or perhaps because) it seems to be an element of performance that represents nothing tangible, it is often in fact burdened with signifying qualities which themselves seem intangible. Theodores argues that Siegel and her colleagues are most vociferous about the loss of styles which signify aspects of American-ness. In Ashton's case his ballets undoubtedly mediate Englishness. The fact that in their day the work of the Ballets Suédois was not considered by the Swedes themselves as representative of national character undoubtedly contributed to the loss of all but one of Börlin's ballets. *Skating Rink* is in fact a quintessentially international ballet, not only because it was the result of a collaboration between a French painter, Fernand Lèger, a Swiss composer, Arthur Honneger, and a Swedish choreographer, Jean Börlin, and took as its libretto a poem by the Italian writer, Riciotto Canudo; but also because its subject – the modernity of the modern city and of mechanisation – was, in the 1920s, endemic to all the leading Western industrialised nations.

Skating Rink, which was first performed by Rolf de Maré's Ballets Suédois at the Théâtre des Champs Elysées in Paris in January 1922, was based on a poem by Canudo which was itself based upon Charlie Chaplin's film *The Rink*. The ballet is set at a roller-skating rink where factory workers and market girls, prostitutes, immigrants and young aristocratic dandies are shown all skating together. The central character in the ballet is called the Poet, or the Madman. He is wealthy but an outsider whose brilliant skating disturbs the atmosphere at the rink. He steals the Young Woman, who is the girlfriend of the Man, an Apache, and the resulting struggle between the Poet and the Apache Man leads inadvertently to her collapse and, possibly, death.[1] The other skaters momentarily seem to register what has happened but then, callously, resume their dancing – such is the blasé indifference of the big city dweller. As the final curtain descends, the Poet is leaving the stage with the limp body of the Young Woman slung over his shoulder while behind them the crowd skate and dance in wild abandon. The Apache Man, alone in the crowd, looks on in despair.

The style of the dancers' reactions throughout the ballet, as Archer and Hodson's research revealed, should be that of silent film actors. At times it is as if they are in a Chaplin comedy. Early on when the Lady's Maid comes on stage, she is clearly not a confident skater and repeatedly appears about to fall over until the Sailor gallantly leaves the circling crowd to catch her and offer her his arm to lean on. Throughout the ballet there are spectacular collisions between skaters, one bringing down the whole corps de ballet in a large heap that spreads right across the stage. Everything is overdone for effect just like a silent comedy. There are other more serious moments when the dancers look like a crowd in a German expressionist film such as *Metropolis* or *The Cabinet of Doctor Caligari*. In packed groups, like 'loose' rugby scrums, dancers take up the angular arm gestures that are indicated in Léger's designs and in photographs of the original production. Millicent Hodson calls these 'cubist gestures' because Léger was a cubist painter, but the effect is highly expressionist. The groups resemble photographs of Dalcroze and Laban movement choirs. Modernity is also exemplified through stylised planar movements dictated by the costumes' construction. As Archer and Hodson write in the Zürich programme, 'The men's jackets are cut and padded so that the torso, oversized and often asymmetrical, remains stable as the legs skate nimbly underneath, in the manner of marionettes. Conversely, the women's skirts are large, stiff geometrical shapes that hold their line as the torso moves freely above' (1995: 15). The result is puppet-like movement which refers to the mechanised motion of the roller-skate and to the modern popular entertainment form the cinema. *Skating Rink* should be seen in relation to other modern ballets and movement experiments – in particular biomechanics developed by the Russian theatre director Meyerhold, Russian machine ballets by Goleizovsky and others (see Souritz, 1990), and the theatre works of

Oscar Schlemmer whose *Triadic Ballet* is contemporary with *Skating Rink*. What is specific to *Skating Rink* is that this interest in the mechanisation of human experience is set in the modern metropolis.

The metropolis exemplifies the process through which the new becomes old with alarming rapidity, while its building sites suggest a disturbing fluidity rather than stability. In this environment during the first few decades of the twentieth century, the social impact of new methods of industrial management and distribution dictated by the needs of mechanisation seemed for many to constitute a disturbing threat to older definitions of individual and national identity. The writers of some reviews of the original production of *Skating Rink* appear to have felt as disoriented and disturbed by the ballet as many at the time were by modernity itself. André Levinson, for example, was scathing about the ballet's 'pathetic urbanism': 'On the asphalt of the skating rink a circle of subordinate, damned souls turn on their roller skates in a uniform movement that is subservient to the machine' (1929: 393). He was particularly critical of Léger, 'high priest of the machine and high commissioner [*garde-chiourge*] of the new slavery' as he called him. The flat, opaque colours of Léger's set and costumes were, for Levinson, as unsubtle as a target in a fairground shooting gallery. The dancers, he states, are walled into this composition which is flat, lifeless and devoid of all constructive logic – a judgement to which I shall return.

Levinson was one of the sources which Henning Rischbieter used for his major 1968 book *Art and the Stage in the Twentieth Century*. While recognising that Levinson was a conservative critic with no understanding of the conceptual basis of Léger's art (1968: 92), Rischbieter nevertheless concludes that Léger's theatre designs 'are still open to the reproach that... on the stage, on backdrops and wings, a super-sized (and hence frequently insensitive) art exhibition took place, in front of which – not helped, but often hindered by it – the play, dance, opera or drama was performed' (1968: 13). Rischbieter might well have come to a rather different conclusion about the avant-garde nature of Léger's ballet designs had he been able to watch Archer and Hodson's reconstruction of *Skating Rink*.

In characteristically pessimistic mode, the German theorist Walter Benjamin wrote in 1940 (in his 'Theses on the Philosophy of History'), 'In every era the attempt must be made anew to wrest tradition away from conformism that is about to overpower it' (1970: 257). Benjamin's aphorism offers insights into the avant-garde intentions of the Ballets

Suédois. Their ballets were not modernist in that they did not constitute a withdrawal from representation in favour of the exploration of formal and expressive qualities for their own sake – the aesthetic formalism advocated by Roger Fry and Clive Bell, and later developed into a modernist theory of visual art by Alfred H. Barr and Clement Greenberg. Ballets like *Skating Rink* and *Relâche* can more usefully be seen as avantgarde. Peter Bürger has argued that, in order to re-establish a connection between art and life, the historical avant-garde of the early years of the twentieth century no longer engaged in a critique of previous art but of art itself as an institution. Avant-gardism constituted an attempt to destroy 'institution art' in order 'to reorganise a new life praxis through art and politics' (Huyssen, 1988: 8). The poet Blaise Cendrars, in his 1924 eulogy for Jean Börlin suggests that the latter's choreography constitutes precisely such an avant-garde destruction of the institution of classical ballet in favour of a reconnection with the ordinary everyday experience of the modern city dweller, 'Billboards and loudspeakers have made you forget the pedagogy of the Académie de Danse, with its bouts of sciatica and measure, bars [of music] and good taste, affectation and virtuosity. When you've forgotten all this you've discovered rhythm, the beautiful rhythm of today, which opens five continents to us: discipline, balance, health, strength, speed' (quoted Häger, 1990: 291). While working on *Skating Rink*, Börlin, Honneger, Léger and de Maré discovered the rhythms and shapes of the popular dances that are quoted in the ballet on visits to working class dance halls.

One aspect of the pedagogy of the Académie de Danse was the classical mime of traditional nineteenth-century ballet which, in *Skating Rink*, Börlin rejected in favour of mime based on the silent cinema. Thus while in 1921 Nijinska and Diaghilev were trying to work out how faithfully to perform Petipa's mime passages in the London production of *The Sleeping Princess*, Léger and Börlin were looking at Charlie Chaplin's film *The Rink*. Levinson wrote of *Skating Rink* that 'the dancers' laborious gesticulations, vain and prolix, are no more than a conversation of deaf mutes who are ignorant of conventional languages' (1929: 393). Whereas for Levinson classical ballet is a means by which the dancer transcends the mundane limits of the physical body to attain a metaphysical ideal, the dancers in *Skating Rink* appear to him 'stuffed carcasses, spineless and resigned, in hopeless bondage to pleasures that are neither joyful nor beautiful' (ibid.). Levinson's description of stuffed carcasses seems particularly telling in the light of Archer and Hodson's discoveries about the stiff jackets worn by the male dancers.

Skating Rink challenges and disrupts in an avant-garde manner the way in which traditional ballet mediates metaphysical meanings, namely ballet's dualistic conception of the individual as subtle spirit and gross corporeality. Börlin and Léger's puppet-like dancers confound the idea of performance as the externalisation of what is private, psychological, and deep within the individual. *Skating Rink* is not about depth but about a play of surfaces and the dancers' bodies become one of many surfaces on which meanings are pictorially and choreographically inscribed. This is exemplified in the way Léger's design for the Madman includes an off-centre black rectangle of grease-paint on the side of his face. It is in this context that Levinson's comments about the dancers being walled into a flat composition are significant. Depth for Levinson signifies individuality. For Léger, the new ballet dancer transcends individualism to become the moving scenery of the new ballet spectacle. Thus he proposed, 'Man becomes a mechanism like everything else: instead of being the end, as he formerly was, he becomes a means... If I destroy the human scale, if my scenery moves around, I obtain the maximum effect, I obtain a whole on the stage that is totally different from the atmosphere in the auditorium' (Léger, 1964: 72). In his second ballet for de Maré and Börlin, *La Création du Monde* (1923), with a libretto by Blaise Cendrars and music by Darius Milhaud, dancers literally became moving scenery as they manipulated flat puppet-like moving props around the stage. In the light of Archer and Hodson's reconstruction of *Skating Rink* it is thus possible to see in Levinson's comments an unsympathetic but nevertheless scrupulous critical response to a ballet which was framing new ways in which subjectivities were embodied in an industrialised and mechanised society.

At that time the silent cinema, which as I have shown was a key referent in *Skating Rink*,[2] played a central role in representing these new ideologies of embodiment. In 1927, the Italian writer Luigi Pirandello acutely analysed the way in which the movie camera mechanised bodies:

[Cinema actors] are acutely aware, with a maddening, indefinable sense of emptiness, that their bodies are so to speak subtracted, suppressed, deprived of their reality, of breath, of voice, of the sound that they make in moving about, to become only a dumb image, which quivers for a moment on the screen and disappears, in silence. (quoted Virilio, 1989: 15)

Paul Virilio cites Pirandello in his study of war and cinema, pointing to the use of cameras for reconnaissance and targeting within modern, mechanised warfare. The troops in the trenches during the 1914-18 war were, he argues, like Pirandello's actors:

Numerous veterans from the 1914-18 war have said to me that although they killed enemy soldiers, at least they did not see whom they were killing, since others had now taken responsibility for seeing in their stead... The soldiers themselves could recognise [their targets] only by the flight-path of their bullets and shells, a kind of telescopic tensing towards an imagined encounter, a 'shaping' of the partner-cum-adversary before his probable fragmentation. (ibid.: 14-15)

Léger, Canudo and Cendrars were all in the army during the 1914-18 war. Léger was a sapper and then a stretcher bearer in the trenches before being invalided out after being gassed in the spring of 1917. His machinist paintings of the city like *Le Pont de bateau* (1919) which are closest to his designs for *Skating Rink* were painted immediately after a series of cubist compositions of soldiers in trenches and with artillery like *Le Soldat á la pipe* (1916). In both these series human beings appear machine-like. In 1921 when he commissioned Léger to design the ballet, Rolf de Maré owned a number of Léger's works including *Le Pont de bateau* and *Le Soldat á la pipe*. It is reasonable to conclude that, rather than producing Rischbeiter's 'super-sized (and hence frequently insensitive) art exhibition' which hindered rather than helped the dancing (Rischbeiter, 1968: 13), Léger and Börlin collaborated to find visual and choreographic imagery with which to explore new forms of subjectivity produced by the mechanisation of human experience. This conclusion has been reached with the benefit of the knowledge which Archer and Hodson have recovered about the ballet *Skating Rink*.

A devil's advocate could still argue that all this academic discussion about the precise meanings of visual and choreographic imagery might be of value from a scholarly, historical point of view, but it does nothing to prove that the reconstruction is any more than an illustrated corpse. In reply to this criticism, I would like to suggest that the reconstruction does more than put the facts straight and put more accurate information about *Skating Rink* back into circulation for scholars. To reconstruct *Skating Rink* in the 1990s is timely and answers specific needs in our postmodern times.

There is considerable interest at the end of the century in some aspects of the intellectual culture of early modernism. Peter Bürger, Andreas Huyssen and others have re-examined the failure of the historical avant-garde in order to theorise the strategies of postmodern artists. The writings of Walter Benjamin and George Simmel, particularly their analysis of urbanism, are being seen as precursors for more recent work in the area of cultural studies. Both are cited in Helen Thomas' new collection *Dance and the City* (1997). Virilio's account of the social impact of mechanised imaging during the First World War presages Jean Baudrillard's claim that the Gulf War did not take place (1995). The heavy, repetitive manual labour of the early twentieth-century production line that is caricatured in Fritz Lang's *Metropolis* (1926) and Charlie Chaplin's *Modern Times* (1936) is remote from present experience, but the sense of disorientation felt then as new social and technological developments undermined the basis on which individuals underst imagine new ones. The reconstructed *Skating Rink* answers present needs by reminding people of the possibility of cultural explorations of new forms of subjectivity.

Notes

1. At first the Poet does not notice that the Young Woman has fallen but is exultant about his victory over the Apache Man. When he does notice he makes a cry which Millicent Hodson wanted the dancer playing the Poet to make cartoon-like, and in her drawing of this moment his mouth crying forms a square. Whether or not one thinks the Young Woman dies depends on how one interprets this cry. Personal communication Millicent Hodson.

2. Chaplin's *The Rink* was the inspiration behind Riciotto Canudo's poem which was used as libretto for the ballet. Rolf de Maré, who financed and directed the Ballet Suédois, was also a keen supporter of film making. Before working on *Skating Rink* Léger and Honneger had previously collaborated with the film maker Abel Gance on the film *La Roue*, part of which was filmed in the Théâtre de Champs Elysées which de Maré had leased as a base for the Ballets Suédois. Börlin later appeared in a film by Gance. Léger's experimental film *Ballet Mechanique* was made with the help of Gerald Murphy, who designed the ballet *Within the Quota* for the Ballets Suédois. *Ballet Mechanique* includes an animated drawing of Charlie Chaplin.

References

Archer, K. and Hodson, M. (1995), 'Skating Rink: cubism on wheels', *Dance Now* Vol. 4 No. 4, pp. 14-18

Baudrillard, J. (1995), *The Gulf War Did Not Take Place*, Bloomington: Indiana University Press

Benjamin, W. (1970), *Illuminations*, transl. Harry Zorn, London: Fontana

Bürger, P. (1984), *Theory of the avant-garde*, Minneapolis: University of Minnesota Press

Häger, B. (1990), *Ballets Suédois*, London: Thames and Hudson

Huyssen, A. (1988), *After the Great Divide: Modernism, Mass Culture and Postmodernism*, London: Macmillan

Léger, F. (1964), *The Function of Painting*, London: Thames & Hudson

Levinson, A. (1929), *La Danse d'Aujourd'hui*, Paris: Editions Duchartre et Van Buggenhoudt

Manning, S. (1993), *Ecstasy and the Demon: Feminism and Nationalism in the Dances of Mary Wigman*, Berkeley, California: University of California Press

Phelan, P. (1997), *Mourning Sex: Performing Public Memories*, London: Routledge

Rischbeiter, H. (ed.) (1968), *Art and the Stage in the Twentieth Century*, Greenwich Connecticut: New York Graphic Society Ltd, (editorial statements and introductions)

Siegel, M. (1972), *Beyond the Vanishing Point: A Critic Looks at Dance*, Boston, Massachusets: Houghton Mifflin

Souritz, E. (1990), *Soviet Choreographers in the 1920s*, transl. L. Visson, ed. S. Banes, Durham, North Carolina: Duke University Press

Theodores, D. (1996), *First We Take Manhattan: Four American Women and the New York School of Dance Criticism*, Amsterdam: Harwood Academic

Thomas, H. (1997) (ed.), *Dance in the City*, London: Macmillan, chapters 9 and 11

Virilio, P. (1989), *War and Cinema: The Logistics of Perception*, London: Verso

Diaghilev's 'Soviet Ballet'
Reconstructing Jakulov's Set Design for *Le Pas d'acier* (1927)

Lesley-Anne Sayers

In 1924–5 Diaghilev expressed the earnest desire to put before his public a ballet that would represent the theatrical and social innovations of post-revolutionary Russia. He commissioned a score from Prokofiev, designs by the Soviet artist George Jakulov and eventually choreography by Massine. The result was *Le Pas d'acier, the Step of Steel*, presented in London and Paris in the summer of 1927. There is a certain irony in the notion of a ballet inspired by the new Soviet republic being produced by Diaghilev's Ballets Russes. The company was a focus point for white Russian *émigrés*, most of whom were far from sympathetic to the Soviet Union, and it was produced only the year after England's General Strike had sent the fear of Bolshevism to new heights in Western Europe.

Although this short-lived ballet was taken seriously by eye-witness historians, Cyril Beaumont and W.A. Propert (Beaumont, 1940: 278–80; Propert, 1931: 56–9), it has largely been ignored by later writers or dismissed as a mere flirtation with Soviet ideas. Since the 1980s, however, the growing body of research into constructivism in the early Soviet theatre and ballet invites renewed interest in this long forgotten work. As with so much of our dance history however, any new study of *Le Pas d'acier* is immediately confronted with the presence of its absence.

With *Le Pas d'acier* we have, as far as I have been able to discover, no notation, no film, no detailed documentary notes from the creators, not a single photograph to show us the set as it looked in performance and very limited possibility in terms of drawing on living memory. Yet going back to material from the creative process that has survived, and to the reviews, we discover a work which has left behind records of a fascinating ambition, and a not-inconsiderable effect.

What has survived is both much more than and much less than a performance. It is clearly not the performance itself, but it relates to it in a variety of complex ways. The primary source material I have gathered relates mainly to the developmental process or to the effect of the work, how it looked to critics and other spectators in the auditorium. I have come to think of such material as aspects of a work, something that is distinct from the performance, and yet obviously relates to the performance. To some extent at least this work can be found through historiography, in terms of cause and effect, as the development and consequences of a particular interaction, collaboration and circumstances. As such it can be used as a means towards identifying and exploring the space and potential space of the work's performance.

In this brief paper I would like to try and present some of the problems and issues that have arisen from my attempt to reconstruct Jakulov's set design, and some of the research findings so far. This is still very much work in progress.

A black–and–white photograph of Jakulov's model is the most frequently reproduced image of this ballet; it is the image of the work to have come down to us through history. Quite why it should be a photograph of the model that has survived and not one of the actual performance set, is one of many puzzles. It invites us, perhaps, to conclude that this is what the performance set looked like, that this model was the final part of the design process, even perhaps built as instructions to the scene builder. But research indicates that the relationship of this model to the performance set is not so straightforward. There are several obvious discrepancies between the model and contemporary descriptions of the set, and my research into the developmental process of the ballet indicates that the model was built quite early on in the ballet's creation, in 1925 (Jakulov, letter to Prokofiev 12 October 1925).

The ballet was first conceived, and the designs and libretto developed by Jakulov and Prokofiev in Paris in 1925, when Jakulov was a prize-winning exhibitor at the International Exhibition. The idea was to produce a ballet concerned with the transformation of Revolutionary Russia, showing the construction effort. The concept of a railway station setting for Act I followed something of a struggle between Jakulov and the Soviet writer Ilya Ehrenburg, who had Diaghilev's ear for a while in the planning stages of the ballet (Jakulov, letter to Koussikov). The Moscow Flea Market had been considered as the setting but was reduced instead to one short scene. At some point the train, shown on the model, was almost undoubtedly dropped from the set design; though the railway station remained in the theme of signals and platforms. The train was of course a vital part of the Russian revolution, bringing news and propaganda out from the towns to the rural communities, and this rhythm and dynamic was I think important to the concept of Act I, which is set in the rural Russian countryside after the revolution. Accompanying a CD recording of the music (Olympia, 1987), are notes which describe the 'merry train racing through the countryside', something that can readily be heard. With the futurists, of course, the train had become a symbol of speed and progress, envisaged not as a static object, but in terms of a new level of consciousness, in terms of movement and dynamism. I have come to think of Jakulov's train rather like the train in *Le Train bleu* as something that has been and gone; but remains thematically significant in understanding the development of *Le Pas d'acier*'s concept and designs.

Many parts of the model can be clearly identified in the reviews, but others appear to have been changed later, or may have been intended to show or explore stage effects. The painted cloud on the gauze for example almost certainly materialised purely as smoke puffing from the pistons in the second act. My research indicates that Jakulov's set came to life through the use of coloured light and the interaction of colour, light and moving structure, something that is difficult to model and would have been difficult to capture in the black and white photography of the day. This may perhaps at least partly explain why it is that we have only the model as a record of the set.

The original model has survived but is in private hands and has proved inaccessible. Fortunately Sotheby's kindly provided me with the colour transparency that was professionally taken of the model when it last came up for auction in 1984. The model was by then battered and broken and has several missing parts, but it gives an idea of the colours used and where it is broken we can see the means of its construction.

In terms of his stage objects Jakulov conforms very much to the language of Russian constructivism, with its wheels, ladders and platforms and use of industrial materials. These were usually realised in wood because unlike steel and other man made materials, wood was plentiful in the war-ravaged Soviet Union of the time. Like other constructivist sets that appeared in the Russian theatre during the 1920s, Jakulov's set was designed to be an adaptable setting with an emphasis on the economy of means; it is not decor, it is performance apparatus, bringing with it a whole new approach not just to the stage space but to the very concept of theatre.

Several of Jakulov's drawings of his designs for the ballet have sur-

Work in progress: a model reconstruction of Jakulov's design of *Le Pas d'acier*, Act II. Photograph by Peter Sayers

vived and in them we can see his concern with an architectural approach to the stage space and also, I think, with space delineated and explored for theatrical, physical and also emotional properties. In one drawing in particular, Jakulov's extraordinary vision of the stage space takes flight. He shows performers ascending to the full height of the space, up and down ladders supported by numerous platforms that intersect with each other across the stage; it is an arrangement of horizontal mass and vertical aspiration. The dancers are drawn like industrious ants involved in some colossal collective enterprise. Ironically it is fairly typical of constructivist design of the period to conjure up on paper architectural visions that were utopian in terms of the possibilities of actually building them at the time, especially on small proscenium stages. Many such wonderful constructivist visions lay unrealised. Yet the spirit, at least, of this drawing was somehow realised in performance, for it is evoked by several critics. Herbert Farjeon for example, wrote (*The Sunday Pictorial*, 1927), 'Le Pas D'Acier is an amazing and exhilarating achievement. The stage is filled with rising tiers and receding vistas of workmen, heaving and hewing, ascending and descending, and exhibiting a kind of automatic ecstacy in their subjugation to the power of steel.'

'Rising tiers and receding vistas' – an effect that was somehow evoked through the use of two basic platforms, gauze and a couple of ladders.

In exploring Jakulov's model many highly theatrical facets begin to emerge, particularly the circus-like potential of adaptable, moving decor, and the potential for burlesque afforded, for example, by revolving doors. Constructivist utilitarian concerns with economy of means and truth to materials did have a playful dimension in the theatre with a love of collapsible scenery giving rise to overt theatricality, an aspect that was, I think, particularly emphasised in Jakulov's designs. The black–and–white photograph of Jakulov's design looks very severe, but in rebuilding the model its playfulness becomes apparent. Everything moves, swivels, revolves, and requires human interaction to bring it to life.

Jakulov had a love of trap doors and theatrical effects. His 'railway signal' for *Le Pas d'acier* set is a good example of this, having not one but two inner revolving doors. On the original model the centre piece of these doors is missing. In my reconstruction I have used steel. I chose steel not because it is the most likely material to have been used on the actual set, but because of its significance as an industrial material and because its reflectivity would interact well with both light and action. I wanted to emphasise, or bring out, the circus-like aspects of the set design. Thematically I would argue that this is 'authentic' and justifiable in terms of the explorative aims of reconstruction, whether or not it is the original material. The development of the reconstruction has been about balancing detailed research leading to knowledge, with the unavoidable but potentially enlivening and interactive use of interpretation and reinvention.

In exploring Jakulov's model, with all its moving parts, it becomes clear just how much a concept of the action is integral to the designs. The big question then has to be how Massine responded to Jakulov's conception, and how far he may have altered its realisation. It is a design after all that not only fills the performance space, but channels and directs choreographic possibilities. For example, the set left no room for entrances other than from the sides, imposing a use of movement going up and down and from side to side rather than backwards and forwards. Massine came to the ballet very late on in its development; the set, music and libretto were all devised without the involvement of a choreographer. Massine clearly made, nevertheless, a powerful use of the restrictions imposed upon him. In the second factory act critics were overwhelmed by his innovative use of up to 45 dancers on stage at work in the factory forge and turning themselves into a variety of complex machine parts, from cogs and pistons to gear wheels, signals and levers.

Jakulov's vision of the ballet extends well beyond the design to the movement itself. In his drawings, the interaction of the set and the dancers is clearly integral to his whole concept of the design. He shows the dancers operating and performing on parts of his apparatus, and his annotations divide the stage space into three planes. He writes, 'the general principle of the construction of the set is a system of moving crankshafts. The movements for the dancers are accompanied by the movements of parts of the set, to give an impression not of abstract ballet movements but of useful work' (Jakulov, undated drawing, translated from Russian). He also describes particular dances including a dance with pedals and dances utilising wheels and various parts of the set. His concern, though, appears to be with the dancers operating the set, rather than with the idea of the dancers becoming machine parts themselves, as in Massine's realisation.

In his drawings Jakulov delineates the stage space into planes or layers and gives details of particular items such as the machine tool with pedals, the wheels which come down on shafts from above, and what he calls 'mock lighting devices coming down from above that rotate and light up'. For the purposes of economy, he writes, the moving devices will be designed to support a series of movements, the number to be kept to a minimum.

When it comes to filling gaps in knowledge and interpreting data, we can, I think, identify essentials of the set design that run through Jakulov's model and drawings, and then appear as realised constructions and effects in the descriptions and evocations of the critics. In each and every drawing, it is as if Jakulov is exploring possible variations to his theme rather than providing detailed records of what was to be built. The drawings that have survived were undoubtedly not meant to be detailed historical records, and it is therefore constantly necessary to interpret them. The task as I have seen it is to discover the essential elements within the drawings, model and spectator experience and then, informed by the existing model, reconstruct a version of the set design.

One of the most notable things about the reviews is a sense of just how important lighting was to the realisation of the set design. The surviving model has a deep red background but the grey decor described by the critics would, of course, respond very well to projected light and could instantly be transformed from cold bare stage to the fiery factory forge also described by the critics. One of the most difficult things in reconstructing the set is, I think, getting the balance right between what should be painted and what should be left to be in someway a receiver or transmitter of light.

Jakulov was throughout his life immensely interested in colour and light. The colour wheels that I have rebuilt from Jakulov's model are fascinating in themselves and relate very obviously to the work of the Delaunays, who were close friends of Jakulov and with whom he was staying in Paris in 1925 when his designs were shown to, and approved by, Diaghilev. These constructions were designed to be operated by the dancers using pedals and beltings to make the disks spin. In one drawing Jakulov shows them mounted on castors with the dancers pedalling while gliding across the stage space.

I have been reluctant to think that these colourful constructions did not appear like this on the performance set, but I have as yet found no evidence for them as painted objects. Even here Jakulov may have been using his model not as a definitive set of instructions but as an exploration of ideas, of theme and variations, as in the drawings. What is vital is the concern with the idea of dynamism. A fascination with movement itself, and also with the idea of transformation, is fundamental not just in the libretto, but in the design itself, realised, I think, largely through the use of light or colour on structure to produce dynamic effect.

One particular puzzle is Jakulov's mock lights, which on the original model are carved in detail out of wood and individually pinned, and in the drawings are described as rotating wheels that light up. But light up how? Through projected light, through reflected light or mechanically? Certainly the critics saw semaphore, flashing lights, signals of all kinds, and the question is I think how best to interpret and realise this essential element of the design in a reconstruction.

The large overhead wheels were introduced only for the second act in the factory. They were designed to rotate on a belting and they moved in time to the dancers' hammering movements and Prokofiev's industrial rhythms, getting faster and faster until the final climax of the ballet. Their supports were probably intended to look like iron, one of the materials observed by the critics. On the model the wheels are painted but I cannot find a source to confirm painted wheels of any kind on the performance set. Yet in spinning the centre wheel around unpainted, it quickly becomes apparent that the choice of structure only becomes meaningful with the addition of paint or light; for it is through the interaction of the structure with colour or light that the movement of the wheel is broken up, like splitting the atom, and the dynamic is made visual.

The first act of the ballet was set in the Russian countryside showing scenes of Russian life in 1920 in the tumult of transformation from the old order to the new. It draws on everyday life and from the legends and stories of the old Russia. The set for Act I has to be particularly versatile, accommodating a wide variety of short individual narrative scenes. In addition to the basic set parts, props were also used such as crossed-over wooden sticks to signify a window. In my reconstruction I wanted to capture the plain grey interior, with the few signifiers of location described by the critics. My theory is that Jakulov revealed the potential of the set gradually, which explains, I think, why the critics saw at first a bare grey set, but by the end of the ballet had been transported to a factory forge and lifted to heights of evocative description.

Into this grey space came a host of characters such as Soldiers, Commissars, Orators, devils dressed as firemen with copper helmets, cats and mice, and former countesses with lampshades for hats forced to barter their colourful but ragged clothes for a sack of flour from a black-marketeer. One little-known photograph shows Woizikovsky, Tchercas and Effimov as the three drunkards. It reveals something of the physical jerks and automatic movement described by the critics. Massine's predilection for angular movement reached new extremes in this ballet; stylistic influences no doubt included movement inspired by current Soviet approaches such as Meyerhold's biomechanics and Foregger's Machine Dances, which Massine would have known about but could not have seen directly. By contrast the photographs of the principals, Massine, Danilova, Lifar and Tchernicheva, show Massine's use of slavic types and movement.

Act II opened with a *pas de deux* 'Le Beguin', 'The Fleeting Romance', danced by Lifar and Tchernicheva. It does not appear to have been directly connected with the factory scenes that followed, almost like a music hall number, or *entr'acte*, in keeping with the revue-like style of the first act. There is some evidence to suggest that it was danced in front of a bright Soviet-red screen.

For the factory scenes wheels and constructions were introduced. Later on the gauze was lit so as to reveal the silhouettes of workers wielding hammers in the forge behind. Much of the power of the factory act clearly depended upon lighting effects, as well as on Massine's choreography. The critics report the powerful effects of flashing and flaming lights, of revolving red, green and white lights flashing down on the triple tier of workers, of signal discs snapping on and off and wheels moving faster and faster until a crescendo finale.

What is perhaps particularly interesting is just how far many of the review descriptions evoke a basic conception that goes right back through the work to Prokofiev and Jakulov's early conception in 1925. In his memoirs Prokofiev notes:

> Sitting in a tiny café on the banks of a river half an hour outside of Paris, Yakulov and I roughly sketched several draft librettos. We assumed that the important thing at this stage was not to provide mere entertainment but to show the new life that had come to the Soviet Union, and primarily the construction effort. It was to be a ballet of construction, with a wielding of hammers big and small, a revolving of transmission belts and flywheels, a flashing of light signals, all leading to a general creative upsurge with the dance groups operating the machines and at the same time depicting the work of the machines choreographically. The idea was Yakulov's who had spent some years in the Soviet Union and described it all most vividly. (Prokofiev, 1960: 65–6)

'The idea was Jakulov's'. I think that the evidence is that this largely was Jakulov's ballet, and one that produced an interesting series of interactions between Soviet ideas and Western perceptions. *Le Pas d'acier* was, I think, very much a work where a Russian constructivist conception met a Western conception of Soviet ideology and constructivism. Part of its significance lies perhaps in that tension and in its possible influence on the development of certain aspects of Massine's later choreography.

At the moment my model-in-progress is simply a site for the exploration of possibilities. But this is, I think, one of the major advantages of using practical reconstruction, even in a limited sense such as here; as a process of exploration. Even the preliminary task of practically rebuilding parts of Jakulov's model has been revealing, a voyage of discovery and surprise; it has extended my understanding of the set well beyond that which came purely from observation. Much of the reconstruction is now concerned with exploring and trying to decipher a brief lighting plan of Jakulov's that has survived, and putting it together with the review descriptions and other contextual material in formulating an overall interpretation of the design.

It seems to me that the challenge afforded by reconstruction of lost works such as this, is not just to interpret surviving material through historiography, but to produce an interpretation that is both authentic in terms of being true to the work (as distinct from the unrepeatable original performance) and alive in terms of exploring and revealing the work's performance potential.

References

Beaumont, C.W. (1940), *The Diaghilev Ballet in London*, London: Putnam

Farjeon, H. *The Sunday Pictorial*, 10 July 1927, p. 9

Jakulov, G. Letter to Koussikov, (1925?) published in French in 'Les Ballets Russes de Serge Diaghilev', L'Ancienne Douanne, auction catalogue, 15 May-15 September 1969, Strasbourg, p. 231.

Jakulov, G. Unpublished letter in Russian to Serge Prokofiev, 12 October 1925, the Prokofiev Archive, London.

Jakulov, G. Drawings from collections held by The Victoria and Albert Theatre Museum, the Kochno Collection of the Archives of the Paris Opera and private collections.

Prokofiev S. 'Ballets', The USSR Ministry of Culture Symphony Orchestra, Olympia, 1987

Prokofiev, S. (1960), *Autobiography, Articles, Reminiscences*, Moscow: Foreign Languages Publishing House

Propert, W.A. (1931), *The Russian Ballet 1921-1929*, London: John Lane The Bodley Head Ltd

After the Event
Reconstructing Ashton's 'Past'

Carol A. Martin

In this paper I want to ask: 'Is the time right to start reconstructing Ashton's past in line with contemporary theoretical debate?' If so, how might this contribute to the reconstruction and understanding of his work, the survival of his legacy?

Over the last five years, certain developments indicate a renewal of interest in Ashton's life and work including some important revivals at the Royal Opera House and the Ashton Conference at Roehampton, Julie Kavanagh's (1996) biography and the planned new edition of David Vaughan's (1977) seminal study. Alastair Macaulay's (1996) paper on gender and community has bravely and sensitively illustrated the potential of a socio-cultural perspective, perhaps even more significant in the light of Kavanagh's research. It is possible that we now know more about Ashton than at any other time.

An increase in sources, however, is just one of the signs that the time is right for a renaissance. Whether we are still in the grip of postmodernism or, as some would suggest, its aftermath, developments such as these have emerged at a time of intense preoccupation with the past. As noted by Roger Copeland, in the dance world at least 'the "Me" Generation has been succeeded by the "Re" Generation' (Copeland, 1994: 18). Ashton and MacMillan revivals at Covent Garden; Massine, Agnes de Mille and Balanchine at Birmingham; *Dark Elegies* and *Stabat Mater* at the Coliseum; *Swan Lake* and *Cinderella* in the West End – these have been some of the most enthusiastically received events in recent British seasons.

With a greater body of knowledge at our disposal and carried on a wave of enthusiasm for revivals, reworkings, restagings and reconstructions, the time *is* right to reconsider Ashton's work. Why then does the future of Ashton scholarship and the legacy it seeks to enrich still seem so insecure? One of the major reasons is to be found in the continued gulf between the study of Ashton and the sophisticated complexities of postmodernist theory. The barrier can and should be challenged and the concept of 'reconstruction' provides ample opportunity to do so. This agenda was the starting point for my recent MA dissertation at the University of Surrey, research through which I sought to illustrate how Ashton scholarship might be brought into dialogue with contemporary debate on the nature of history. For this paper, I have drawn on my research in order to present a different way of looking at Ashton's early career.

I proceed from a theoretical perspective drawn from the work of the American theorist/historian Hayden White which focuses on two main issues. Firstly, the distinction he makes between 'event' and 'fact', leading to the argument that whilst events actually happened, their traces or 'facts' are constructed and history reconstructed from (some of) the facts. The distinction has been interpreted by some as a denial of the past, however, on closer scrutiny, the argument would seem not that the past never happened but that we do not, and never have had, direct access to it. What we do have access to are a number of facts. Linda Hutcheon puts the issue succinctly when she states 'All past "events" are potential historical "facts", but the ones that become facts are those chosen to be narrated' (Hutcheon, 1989: 75). In his early text, *Metahistory: The Historical Imagination in Nineteenth Century Europe*, the process is theorised by White as a 'transformation' from the 'chronicle' to the 'story' 'effected by the characterisation of <u>some</u> events in the chronicle [my underline]' (White, 1973: 5).

This leads me to the second issue I want to consider: White's notion of the historical work as 'narrative prose discourse' which is 'as much invented – or imagined – as found' (White, 1978: 82). Here White points to the contextualisation of facts through which historians construct 'meaning'. The argument is addressed by Keith Jenkins (1995), whose interpretation of White's work identifies some of the complexities involved. In Jenkins' understanding, the problem for the historian is that whilst 'facts' can be found in the historicised record or archive, the background or context against which these become meaningful can never be found in any definitive sense. Thus, ultimately, the context has to be invented or imagined and it is in this aspect that narrative plays a vital role.

How might White's claims be used to reconstruct a context for Ashton's work in the period 1926-35? I take as my starting point a comment made by Ashton himself in a letter to Marie Rambert written in 1935. The letter is one of two discovered by Jane Pritchard and discussed in her paper at the Ashton Conference. I thank her for sharing them with us.

The letter begins, 'Dearest Mim, I have come to the conclusion that civil war has broken out in the world of ballet, and there is nothing more destructive in the world than civil war, much worse than a foreign invasion' (Ashton cited in Pritchard 1996: 110). The notion of a 'civil war' during the early years of English ballet seems an interesting alternative to more traditional narratives of community and pioneering spirit. Ashton seems to be warning against the potentially devastating consequences of 'fighting amongst the ranks' as English ballet struggles to stem the flow of visiting Russian stars. With this in mind, I have identified four communities which might be interpreted as rival 'factions' in an English ballet 'civil war' (Table 1). Reading from left to right, the names will be familiar: The Ballet Club, based at the Mercury Theatre; Ballet in Theatreland (or the commercial theatre), spread over selected West End venues; The Camargo Society, spread over selected London theatres and The Vic-Wells Ballet based at the Sadler's Wells and Old Vic theatres.

A narrative strategy is implicit in the selection of chronological parameters which begin with Ashton's debut work for Rambert, *A Tragedy of Fashion* (1926) and end in the year he joined the Vic-Wells Ballet. Thus I am already setting out to plot a story of 'defection' from one company to another and, simultaneously, a change of partnership from Ashton/Rambert to Ashton/de Valois. Reading from left to right, the four communities represent Ashton's 'career ladder' from the tiny Mercury stage to the newly-opened Sadler's Wells Theatre. In geographical terms, they mark a route across London from Notting Hill Gate, to the West End and on to Islington; a journey several other Rambert 'discoveries' were to make. As can be seen, there are various time overlaps which reinforce the notion of competition and rivalry. From 1931 to 1933 Ashton's time and energy as both dancer and choreographer were in demand from all four 'factions', freelance years which must have been rewarding but difficult to co-ordinate and immensely tiring. It is possible that this was a major factor in his decision, in 1935, to become a permanent member (and resident choreographer) of de Valois' company.

Since my concern in this chart is mainly with the wider picture, I have done no more than outline some of the fundamental facilities, legacies and contributions upon which each of these communities is based. These are interpretations based on a selection of 'facts' such as geographical location, company members, repertoire and so on, which can be checked as true or false against more detailed accounts in the archive. However the chart illustrates White's argument that whilst these facts can be empirically validated, the context or 'whole' cannot, and this applies to each of the four communities as well as the 'whole' picture. Whether or not these communities constitute rival factions in a battle for supremacy cannot be proven 'true' or 'false'. Such an interpretation can only be judged against others. As Keith Jenkins points out, 'a true interpretation is an oxymoron' (Jenkins, 1995: 23). At the same time, it is necessary to note that whilst I have allowed myself a level of invention and imagination, the civil war metaphor is not mine but Ashton's. On one level, it is a 'fact' that Ashton perceived a civil war in English ballet of around 1935. Thus this reading presents a prime example of the fascinating balance between finding and inventing, between fact and fiction. From a 'post-ist' perspective, the question is not whether this *was* a 'true' picture but whether it *is* an acceptable one.

Having identified four separate organisations as rival factions competing for audiences and artists, it is possible to draw up the following list of potential 'battle-lines' or conflicts:

The Ballet Club	versus	Ballet in Theatreland
The Ballet Club	versus	the Camargo Society
The Ballet Club	versus	The Vic-Wells Ballet
Ballet in Theatreland	versus	The Camargo Society
Ballet in Theatreland	versus	The Vic-Wells Ballet
The Camargo Society	versus	The Vic-Wells Ballet

Some of these tensions have been considered in writings on the period. The rivalry between the companies under Rambert and de Valois is, perhaps, the most familiar. Conflict between the ballet organisations and the commercial theatre has received far less attention, possibly because the West End has not been perceived as an equal player but rather as a necessary 'bread and butter' earner. The relationship between the Camargo Society and the Vic-Wells Ballet has, generally, been interpreted as one of alliance, although one could argue that from 1931 to 1933 the Society drew on the very same resources needed by de Valois' company and thus was a competitor. Of equal interest is the Camargo Society's destructive influence on The Ballet Club. It is within the context of the Society, where Ashton and de Valois were more directly involved than Rambert, that one can detect the beginning of Ashton's 'defection' to Sadler's Wells. In many ways the battle for Ashton was undertaken within this brief but significant 'interregnum'.

In Table 2 I look more closely at Ashton's relationship with each of the four factions through a choreochronicle, drawn from the extensive appendices in David Vaughan's text. The distribution of these ballets across the four different contexts is significant, indicating that Ashton spent much of his time working outside the embryonic ballet world. Between 1931 and 1933 Ashton was working for all four factions. I choose to focus on these years since they illustrate the narrative content in the historicised record. A breakdown of Ashton's output during this three-year period reads as follows:

Ballet in Theatreland	10 productions
The Ballet Club	7 productions
The Camargo Society	4 productions
The Vic-Wells Ballet	2 productions

The significance of the period has, generally, been (re)constructed in exactly the reverse order with writings on the Vic-Wells Ballet dominating the ballet history archive. In recent articles Kathrine Sorley Walker (1995), Angela Kane and Jane Pritchard (1994) have gone some way to elevating the status of the Camargo Society but Rambert's company and the commercial theatre have been, and remain, marginalised. This is confirmed when one considers what has survived from Ashton's 1931-3 repertoire. Only two ballets are still performed, both of which belong to the later organisations; *Façade* (1931) for the Camargo Society and *Les Rendezvous* (1933) for the Vic-Wells Ballet. The body of work created for the Ballet Club, the commercial theatre and film contexts, has been rendered absent from the Ashton canon. Chapters on the cultural significance of Ashton's film and revue choreography have, as far as I know, yet to be written. Similarly 'Ashton and Rambert' or 'Ashton and de Valois' have overshadowed relationships such as 'Ashton and Charles B. Cochran' or 'Ashton and Buddy Bradley'.

A breakdown of the year 1932 alone is also revealing:

Ballet in Theatreland	5 productions
The Ballet Club	2 productions
The Camargo Society	1 production (with Buddy Bradley)
The Vic-Wells Ballet	No productions

These facts can be interpreted in a number of ways. First and foremost they seem to indicate that, despite the developments in English ballet, Ashton was occupied elsewhere. This prompts questions as to why, at such a critical moment, Ashton seems to have temporarily abandoned ship. Ballet historians have pointed to the obvious financial considerations; the commercial theatre paid far better wages. However the pattern of distribution makes it possible to challenge the notion that this was (merely) the 'bread and butter' work which supported more significant (i.e. 'high art') ventures. As noted by David Vaughan, many of these dances or arrangements received excellent notices and one might add that they would have been seen by far larger audiences than the gathered elite at the Mercury or Sadler's Wells. This work was seen and enjoyed by many and it is possible that Ashton enjoyed, rather than suffered, working in the West End. The status gained through this exposure and the respite from the competing demands of two equally determined women, must have had its own rewards. This reading becomes even more plausible when one considers that in the previous year, 1931, he had been obliged to try and keep everyone happy, producing three ballets each for Rambert and the Camargo Society and his first ever for de Valois. Whether this was an *annus mirabilis* or *annus horribilis* is debatable, however it appears that in 1932 Ashton kept his distance from all three ballet factions.

Ashton's metaphor of civil war is developed throughout his letter to Rambert in which he offers her the following advice:

> I think that you should go slowly in a neutral way & watch the results of the warfare & like America step in at the right moment I would not enter the guerrilla & risk a defeat because Sadler's Wells & Markova have more ammunition with which to fight, & now I see that Leon [Woizikovsky] has also a company & altogether there is too much activity. (Ashton cited in Pritchard, 1996: 110)

The historian in need of a paradigm for the study of early English ballet as 'civil war' need look no further than Ashton's *Façade* (1931). Produced under the aegis of the Camargo Society, subsequently taken into the repertoire of Rambert's company and then acquired (or given) to the Vic-Wells Ballet for the 1935-6 season, this work occupies a somewhat uneasy, albeit successful role in English ballet history. Ashton, of course, was obliged to offer some explanation as to why a ballet paid for by Rambert and created on Ballet Club dancers (with the exception of Lydia Lopokova) was being given to de Valois. At the centre of his letter Ashton explains, 'I hope that you are not too upset about Façade but that is not really my doing but Willie [Walton] who wants royalties' and goes on to say 'For my part it also gives me a good dancing part to hold my own against Bobbie & Harold' (Ashton cited in Pritchard, 1996: 110). Ashton 'passes the buck', however the second comment is of equal significance, reminding us that at this time he was still in pursuit of a dancing career. As the references to Robert Helpmann and Harold Turner indicate, in addition to conflict between rival factions the civil war narrative has the potential to include rivalries between dancers.

Having outlined this picture of confrontation, conflict and competition, my intention has been to reconstruct an alternative context for the study and interpretation of familiar events, or 'facts', concerning Ashton's early career. The research draws on what White would term the 'already written', that is, the Ashton archive developed by a generation of historians and archivists from within the modernist tradition. I am not for one moment suggesting that this project be abandoned. As many of us are aware, now is the time to collate and document the wealth of 'first hand' knowledge and experience still available. Discussion panels at the Ashton Conference and 'Ballroom Blitz '97', have only re-emphasised the urgency. However, there is no reason to assume that new perspectives and alternative lines of enquiry cannot be undertaken simultaneously. Such diversification could well lead to the creation of a dynamic dialogue between the two. It is within this discursive 'space' that Ashton scholarship, and the study of British ballet in general, might achieve a new lease of life. I am thinking here of the dance undergraduates I teach for whom early English ballet seems to hold little or no interest. Part of the reason lies in the lack of scores and video sources and yet these same difficulties do not, in my experience, dampen enthusiasm for the study of, for example, nineteenth-century Romantic ballet or the Ballets Russes. Another possible reason for this lack of interest can be identified in the perceived 'unrelatedness' between the study of British ballet and the challenging array of theoretical perspectives which have enriched other areas of dance scholarship. The gulf is particularly evident when one considers how defenceless ballet scholarship has been against the onslaught of feminist critiques. White's insistence on the historical work, however revisionist, as 'narrative prose discourse' has, I believe, the potential to reclaim ballet from the grip of feminist politics.

The next step in an enquiry such as I have outlined would be to consider ways in which it might contribute to our understanding of Ashton's works. A 'civil war' narrative might, for example, be of significance when looking at subject matter, the choice of dancers and the roles Ashton created for himself. His largely unfulfilled ambitions as a dancer

might be brought alongside the more familiar interpretation of a choreographic apprenticeship. The demand for Ashton as a dancer, his position
within a small but expanding group of British male dancers, could lead to
much-needed research into Ashton's choreography for men. In the light
of Julie Kavanagh's research on Ashton's sexuality, the potential for new
readings would seem significant.

In making these suggestions I am, of course, ignoring a fundamental
problem. Few of Ashton's early ballets have survived and interest in
reviving them has not been strong. It is not possible in this paper to go
into the numerous theoretical and practical issues facing such a project.
What then is the point of my reconstruction if the works I seek to make
sense of have not survived? One possibility is that just as revivals of
Ashton's work have initiated renewed interest in the study of their historical context, the reverse might also be possible. The reconstruction of
'lost' Ashton works could well come from a more diverse and critical
scholarship. However, it is necessary to point out that the kind of radical
perspective I have proposed for the reconstruction of context, could
hardly be employed to make sense of a positivist reconstruction of a
dance text. In other words, having raised the distinction between events
and facts and denied the possibility of direct access to the past as it was,
notions of 'finding' or reclaiming the 'original', the 'authentic' or the
'truth' can no longer be sustained.

An alternative starting point might be the drawing of a parallel between history and dance performance. The first performance of a ballet
becomes a historical event, which, like all other historical events, happened, finished and is over – in other words, is history. Similarly, White's
notion of 'facts' as constructed will have significance in relation to the
identification and interpretation of 'traces' of the dance. In place of the
traditional emphasis on authenticity, first casts and the past 'as it was', a
'post-ist' reconstructor would need to address alternative issues such as
the number of facts needed to reconstruct a lost dance, the significance of
contradictory facts, ways of acknowledging the contemporary performance context and identifying criteria to replace notions of 'truth'. These
are some which come to mind but perhaps I should add another: would
permission ever be obtained to undertake a radical reconstruction of an
Ashton ballet?

In her article 'Reconstruction and its Problems', Sarah Rubidge (1995)
asks whether a more radical type of approach to reconstruction might
render the historical modern dance canon more relevant to contemporary

audiences. She notes, however, the particular problem of reconstructing the recent past. As with the work of Graham, Humphrey, Hawkins, Sokolow et al, Ashton's canon remains in the collective memory of those who have spent a lifetime performing, watching, coaching, reviewing and studying his work. It is *still* difficult to find an Ashton review which does not mention the original cast or make comparisons (usually unfavourable ones) to the 'original' production. Such knowledge and experience is the vital source material for future study but as more of us are able to say 'I was not there', the authenticity perspective will continue to become more problematic. Ultimately we are likely to ask whether the way forward is, as some would argue, backwards.

To conclude, in this paper I have outlined a theoretical perspective for the reconstruction of Ashton history and illustrated ways in which it might enliven Ashton scholarship and initiate the regeneration of his legacy. Different ways of looking, whether rejected, ridiculed or respected, can strengthen Ashton scholarship even as they seem to challenge it. The challenge can and should be met. The task will fall to those who, like me, have a passion for Ashton's work without having known him or seen his beloved first casts. For us, a post-Ashton generation entering the third millenium, reconstruction promises that – after the event – we can still participate in the making of Ashton history.

References

Copeland, R. (1994), 'Reflections on Revival and Reconstruction', *Dance Theatre Journal* Vol. 11 No. 3, pp. 18-20

Hutcheon, L. (1989), *The Politics of Postmodernism*, London and New York: Routledge

Jenkins, K. (1995), *On "What is History": from Carr & Elton to Rorty & White*, London and New York: Routledge

Kane, A. & Pritchard, J. (1994) The Camargo Society: Part 1. *Dance Research* Vol.1 XII No.2, Autumn 1994, pp. 21-65

Kavanagh, J. (1996), *Secret Muses, The Life of Frederick Ashton*, London: Faber & Faber

Macaulay, A. (1996), 'Gender, Sexuality, Community' in *Following in Sir Fred's Steps: Ashton's Legacy*, ed. Jordan, S. and Grau, A., London: Dance Books, pp. 115-26

Pritchard, J. (1996), 'Two letters' in *Following in Sir Fred's Steps: Ashton's Legacy*, ed. Jordan, S. and Grau, A., London: Dance Books, pp. 101-14

Rubidge, S. (1995), 'Reconstruction and its Problems', *Dance Theatre Journal* Vol. 12 No. 1, pp. 31-33

Sorley Walker, K. (1995) The Camargo Society, *Dance Chronicle*, Vol.18 No.1, pp. 1-114

Vaughan, D. (1977), *Frederick Ashton and His Ballets*, London: A. & C. Black

White, H. (1973), *Metahistory: The Historical Imagination in Nineteenth Century Europe*, Baltimore: John Hopkins University Press

White, H. (1978), *Tropics of Discourse*, Baltimore: John Hopkins University Press

TABLE 1: 'Raising the Flag' or 'Civil War'? English Ballet 1926-1935

FACTION 1: (1926-1935) THE BALLET CLUB	FACTION 2: (1926-1935) BALLET IN THEATRELAND	FACTION 3: (1930-1933) THE CAMARGO SOCIETY	FACTION 4: (1931-1935) THE VIC-WELLS BALLET
Home: The Mercury Theatre	Home: London & Regional Theatres	Home: Selected London Theatres	Home: Sadler's Wells/ Old Vic
Concern: English Ballet	Concern: English Theatre	Concern: English Ballet (Production)	Concern: English Ballet
A community based on: - the legacies of Music Hall Ballet, Russian Ballet & EnglishTheatre - Rambert's school - acquisition of the Mercury site - Rambert's contacts in ballet/theatre - collaboration between composers, designers, choreographers & dancers - the dimensions of the Mercury stage -Rambert/Ashton relationship - contributions by guest artists - a growing ballet audience - the existence of Factions 2, 3 & 4	A community based on: - the traditions of drama, opera, film & the popular stage including: musical comedy revue burlesque cabaret variety theatre - collaboration between writers, composers, designers, choreogra- phers, dance arrangers, artists, impresarios, directors, producers, film crews, promoters etc. - growing theatre audience in London - the existence of Factions 1, 3 & 4	A community based on: - the need to fill the vacuum left by the death of Diaghilev - the concept of an English Ballet - the formation of a committee - the legacies of Music Hall Ballet, Russian Ballet & English Theatre - the collaboration and generosity of leading figures in music, art, design & ballet in London Society - the financial expertise of Maynard Keynes - the choreographic contributions of de Valois & Ashton - contributions by guest artists - core of dancers from Factions 1 & 4 - the existence and co- operation of Factions 1, 2 & 4	A community based on: - de Valois' school - de Valois/Lilian Baylis association - the legacies of Music Hall Ballet, Russian Ballet & English Theatre - de Valois status as dancer and choreogra- pher - contribution of guest artists - corps de ballet drawn from school - dancers/ choreogra- phers from Faction 1 - de Valois/Ashton/ Lambert/Fedorovitch collaborations - existence of Factions 1, 2 & 3 - the legacy of Faction 3 - a growing ballet audience
REPERTOIRE FOUNDATIONS Fokine revivals, abbreviations of Petipa 'classics' and new works by Ashton, Salaman, Howard & Tudor		REPERTOIRE FOUNDATIONS Fokine revivals, Petipa 'classics', new works by Ashton & de Valois	REPERTOIRE FOUNDATIONS New works by de Valois & Ashton, ballets acquired from Faction 3, revivals of Petipa 'classics' by Sergeyev

TABLE 2: Ashton Choreography and Performance 1926-1935
(Vaughan, 1977)

* Productions in which Ashton also performed

For Marie Rambert Dancers, Ballet Club & Ballet Rambert 1926-1935	For Opera, Drama, Film & The Commercial Theatre	For The Camargo Society & Vic-Wells Ballet 1930-1935
*A Tragedy of Fashion (1926) (Marie Rambert Dancers)	1926 Riverside Nights revue, prod. N. Playfair	THE CAMARGO SOCIETY
*Pas de Deux (1926)	1927 The Fairy Queen prod. D. Arundell	Pomona (1930)
*Suite de Danse (1927)	1929 Jew Süss prod. M. Lang & R. Denham	*Façade (1931)
*Argentine Dance (1927)	1930 *Marriage à la Mode prod. N. Playfair	A Day in a Southern Port (1931)
Nymphs and Shepherds (1928)	*A Masque of Poetry and Music: 'Beauty, Truth & Rarity' prod. G. Rylands	*The Lord of Burleigh (1931)
*Leda (1928) (chor. Ashton & Rambert)	1931 Cabaret Français details unknown	*High Yellow (1932) (chor. Ashton & B.Bradley)
*Capriol Suite (1930)	excerpts from Faust opera by J. Barbier & M. Carré	
*Saudade do Brésil (1930)	1932 Dance Pretty Lady film, prod. B. Woolfe (filmed 1931)	THE VIC-WELLS BALLET
*Mazurka des Hussars (1930)	The Cat and the Fiddle revue, prod. C.B. Cochran	Regatta (1931)
A Florentine Picture (1930)	*Magic Nights revue, prod. C.B. Cochran	Les Rendezvous (1933)
*La Péri (1931) (Ballet Club)	A Kiss in Spring comedy, prod. O. Stoll	Le Baiser de La Fée (1935)
*Mercury (1931)	Ballyhoo revue, pres. L. Barton	
*The Lady of Shalott (1931)	How D'You Do? Revue by Macrae, Byng, Farjeon et al	Key:
Pompette (1932)	After Dark revue, prod. K. Diffield, pres. by R. Jeans	prod. = produced by
*Foyer de Danse (1932)	Gay Hussar musical play, prod. J. Wylie	chor. = choreography by
*Les Masques (1933)	*Nursery Murmurs details unknown	pres. = presented by
Pavane Pour une Infante Défunte (1933)	1934 Four Saints in Three Acts words G. Stein, prod. J. Houseman	dir. = directed by
*Mephisto Valse (1934)	*Jill Darling! Musical comedy, prod. W. Mollison	
*Valentine's Eve (1935) (Ballet Rambert)	Escape Me Never film, prod. H. Wilcox, dir. P. Czinner, (filmed December 1934)	
	The Flying Trapeze play, prod. E. Charell	
	Round About Regent Street revue, prod. G. Black	
	*Follow the Sun revue, prod. C.B. Cochran	

Inside Artistry:
The George Balanchine Foundation Video Archives

Nancy Reynolds

In 1995 under the auspices of the George Balanchine Foundation, I began a video programme to retrieve fragments of Balanchine choreography no longer performed (and thus in danger of being lost or forgotten), and to preserve the coaching and interpretations of Balanchine roles by those who worked directly with him – preferably those on whom the roles were created. These taping sessions would not consist of interviews per se, although interviews would be part of the process; I felt there were plenty of interviews and oral histories out there already. What I wanted was to capture the body language of Balanchine's dancers as they passed on their roles to dancers of today. I felt this would convey far more informa- tion than purely verbal discourse. I also suspected that dancers, who are sometimes inhibited when expressing ideas about dance in words, would lose themselves in the teaching process and in so doing, impart not only the choreography itself but the nuances of interpretation and phrasing, including the motivations behind the steps, in a way that simply would not happen in face-to-face interviews.

Today, more than 100 hours of videotape later, Dame Alicia Markova, Maria Tallchief, Frederic Franklin, Marie-Jeanne, Patricia Wilde,Melisa Hayden, Alicia Alonso and Todd Bolender, among others, have examined in depth some of the gems of the Balanchine repertory for the Founda- tion's video cameras (more detailed specifications of the programme will be found at the end of this essay). Even so, I feel we have barely begun to scratch the surface of what is possible, because the project is completely open-ended, and as long as there is a Balanchine dancer around with something interesting to say, I hope to be around myself to capture it.

At the outset I assumed the project needed little defense. Who could possibly think it a bad idea? However among the many, many things that I have learned over the past six years, one is that not everyone agreed with me. 'Balanchine abandoned or changed many of his works; what right have you to exhume them?,' goes one line of thinking, or, 'Why should we care about what Balanchine himself discarded?' or, 'There are so many versions of Balanchine ballets around, which he either changed deliberately or which changed inadvertently over the years; how will you arrive at the authentic version?' Rephrased, the question becomes 'What will you do if two 'authorities' disagree?' There also seemed to be a political worry – would today's artistic directors, busily preparing their Balanchine programmes, not be offended by my trying to establish the 'correct' Balanchine style, implicitly showing up all the things they were doing wrong? The illustrious older dancers, our teachers and coaches, sometimes wondered whether they should correct today's performers, knowing that things are done differently now. They were also hesitant about interfering, even for an afternoon, with ideas another artist might have formulated over a period of years.

The answer to all of these concerns, it seems to me, is that Balanchine is now history, and what he did now belongs to all of us. It is fair game for exploration in any way we choose. On the tapes we document variant versions without comment, knowing that there is no absolute Balanchine. It is for artistic directors – not the Balanchine Foundation – to decide how to present Balanchine on stage in the future. To the coaches I say, 'I am looking only for your interpretation, what you think Balanchine wanted from you. Please do not worry about what other people are doing.' The young dancers are told that their work with the coaches is only for the purposes of the tape; it is up to them whether they carry a new viewpoint over to their performances.

At the beginning, the historian in me knew very well that two of the most lustrous dancers of the century had unique information about older works; Dame Alicia about *Rossignol* and Frederic Franklin about the original *Mozartiana* – and thus, without necessarily intending to, I gravitated toward the older set; the septua- and octogenarians. Once I realised this was happening, it seemed logical – with apologies – to save those in their forties, fifties, and sixties for later. (I have spent quite a bit of time explaining why Suzanne Farrell has not yet been a subject of our tapes!) The sense of urgency engendered by working with the older dancers became even more acute when Toumanova died; she and I had had several telephone conversations, and she had agreed to help with *Mozartiana*, but I did not get back to her in time. Now I feel positively hounded by the sense of universal clocks ticking all around me.

Incidentally, working with Toumanova would have presented quite a challenge, since I do not believe she would have allowed herself to be photographed. I am sure we could have handled this in some way or other, as my philosophy has been to put the coaches first and try to accommodate them in every way possible. Without them there would be no project; and I have too often seen their experience taken for granted, ignored, or wasted. Dame Alicia did not want a pianist, so we coped with finding specified measures in the middle of a CD (this can be quite nerve-wracking when you know she is waiting!). Todd Bolender feared he could no longer demonstrate, so I suggested he work out his ideas on an assistant and bring him to New York – but I had to make sure the assistant did not become the center of attention, as New York City Ballet's Albert Evans had already agreed to restudy the role with Todd. Maria Tallchief felt she could not teach, only coach, so I had to find dancers for her who already knew the roles. For Freddie Franklin we had a pianist tape the score observing the cuts as he remembered them, since two years of searching, including advertising and the Internet, failed to unearth the Ballet Russe scores of *Mozartiana* and *Le Baiser de la fée*; Freddie himself, in essence, supplied the score, humming it to the pianist, who then taped 'his' version. For Marie-Jeanne the pianist memorised the metronome markings from the recording used for the original *Concerto Barocco*, with tempos varying greatly from what we hear today.

As for format, I knew I wanted to show process – the mastery or re-creation of the choreography as it was occurring – and to that end I wanted a rehearsal atmosphere, where correction and repetition were expected events. The tapes were not to be in any way confused with performance (indeed, I suspect that the excerpts of lost choreography we have re-created will never be part of a performable work), and so both dancers and coaches were asked to wear practice clothes and street make-up. We hired rehearsal pianists, so we could stop and start as often as needed, and we rented ballet studios rather than television sound stages, which we felt would look too antiseptic (they also lack a horizon line, which can render movements strangely weightless). Using studios however meant we had to cope with the vagaries of the weather and certain urban intrusions such as drilling on the sidewalks below or fire alarms. With Dame Alicia we worked in the evening, which eliminated some of the noise and light problems but stretched the shoot over many more days and required negotiating with video technicians who had four or eight hour minimums.

We deliberated how best to capture process, primarily whether information could be better conveyed by teaching the choreography from scratch or by coaching dancers who already knew the steps (although they might know a somewhat different version and find it difficult to adapt to the immediate circumstances). With teaching the learning process goes more slowly, of course, thereby perhaps providing fuller detail and greater knowledge of danger spots, which can be illuminating. However there is less time to absorb and polish, to assimilate the corrections and to show the 'before' and 'after'. There was also the question of whether to use young or seasoned dancers. The youngsters 'stubbed their toes' more often, which revealed interesting hidden problems, while the mature dancers could more readily convey the nuances of the coach's teaching. For example, Patricia Wilde used an apprentice dancer with little previous rehearsal for the difficult the *pas de deux* from *Raymonda Variations*. Several hours of struggle showed the pitfalls very clearly (I had never realised, for instance, that the ballerina is off-balance throughout), but we were never given a run-through that showed the full magic of the dance, whereas in *Scotch Symphony*, Judith Fugate remade herself before our very eyes, processing Tallchief's corrections and stylistically reinterpreting the *pas de deux* in a breathtaking manner over the course of just two afternoons. In fact we devoted part of the interview afterwards to enumerating to some of the difficulties – such as catches in mid-*pirouette* or partnering with one hand – since they had been so effortlessly handled as to be unapparent during the superbly executed dance sequences. I believe the jury is still out on which is the better method. One approach we tried and discarded was that of being fly on the wall in a company rehearsal; the results were too fragmentary to be of use. So for the moment, all of our taping sessions are staged for the camera.

As a practised Balanchine watcher, I could more or less trust my own instincts as to the content of the tapes. On the technical side however I started from ground zero. I originally thought, in the manner of company rehearsal tapes, it would be sufficient to set up a videocamera in the front of the room, make sure everybody was in the picture, and shoot away. Not so! We first had to decide what kind of equipment to use. Since the tapes have been deposited in libraries and are, we hope, destined for a long life, we invested in broadcast-quality equipment, not because we will ever broadcast – we do not have the rights, among other things – but for better quality and durability. In the beginning, much conscientious consultation led us to Alan Lewis, Director of Sound and Video for the National Archives in Washington, among other people, who assured us that the only truly durable medium was 35-millimeter black-and-white film (it would withstand World War III, he said). This was obviously impractical for a number of reasons (notably cost and flexibility) and we eventually decided on Beta tape (the same as is used in network TV broadcasting), with the notion of upgrading to digital when the market sorted itself out. We have now switched to digital in the editing process, and I assume we will digitise early masters as the technology becomes more affordable and more uniform. There were many other considerations, chief among them how to shoot. The wide-angle 'record' approach would not give sufficient authority to the coaching figure or sufficient interest to the tape as a whole, yet we were certainly not about to go in for a lot of close-ups that cut off the feet! No distortion of the choreography was to be allowed. So the camera is on wheels and can zoom in and pull back with ease; no trick angles, but some variety.

A problem that I did not anticipate was that of sound. On record tapes, where the microphone is attached to or is part of the camera, verbal discourse can be unintelligible; we found we needed more specialised equipment. However miking the dancers individually proved impossible. Most complained that body mikes stuck out in the wrong places or constricted their movements, and even if that hurdle were to be overcome, we had to face the fact that dancers' sweat can cause short circuits (we have it on good authority that the most effective insulation against this problem is a condom, but we cannot say we know this from experience). So at the moment we are using a body mike for the coach and a boom (shotgun) mike to follow the dancers around – for we want them, too, to be a part of the dialogue. Although we have lights, we keep them as low as possible; I believe one of the reasons we have achieved such relative spontaneity in the tapes is that the dancers do not have a lot of hot lights shining in their faces.

About the dancers: Although we have had wonderful co-operation from such outstanding artists as Nikolaj Hübbe, Damian Woetzel, Judith Fugate, Peter Boal, Wendy Whelan and others from the New York City Ballet, I am eager that the project not be seen as orientated exclusively towards New York, since we know that there are dancers around the world who are accomplished Balanchine performers. I would like to celebrate and acknowledge this by actively seeking other venues and companies, as compatible with the wishes of the coaches (many of whom, however, would rather be in New York). Thus we have also done shoots in London, Cannes, Texas, Pittsburgh, Seattle, Kansas City and Miami. I might add that scheduling dancers, which I thought would be a simple matter – there are so many dancers, after all – has turned out to be one of our biggest nightmares. They are either too busy rehearsing and perform- ing, on layoff and 'out of shape,' or on gigs – that is, when they are not injured. One dancer told me her feet had become too tender for virtuoso parts just two weeks after her season ended. Impossible!

So we come to the stage that I blissfully lived most of my life without a suspicion of its existence – video-editing. I will not go into the labori- ousness of the process, but will merely mention that we decided to get into editing – which is both expensive and time-consuming – because we felt that dumping, say, ten hours of raw footage into a library was indul- gent, and that nobody, except perhaps a lone doctoral student, would ever watch the tapes! We also wanted to protect the artists – not to immortalise mistakes and 'off' moments and also not to preserve chore- ography wrongly executed. (This happened often when the dancers were learning the parts from scratch; if something were performed to the wrong music or off the beat, it seemed pointless, if not downright mis- leading, to leave it in.) This means however that Dame Alicia's or Maria Tallchief's vision is filtered through my eye – and that of my expert editor Virginia Brooks – so I cannot say it is presented 100% without comment, much as I would like to. Throughout the editing process, preserving the integrity of the choreography is the uppermost priority. To give you an idea of the number of decisions that have to be made, for the Markova project, we shot seven hours of tape to record a three minute variation. This was edited down to 116 minutes including interviews. Leaving Markova on the cutting room floor can be a wrenching experience.

The Foundation has now completed the editing of fourteen tapes and these have been deposited in the Dance Division of the New York Public Library for the Performing Arts. We have embarked on a project to dis- seminate copies at cost to research libraries worldwide, where they are available for on-site viewing on a nonrestrictive basis – a pioneering exercise, I believe, in making 'unique' material available in more than one location. We do not have the right to sell them; one of our earliest decisions was not to travel the commercial route. Firstly I do not think there is that much demand for these tapes, but, even more importantly, we did not want to take the time to negotiate commercial rights. We wanted to get these octogenarians on tape while they were still able to tell the tale, and that has been the motivation behind virtually all our thinking.

So, other than providing me with an enthralling personal experience, why are we doing these tapes? Some of the answers are too obvious to need mentioning, but here are some others that emerged more slowly, yielding results that I did not anticipate at the beginning:

We have some of Balanchine's matchless interpreters reflecting on roles he created on them, which undoubtedly provided some of the most meaningful moments of their lives. At the same time we are giving a platform to some of our older dancers, our 'national treasures', too often shockingly neglected in their post-performance years.

Through the participation of several generations of Balanchine dancers, we are able gain an unparalleled sense of the evolution of 'Balanchine style' – and evolve it did.

We are producing a new tool for approaching and analysing Balanchine's work. Although we know we are only getting someone else's ideas about what Balanchine thought and can never truly penetrate his creative process, we may gain insight into why he did certain things, or at least raise new questions.

It is well known that Balanchine said little in rehearsals; he demonstrated what he wanted very tellingly, then let the dancer find his own way. So we will probably not uncover verbal pearls of wisdom with these tapes. Balanchine inhabited a world where words were less important than some other things. Lincoln Kirstein once wrote that 'only a dancer dancing can say for him, what he says to them' (*Choreography by George Balanchine*, 1984: 14). With these tapes I believe and hope in some small way we are talking Balanchine's language.

References

Choreography by George Balanchine: A Catalogue of Works, (1984), New York: Viking, p. 14

The George Balanchine Foundation Video Archives
Choreography by George Balanchine

• *indicates master tape in the New York Public Library for the Performing Arts*

Archive of lost choreography

Dame Alicia Markova recreating excerpts from *Le Chant du Rossignol* •
[Nightingale variation; excerpts from pas de deux of Nightingale and
Death]

Music:	Igor Stravinsky
Dancer:	Iohna Loots [Royal Ballet School]
Advisors:	Millicent Hodson, Kenneth Archer
Taped:	January 30-February 3, 1995, London; 116 minutes

Frederic Franklin recreating a male solo from *Raymonda* (1946) •

Music:	Alexander Glazounov
Dancer:	Nikolaj Hübbe [New York City Ballet]
Interviewer:	Nancy Reynolds
Taped:	May 19, 1997, New York City; 55 minutes

Frederic Franklin recreating excerpts from *Mozartiana* (1945), with
Sonja Tyven and Robert Lindgren

Music:	Peter Ilyitch Tschaikovsky
Dancers:	Lilyan Vigo [Southern Ballet Theatre], James Fayette [New York City Ballet], students from North Carolina School of the Arts
Interviewer:	Nancy Reynolds
Taped:	September 9-24, 1996, Winston-Salem, North Carolina; 68 minutes

Frederic Franklin recreating two pas de deux from *Le Baiser de la Fée*
(1940), with Maria Tallchief and Vida Brown [2 tapes] •

Music:	Igor Stravinsky
Dancers:	Nichol Hlinka, Nikolaj Hübbe, Lourdes Lopez [New York City Ballet]

Interviewer: Jack Anderson
Taped: October 21 and November 18, 1996, January 29, 1997, New
             York City; 80 minutes; 101 minutes

Frederic Franklin recreating female solos from *Raymonda* (1946), with
later Balanchine variations to the same music from *Pas de Dix,
Raymonda Variations,* and *Cortège Hongrois*

Music: Alexander Glazounov
Dancers: Peter Boal, corps members of New York City Ballet
Interviewer: Mindy Aloff
Taped: September 13-14, 1998, New York City; 90 minutes

Frederic Franklin recreating two pas de deux and Stanley Zompakos
recreating the Gigue from *Mozartiana* (1945)

Music: Peter Ilyitch Tschaikovsky
Dancers: Julie Kent [American Ballet Theater], Nikolaj Hübbe [New
             York City Ballet], Christopher Barksdale [Kansas City Ballet]
Interviewer: Nancy Reynolds
Taped: January 24, 2000, New York City, and May 5, 2000, Kansas
             City *[to be edited]*

Todd Bolender recreating *Renard*

Music: Igor Stravinsky
Dancers: Christopher Barksdale, Andrew Carr, Sean Duus, Denise
             Small [Kansas City Ballet]
Interviewer: Nancy Reynolds
Taped: May 4-5, 2000, Kansas City *[to be edited]*

Interpreters Archive

Maria Tallchief coaching excerpts from *Firebird* and *Orpheus* [Firebird
Berceuse; Eurydice's solo] •

Music: Igor Stravinsky
Dancer: Heléne Alexopoulos [New York City Ballet]
Interviewers: Arlene Croce, Nancy Reynolds
Taped: June 27, 1995, New York City; 82 minutes

Maria Tallchief coaching ballerina variation, 1st movement, from
Symphony in C •

Music: Georges Bizet
Dancer: Jennie Somogyi [New York City Ballet]
Interviewers:Arlene Croce, Nancy Reynolds
Taped: June 28, 1995, New York City; 77 minutes

Maria Tallchief coaching excerpts from *Pas de Dix* [ballerina variation;
excerpt from finale] •

Music: Alexander Glazounov
Dancer: Jennie Somogyi [New York City Ballet]
Interviewers:Arlene Croce, Nancy Reynolds
Taped: June 28, 1995, New York City; 86 minutes

Maria Tallchief coaching excerpts from George Balanchine's *The
Nutcracker* • [Sugar Plum Fairy variation (partial); pas de deux]

Music: Peter Ilyitch Tschaikovsky
Dancers: Jennie Somogyi, Wendy Whelan, Damian Woetzel [New York
             City Ballet]
Interviewers:Arlene Croce, Francis Mason, Nancy Reynolds
Taped: June 28, 1995, and April 15, 1996, New York City; 110
             minutes

Maria Tallchief coaching the pas de deux from *Scotch Symphony* •

Music: Felix Mendelssohn
Dancers: Judith Fugate, Peter Boal [New York City Ballet]
Interviewers:Francis Mason, Nancy Reynolds
Taped: April 14-15, 1996, New York City; 109 minutes

Maria Tallchief coaching 'Sanguinic' variation from *The Four
Temperaments* and Sylvia: Pas de Deux [ballerina solo] •

Music: Paul Hindemith, Léo Delibes
Dancers: Wendy Whelan, Damian Woetzel, Judith Fugate [New York
             City Ballet]
Interviewers: Francis Mason, Nancy Reynolds
Taped: April 14-15, 1996, New York City; 112 minutes

Patricia Wilde coaching excerpts from *Raymonda Variations* [2 ballerina variations; pas de deux] •

Music: Alexander Glazounov
Dancers: Laura Desiree, Blythe Turner, Stanko Milov [Pittsburgh Ballet Theatre]
Interviewer: Nancy Goldner
Taped: May 23-24, 1996, Pittsburgh; 120 minutes

Patricia Wilde coaching excerpts from *Square Danc*e [pas de deux from 1st movement; excerpts from 'girls dance'; finale] •

Music: Antonio Vivaldi, Arcangelo Corelli
Dancers: Laura Desiree, Alexander Nagiba [Pittsburgh Ballet Theatre]
Interviewer: Nancy Goldner
Taped: May 24, 1996, Pittsburgh; 70 minutes

Marie-Jeanne coaching *Concerto Barocco*, with John Taras, Suki Schorer, and Merrill Ashley •

Music: Johann Sebastian Bach
Dancers: Students from School of American Ballet
Interviewers: Stephanie Jordan, Nancy Reynolds
Taped: June 16-17, 1996, New York City; 116 minutes

Maria Tallchief coaching excerpts from *Apollo, Firebird,* and *Swan Lake,* with Paul Mejia [2 tapes]

Music: Igor Stravinsky, Peter Ilyitch Tschaikovsky
Dancers: Maria Terezia Balogh, Maria Thomas, Todd Edson, Michael Clark [Fort Worth Dallas Ballet]
Interviewer: Nancy Goldner
Taped: May 31-June 1, 1997, Fort Worth, Texas; 101 minutes; 107 minutes

Alicia Alonso coaching excerpts from *Theme and Variations* •

Music: Peter Ilyitch Tschaikovsky
Dancers: Paloma Herrera, Angel Corella [American Ballet Theatre]
Interviewer: Doris Hering
Taped: January 29-30, 1998, New York City; 86 minutes

Todd Bolender coaching 'Phlegmatic' variation from *The Four Temperaments*

Music: Paul Hindemith
Dancers: Albert Evans [New York City Ballet], with Christopher
             Barksdale [Kansas City Ballet]
Interviewer: Robert Greskovic
Taped: September 15, 1997, New York City; 113 minutes

Maria Tallchief coaching excerpts from *Pas de Dix* and *Allegro Brillante*
Marjorie Tallchief coaching a variation from *Pas de Trois* (Minkus)

Music: Alexander Glazounov, Peter Ilyitch Tschaikovsky, Léon
             Minkus
Dancers: Iliana Lopez, Franklin Gamero, Deanna Seay, Mikhail
             Nikitine, Melanie Atkins [Miami City Ballet]
Interviewer: Jordan Levin
Taped: January 18-19, 1999, Miami Beach, Florida *[to be edited]*

Allegra Kent coaching excerpts from *Bugaku* and *La Sonnambula*

Music: Toshiro Mayuzumi, Vittorio Rieti (after Bellini)
Dancers: Janie Taylor, Albert Evans, Peter Boal [New York City Ballet]
Interviewer: Robert Gottlieb
Taped: October 17-18, 1999 *[to be edited]*

Melissa Hayden coaching excerpts from *Stars and Stripes* and *Donizetti Variations*

Music: John Philip Sousa (arr. Hershy Kay), Gaetano Donizetti
Dancers: Gillian Murphy [American Ballet Theater], Charles Askegard,
             Peter Boal [New York City Ballet]
Interviewer: Nancy Reynolds
Taped: November 16-17 and 22-23, 1999, New York City *[to be
             edited]*

Melissa Hayden coaching excerpts from *Episodes* and *Agon*

Music: Anton Webern, Igor Stravinsky
Dancers: Lisa Apple, Jeff Stanton, Louise Nadeau, Oleg Gorboulev,
             Christophe Maraval [Pacific Northwest Ballet]

Interviewer: Francia Russell
Taped: April 1-2, 2000 *[to be edited]*

Karen von Aroldingen coaching excerpts from *Davidsbündertänze*

Music: Robert Schumann
Dancers: Charles Askegard, Jenifer Ringer [New York City Ballet]
Interviewer: Anna Kisselgoff
Taped: October 29–30, 2000, New York City *[to be edited]*

Rosella Hightower and Marina Eglevsky coaching *Pas de Trois* (Minkus)

Music: Léon Minkus
Dancers: Eugénie Andrin, Yuka Omori [École Supérieure de Danse de
                Cannes], Peter Lewton [formerly Les Ballets de Monte-Carlo]
Interviewer: Nancy Reynolds
Taped: November 4–5, Cannes, France *[to be edited]*

Is Authenticity to be Had?

Ann Hutchinson Guest

Preservation is concerned both with the recording of a dance work and also with the production, the bringing to life from that recording. Concerning the latter, I would like first to consider the use of terminology.

1. Revival of Past Works

I use the term 'revival' when someone brings to life a choreographic work which has been recorded in movement notation, comparable to a musician bringing a music composition to life from the notated music score.

2. Reproduction

This would seem an appropriate term for works reproduced from film/video. Can the viewer separate the structure of the piece, the choreographic work, from the performance? The 'learner' too readily takes on the mannerisms and expression of the performers seen on screen. There is not the accuracy of the notated score nor the leeway for personal interpretation which the notated form allows.

3. Reconstruction

Constructing a work anew from all available sources of information, aiming for the result to be as close as possible to the original. Millicent Hodson and Kenneth Archer's *Le Sacre du printemps* and *Jeux*, for example, fall into this category. The term 'reconstitution' might also be appropriate here.

4. Re-creation

This term is suitable for a work created on the general story or basic idea of a ballet, now lost. Dolin's *Pas de quatre* and Joffrey's *Pas des déesses* are good examples; they re-created the choreography using the original music and idea.

5. Restaging

What does 'staging a dance work' mean? Arranging the *mise-en-scène* as in the court scenes in *Swan Lake*? Or does it mean putting it on stage, producing it? This term is used but the meaning is not clearly defined.

6. Reworked

If choreography is reworked, is it by the choreographer or by some other person? This difference needs to be indicated clearly.

Programme Credits

The choice of term to use for the programme credit is of vital importance. A truly authentic work is that notated by the choreographer him or herself. When the choreographer is deceased, the most authentic score is that written in collaboration with the choreographer. Revivals from such scores can still be called 'Choreography by X'. When versions are handed down by memory, or pieced together, at what point can they no longer be fully attributed to the initial choreographer? When should the wording become 'Based on the choreography of X?' The programme note must be very clear on the attribution. For example, Nijinsky's *Jeux* should be listed as 'Choreography by Millicent Hodson based on the existing evidence of Nijinsky's original ballet' – a mouthful, but honest. The memory-based versions of Nijinsky's *L'Après-midi d'un faune* should have a statement such as 'Memory-based version derived from Nijinsky's original ballet', or in other instances it might be 'Choreography by X inspired by Nijinsky's original', and so on, to fit the particular situation.

Revival of Past Works

My own experience in reviving works of the past has included the following:
1. Fanny Elssler's *Cachucha*,
   recorded by F.A. Zorn in his notation system.
   Lack of details in the original stick-figure notation resulted in the need to create transitions and to add style. For my revival I turned to a Spanish dance expert to check the style, particularly the arms; in certain places I could not believe that Elssler held her arms static for eight measures.
2. Saint-Léon's 'Pas de six' from *La Vivandière*, recorded in his own notation.

Saint-Léon was adept in his system; he gave much detail but was not a trained notator. He apparently analysed the steps in slow motion, thus providing detailed leg gestures impossible to perform at the speed required by the music. This ballet has proved to be technically difficult for today's dancers; they need training in what is now known as the 'Bournonville style', a style more familiar to those trained in the Cecchetti method, for example, in performing the undercurve *chassé* step.

3. Nijinsky's *L'Après-midi d'un faune*, recorded in his own notation system.. Nijinsky provided very specific detail. Dancers have difficulty coping with the exact, spare and very self-contained movement. Once the framework is mastered, the inner meaning, the motivation has to be discovered to produce the subtle expressiveness in the unfolding of the action.

Two questions arise:

Modifications. For revivals an important question is: can the original work be brought to life *without modification* and be fully appreciated by today's audiences? Yes, if we go by the example of the Joffrey Ballet and the Sadler's Wells Royal Ballet's productions of *La Vivandière*, both of which were well received and relished for their simplicity and clarity. Can today's dance artists rise to the challenge of finding their own interpretation without changing any of the 'notes'? Can they achieve the dance equivalent of Mitsuko Uchida's very personal and deep rendition of Mozart's Piano Sonata in D (KV311)? To what extent should a historical or 'period' piece be 'updated' to meet the tastes of present-day audiences? To what extent is imposing one's own ideas and preferences considered artistic licence and hence acceptable? For example there is the work of Pierre Lacotte and Dinna Björn, both of whom use their researches into old notation scores as points of departure. Is this freer approach made clear in the programme credits?

Time is the enemy. Meticulous research into old sources requires time. I have been fortunate; I have had no pressure and I have had students on hand with whom to work. Inadequate rehearsal time has in the past been the reason for simplifying floor plans and eliminating movements in canon, as had happened to one of Balanchine's ballets. If difficult movements are encountered, do dancers take up the challenge? Do they find extra time to practise on their own? Too often ballerinas feel they have the right to modify the material to suit themselves – the easy way out. In

Naples, Eric Vu An took for granted that I would allow him to improve on Nijinsky's choreography for *Faune*. No sir!

Before I go on to question 2, I would like to discuss excerpts of the same passages from two different productions, first of the *Pas de six* from *La Vivandière*, then from Nijinsky's ballet *L'Après-midi d'un faune*. The *Pas de six* productions were both derived from the same source; the notation score written by the choreographer himself, Arthur Saint-Léon. The first is from my production of this ballet for the Zürich Opera company, the second from the production by Pierre Lacotte for the Kirov Ballet. Apart from the obvious differences in style, the following points of divergence in the latter version should be observed:

The first *Pas de cinq*
In my production, the circular patterns require the two end dancers first to make a complete circle around the inner girl before retracing the circle with backward steps; later each girl circles around her partner while still facing front. In contrast to this the Kirov dancers turn around themselves in both of these passages. At the conclusion of this section the travelling turning steps and manner of their exit are different.

Fanny's Solo into the Second *Pas de cinq*
As she progresses across the front of the stage with delicate steps on pointe, accompanied by arm gestures opening toward the audience, her footwork describes small semi-circles. In contrast the Kirov dancer performs *enchaîné* turns in uneven timing on a straight path. Her *port de bras* is different as is her footwork in the change into repeating the passage to the other side. At the conclusion of her solo, Arthur enters with the four corps girls. This entrance is markedly different; Saint-Léon notated the entrance as coming from the upstage right corner, the dancers moving in line with their backs to the audience. This stage placement makes the subsequent floor plans follow logically. In the Kirov version the five dancers enter from upstage left facing the audience, so the directions of their subsequent travelling had to be altered. How all six dancers get into one file in centre stage is different as are their alignments as they face different directions. An important moment, quite clear in Saint-Léon's floor plan, is the circling *bourrée* around the male dancer and the pose taken – if briefly – by all six dancers prior to the *adage*. The circle around the male dancer and the ending pose are both missing in the Kirov version.

Adage pas de deux
Saint-Léon showed only very simple *ports de bras* during this section; the Kirov ballerina employs flowery arm gestures. The corps has only a few movements to perform, being still most of the time. However they respond to the moment when Fanny performs a low *chassé* step into fourth *plié* in relationship to them. The movements of the Kirov corps are more elaborate and the relationship to Fanny is lacking, indeed they perform an *arabesque* facing away from her at one point. Fanny's backward steps walking around behind Arthur toward the end of this *adage* provide an intimate and unusual lead into the swivel on pointe with her leg in second *en dedans* and then *en dehors*. The Kirov lead into this turn in second is merely a 'getting there' link. The movements into the final pose and the height of Fanny's *arabesque* are different; Saint-Léon wrote an upright *arabesque* for Fanny so that her leg does not cover her partner's face. It is sad that the present-day desire for exaggeration seems to demand high extensions and a *penché* torso.

Do these differences result from lack of time to study the original score in depth and carefully work out the movements? Was it lack of time that prevented rehearsing the more intricate manoeuvres? Some of the most charming moments in the ballet require patient rehearsing.

In the case of Nijinsky's *L'Après-midi d'un faune*, my production is based on the ballet as Nijinsky himself wrote it down. Three excerpts from his version are compared with the same sequences in the memory-based version as danced at the Paris Opéra with Charles Jude as the faun.

The Opening Section on the Rock; Entrance of the Nymphs
Nijinsky's choreography is simple, the mood is contemplative, the faun is lying dreamily on the rock. Twice the faun interrupts what he is doing to look back into the wings from where the nymphs come as though he is anticipating their arrival. He merely looks at one bunch of grapes and then another. In contrast, the memory-based version shows a restless faun taking jerky poses; he make little use of the flute, and 'devours' the grapes. Throughout the ballet the greatest differences between Nijinsky's and other versions lie in the actions of the supporting nymphs; when and how they enter and what they do. Nijinsky provides a logical development and gives the nymphs individuality. The first three nymphs are each different; after they enter they have a little dialogue before continuing to their places. The leading nymph enters when four of her attendants

are in place. The last two nymphs enter late, their heads bowed in shame. The leading nymph watches them move into place before she begins to unveil. These meaningful details, 'human' though abstractly couched in the ballet, are missing in the memory-based version.

The Encounter; the Duet
Nijinsky's idea was that encountering the faun is a surprise for the leading nymph; she has not seen him until that moment. As the faun's feelings are aroused he paws the ground before taking off for his one big leap. Memory versions passed on the idea that the nymph has already seen the faun and walks up to him; he responds with an overhead 'chop' of his arms near her head. Before his big leap he reacts to her presence with high prancing steps and a backward low aggressive preparation. Nijinsky wrote no contact between the faun and the leading nymph except for the one unexpected and momentary elbow link. Aware that the other nymphs have entered and are observing, the leading nymph quickly withdraws her arm and leaves. The nymphs then follow her, exiting with individual movements. The memory version provides the faun with arm positions that enclose the leading nymph; the elbow link is slow and readily entered into. There is no entrance of the other nymphs.

Return to the Rock
The last of the nymphs having gone, the faun, absorbed in the leading nymph's dress, walks slowly, as though in another world, directly back to the rock. During his ascent he is focussed on the dress. Kneeling at the top, he takes one last look back toward the wings, lifts the dress to smell it, then lays it down and lies on it. The memory version incorporates a to-and-fro walk with exaggerated heel-first steps. Walking up the steps includes a *relevé* on each step. Accents in the music are echoed by staccato arm movements; there is no savouring the scent of the dress. The final moments include a fairly explicit spasm.

These are only a few of the very noticeable differences. Is it surprising that memory cannot be relied on? When Nijinsky returned to the Diaghilev company in 1916 he refused to dance in *Faune* because it had become so changed, and 1916 was only four years after its creation. Subsequently, as the details of the supporting nymphs' movements became lost and their parts curtailed and stereotyped, the need must have been felt to augment and overemphasise the movements of the two leading rôles. The quality and overall expression of the ballet suffered accordingly.

Standards

What do academic standards demand in a serious revival of a choreographic work? What are we giving the audience? Does the younger generation know how much they are being shortchanged? Do they believe that what they are seeing is *it*? The authentic work? Is authenticity being given first consideration? It is significant that the Balanchine Foundation's policy appears to be that, as long as there are dancers around who performed in the work, in other words, had the physical experience, there is no need to refer to the Labanotation score. There have been admissions by these custodians that memory is failing. Where does the responsibility lie? Who cares? The coinage of our dance heritage is getting sadly debased!

Dance historians! The past is now! I call on you to rest awhile from labours focussed on past centuries and concentrate now on preserving the present for the future.

Issues of Authenticity and Identity in the Restaging of Paul Taylor's *Airs*

Angela Kane

In this paper, I shall first identify some general issues in the restaging of works by the American choreographer, Paul Taylor. Then, by focusing on one of his dances, *Airs* (1978), I aim to demonstrate how these issues impinge upon and are manifest in subsequent performances.

Before addressing the work of Paul Taylor specifically, it is important to align the political and aesthetic significance of restaging his choreography alongside such general issues as authenticity and identity – and inevitably, this has prompted an initial consideration of terminology.

At a previous conference, 'Dance ReConstructed', held at Rutgers University in 1992,[1] the distinctiveness and/or synonymy of the terms 'revival', 'reconstruction' and 'restaging' emerged as an issue in itself. During a keynote panel, Susan Manning proposed that: 'when we use the term "revival", we mean work where there is a major reliance on oral kinesthetic transmission. ...When we use [the term] reconstruction, we usually mean primary reliance on non-oral, non-kinesthetic sources, either a notated score or visual documentation.' (Palfrey, 1993: 15)

A similar distinction of terms has been made between the subsequent staging of works which have survived in repertory and the retrieval of 'lost' works from an earlier period. However, if we draw upon recent expositions in the areas of New History and Early Music which have challenged the traditional paradigm of the past as an actual – and, therefore, retrievable – reality, it could be argued that *any* subsequent staging is a new version – and thus a contemporary *con*struction, shaped by present-day epistemology and taste. Therefore, there is a crucial distinction to be made between a historically-accurate performance and an authentic performance which reflects late twentieth-century sensibilities.

In this paper, the terms 'revival' and 'restaging' will be used to differentiate between new versions of Taylor's choreography as performed by his own group of dancers (that is, a revival) and restagings for other companies. Since the works selected by these other companies have been exclusively works which have survived continuously in Taylor's own repertory, the issue of authenticity is of secondary importance to that of identity.

This issue of identity raises the question of the 'dance text'. Although the musicologist and performer Richard Taruskin distinguishes the text of a musical work – the physical, objectified score – from the 'act' of performance,[2] I would argue that the notation score is only one of many texts which contribute to our reading of dances. Moreover, there is a dialectical relationship between first and subsequent performances of a dance work and, thus, there will be multiple texts which originate in and are determined by performance.

The idea that the dance text is embodied in performance is particularly relevant to Taylor's choreography. Since 1992 his company has been involved in a Repertory Preservation Project, funded in part by a grant of $850,000 from the National Endowment for the Arts. The aim of this project has been to document over 30 of Taylor's dances on film and in notation,[3] and to establish an archive for these multiple texts, along with other primary sources such as transcripts of interviews with former dancers and collaborators, newspaper clippings and Taylor's personal correspondence and yearbooks.

A major part of the project, however, has been to 're-create and restore the works in danger of being lost'[4] and this has been achieved through revivals by Taylor's present group of dancers and through the founding of a second, smaller company, Taylor 2.

Of equal significance is Taylor's own view of the past and of repertory. Several of his works created during the last decade reveal an historical awareness. The most overt 'period' pieces are the trilogy *Company B* (1991), *Field of Grass* (1993) and *Funny Papers* (1995)[5], and the recent *Eventide* (1997). Another historical dimension can be seen in *Kith and Kin* (1987), which features contrasting dances for a family spanning three generations. Yet other references to the past are evident in *Danbury Mix* (1988) and *Fact & Fancy* (1991), where Taylor makes autobiographical references in both works to earlier choreography. Also, even prior to the Repertory Preservation Project, Taylor was actively involved in reconstructing his original solo in George Balanchine's *Episodes* (1959) and the solo, *Epic*, from his 1957 concert, *Seven New Dances*.

Notwithstanding these examples, Taylor's attitude to preserving earlier work has to be seen within the context of his current choreographic concerns. As a living – and still prolific – choreographer, his main interest is in the creative process rather than as curator of already complete works. As he explains:

> I do revivals every year. I bring something back that we haven't done for a long time. I'm not wild about seeing any of them, really, because I'm always more interested in whatever the new baby is. It's just more alive. A revival – I feel they're very important – we do a lot of them... because I think it should be interesting to view these older works alongside newer pieces. It's like a retrospective, you can see where things came from or started or were dropped. (Philip, 1987: 146)

Taylor's concept of repertory as retrospective was evident in his 1997 New York season from 25 February to 9 March at City Centre, New York City. The two-week season included three revivals; *Polaris* (1976), *Dust* (1977) and *Brandenburgs* (1988), the latter with redesigned costumes, together with two new works, *Prime Numbers* and *Eventide*. Taylor went on to create another new work, *Piazzolla Caldera*, for the American Dance Festival in June 1997.

When considering the identity of a dance work, an important distinction needs to be made between revivals by Taylor's company, re-created under his direction, and restagings for other companies. Many of his works have been staged for both modern dance and ballet companies, in America and abroad. They have been staged in different locations, at a particular point in time – and often with two or more companies performing the same work concurrently. Moreover, when non-Taylor dancers perform his choreography, they will inevitably bring different training and performance styles to the work.

The first of Taylor's work to be staged for another company was *Aureole*, performed by the Royal Danish Ballet in 1968. As with most subsequent stagings of his choreography, economics rather than aesthetics persuaded him to licence his work to other companies. As he writes in his autobiography, *Private Domain*:

> Selling *Aureole* meant risking child abuse. But the Royal Danish Ballet wasn't to get exclusive rights and, with luck, might keep it in its rep. for only one season... So, since we needed the income, I'd reluctantly gone along with the plan. (Taylor, 1987: 300–1)

Although this first restaging of Taylor's work was the result of economic pragmatism, it implicitly involved an important aesthetic issue, that of 'otherness'. For the first time, the identity and ownership of *Aureole* were called into question and, by Taylor's own admission: 'As aped by the Danes, the steps come out looking like those of an ostrich with lumbago.' (ibid.: 301)

> All of them are trying to break second-nature ballet habits and are floundering in a sea of ballet don'ts. (ibid.: 302)

Ironically, since the early 1960s – and most noticeably since the creation of *Aureole* in 1962 – several critics have referred to Taylor's choreography as classical because of the formal, virtuosic elements in works such as *Aureole*, *Airs*, *Arden Court* (1981) and *Mercuric Tidings* (1982). Yet he has resisted such classification: 'I know that people keep saying some of my recent work is balletic… If you look at some of the steps, we might share the occasional *sauté*, but they see it as ballet because of an overall lyrical feeling.' (Ulrich, 1988)

In another interview, he continued: 'I think people get lyricism and ballet mixed up together.' (Berman, 1988)

It is an important distinction. Although the shaping of the upper body and arms in some of Taylor's work is similar to classical ballet's *port de bras*, the degree of torso bend and torsion and the use of gravity undoubtedly are not. For example, the classical *écarté* position is extended to the extreme – often with the torso inclined from the vertical – and this can be seen most clearly in the fifth movement adagio for the four women in *Airs*. Also, in Taylor's work, transference of body weight is accomplished through the undercurve. Again this is evident in the opening section of the quartet when the women, performing as two pairs in canon on the upstage-right/downstage-left diagonal, slide first into fourth position *plié* and then step *croisé* into fourth *relevé*. Significantly, the *plié* movement is initiated by a soft torso contraction and the *relevé* by a release.

From my own interviews with Taylor I know at first-hand how querulous he can be about the use of contraction in his work. Clearly, he wants to avoid any comparison with Martha Graham (in whose company he performed between 1955 and 1962) and I would argue that the Taylor contraction *is* different from Graham's. In his choreography, the contraction is seldom used as a dramatic statement in itself. More often, it initiates a sustained, larger movement of the whole torso, thus producing a concave body shape in which the shoulders and neck form part of the upper curve – unlike a Graham contraction where the upper and middle spine create a counter-tension.

The contraction and spiral are fundamental to Taylor's style and, together with a sense of weight and undercurve, they are the least understood movements in restagings of his work.

Another important aspect of Taylor's style is his musicality. He tends to focus on the larger musical structure of his accompaniment, often cross-phrasing several bars of music rather than following the detail of individual lines. This has proved particularly difficult for classical ballet dancers in works such as *Airs* because of their tendency not only to move in evenly-metred phrases but also to emphasise certain positions en route in order to correspond with the music's dominant accents.

Thus, identity in the restaging of Taylor's work is a question not of *what* is danced, but *how* it is danced.

At this point, I should like to mention another issue which has emerged as a result of restaging Taylor's work. Despite his dissatisfaction with the performance of *Aureole* by the Royal Danish Ballet, that experience did not deter him from licensing this work, and very soon others, to scores of dance companies. There has been a marked tendency for staging Taylor's plotless lyrical works such as *Aureole, Airs, Arden Court* and *Esplanade* (1975), and most particularly by classical ballet companies. In fact, until the success of *Company B* in the early 1990s, *Aureole* was the most popular work for restaging by other companies – and a majority of them ballet companies. Conversely, with the exception of *Speaking in Tongues* (1988), staged by the Paris Opéra and Teatro alla Scala, Milan and *Le Sacre du printemps (The Rehearsal)* (1980), staged by the Paris Opéra and the Maggio Musicale company in Florence, Taylor's dark, dramatic works have not had the same appeal. Furthermore, for many years now, works with an essentially 'Americana' theme such as *Big Bertha* (1970) and *From Sea to Shining Sea* (1965) have not been performed outside the United States, even by Taylor's own company.

This raises an important issue regarding the concept of the Taylor corpus. For example, works which have been included in the repertory of British companies – *Three Epitaphs* (1956), *Esplanade, Cloven Kingdom* (1976) and *Arden Court* by London Contemporary Dance Theatre, *Aureole* by the English National Ballet and *Airs* by both the Birmingham Royal Ballet and Rambert Dance Company – are indicative of the narrow range of Taylor's work which is seen on an international scale. In the case of Britain's perspective on Taylor, this is particularly significant because, although the Paul Taylor Dance Company performed here regularly between 1964 and 1973, there was then a considerable gap before the company returned to London again in 1989. Thus, for 16 years, certain aspects of the Taylor corpus – and of his continued creativity during this time – went unseen. I believe, too, that it is because relatively few of Taylor's works were seen on a regular basis in Britain that some writers – myself included – perpetuated the notion that Taylor's work can be divided too simplistically into 'dark' and 'light' categories and that his vocabulary is limited. And even though the Taylor company brought a wide range of its repertory to London in 1989 and again in 1991, there are still certain key works – such as *Polaris*, *Dust* and *Le Sacre de printemps (The Rehearsal)* – which have never been performed in this country.*

Different exposure to Taylor's work inevitably determines different conceptions of his corpus. Therefore it is important to point out that, despite the exemplary efforts being made to capture his choreography through the Repertory Preservation Project, it will be present-day preferences and practices which will shape future perceptions of the Taylor corpus – and, thus, any future concept of a Taylor canon.

I should like to end this paper with a quotation from George Orwell's *Nineteen Eighty-Four*: ' "Who controls the past," ran the Party slogan, "controls the future: who controls the present controls the past." ' (Orwell, 1990: 37).[6] It is a maxim which could be applied very appropriately to today's dance reconstructors, artists and scholars.

Notes

1. The conference was held at Rutgers University, New Brunswick, New Jersey on 16-17 October 1992.
2. For a fuller discussion of Taruskin's differentiation, see *Text and Act: Essays on Music and Performance* (1995), New York: Oxford University Press.
3. It is important to locate these works within the context of the complete Taylor corpus: he recently created his 100th work. Moreover, a majority of Taylor's dances have been documented in Labanotation.
4. *Repertory Preservation Project – The Case for Support*, p6. The main aims of the project were first made public in this report, prepared for the Paul Taylor Dance Company by C.W. Shaver and Company and dated 1 April 1993.
5. In 1996 Taylor combined these three works to create *The Wrecker's Ball* for television. Together, they form a chronological commentary on American

popular culture during the 1940s (*Company B*), 1950s (*Funny Papers*) and 1960s (*Field of Grass*).

6. I am indebted to Keith Jenkins for this quotation. It was his reference to Orwell's novel in *Re-thinking History* (1991) London: Routledge, p.18 which prompted me to re-read *Nineteen Eighty-Four* and to realise the important historical parallel in dance reconstruction.

References

Berman, J. (1988), 'Paul Taylor: Still Battling With Ballet', *New York Newsday*, 3 April

Manning, S. (1993), Conference Proceedings, 'Perspectives in Reconstruction', in *The Proceedings of 'Dance ReConstructed'* by Barbara Palfry with Claudia Gitelman and Patricia Mayer, eds. New Jersey: Rutgers, p. 15

Orwell, G. (1990), *Nineteen Eighty-Four*, London: Penguin Books, p. 37 (first published by Martin Secker & Warburg Ltd. in 1949)

Philip, R. (1987), 'Revivals – Wish Book of Danceworks We'd Like to See Again', *Dance magazine* Vol. 61 No. 6, p. 1469

Taylor, P. (1987), *Private Domain*, New York: Alfred A. Knopf, pp. 300-1

Ulrich, A. (1988), 'Taylor-made', *San Francisco Examiner*, 23 October

*Postscript

Le Sacre de printemps (The Rehearsal) was performed at the Sadler's Wells Theatre, London, in November 2000.

Freeze Frame or Fast Forward?

Notating Ashton's *La Fille mal gardée* using video
as a primary source

Michele Braban

This paper focuses on my experience of writing a Benesh notation score using video as a primary source. I shall put forward questions which arose in my own mind, but to which I must admit I have no firm solutions, and raise other side issues concerning professional responsibilities with regard to preserving the integrity of a dance work. In addition to addressing the problems of working from video as a notator, I hope my paper will illustrate that, to document a dance work truly, co-operation between a host of dance professionals is essential.

For a two-year period from 1990 I was engaged by the Royal Ballet on a part-time basis specifically to produce a master score for the Ashton classic, *La Fille mal gardée*. I was initially given two videos to work from – the most recent dress rehearsal video at the time and an archive video with Nadia Nerina and David Blair in the lead roles which dated back to 1960, the year in which the work was choreographed. In addition to this, I had access to the original notation score written in 1963 by Elphine Allen. The task before me was to write a master score of the original *Fille* as choreographed by Ashton in 1960 but also to note (on the opposite page perhaps) what was currently being danced by the Royal Ballet.

However, a short while after I began work on the project, I realised how massive a task this would be. I was being confronted with quite major differences between the original and current versions and realised that the process was going to be extremely time consuming. I began thinking... Somehow I needed to make the project financially viable for the Royal Ballet and yet produce a score that could be used efficiently in the rehearsal studio. After consultation with Grant Coyle, principal notator at the Royal Ballet, it was agreed that I should change my objective and write the current version as danced by the Royal Ballet, leaving the original score by Allen as a record of the original work.

Why was there a need to write another score when one already existed? As I have already said, Allen's score was written in 1963. This was at the very beginnings of the notation and naturally the system has evolved much during the intervening years. With the pressures of limited time available for company rehearsals, choreologists must be able to access scores quickly and efficiently and therefore an updated version of the score was desirable.

Although much of Allen's score was comprehensively written, some sections were lacking in information, particularly the group sections. This is not so surprising when one learns of the circumstances under which the score was written. I quote from a letter which I have received from Allen on her experience of notating *Fille*:

> I was asked to notate it when it was being taught to the Royal Ballet Touring Company and I can't remember if that was the end of 1962 or the beginning of 1963. I travelled around with them for a few weeks while it was being taught … [and] … certainly remember notating it in the dressing rooms between rehearsals and performances and even between acts. I have no idea how long I was able to work on it solely because I also did several other ballets while with them as well as the dancing. When I was back in London I was given permission to go to the basement workshop of someone who had all the films of the company dress rehearsals. Here I would view the film of the original dress rehearsal to check the differences between the two versions (some because of different size stages) … Have they given you a copy of that original film? I would love to see it again now to see just how much the ballet has changed over the years. It may actually have changed less in Australia than in London (when visiting artists come out they often say some of the solos are not the same now).

Which in fact brings me right back to one of the first points made, that a revised score was necessary because the current version as danced by the Royal Ballet was really quite different in places to the original.

When I began work on the project one of the first major differences I encountered concerned the timing of movements. For the 1960 video the piano accompaniment was in fact dubbed. However, possibly due to the technical capabilities of the equipment at the time, movement and music did not correspond. Thus with respect to timing, this video was of little use to me. I therefore had to rely on the recent dress rehearsal video which also caused problems. Not everyone dances full-out in dress rehearsals and maybe this was the first performance for the lead dancers. I struggled on for some time but realised I needed another source for comparative purposes. I was then given yet another video, this time the 1981 televised version with Lesley Collier in the lead role. This at least gave me a choice of two video versions and the original notated score. However, musical problems were still encountered which will be evident as we look at specific sections of the ballet.

Ribbon *Pas de Deux* – Act 1, Scene 1
Cat's Cradle – positions of the legs (repeated twice)

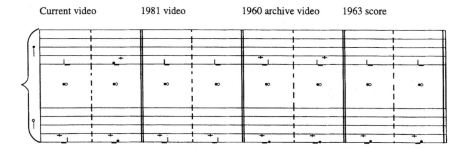

This example questions the leg position Ashton may have preferred in order to complement the Cat's Cradle ribbon position. Did he prefer an open or a crossed position, *tendu* in front or behind? It is interesting to note that the photograph, although not a reliable source on its own, shows an open *tendu* in front position for Lise which corresponds to the first Cat's Cradle position in the 1960 archive video. However, all other versions differ from this.

Nadia Nerina and David Blair: notation of the photograph published in *Frederick Ashton and his Ballets*, David Vaughan, 1977.

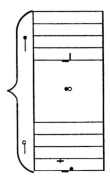

Bourrées over ribbon

1960 archive video	R L R L	kiss	R L R L
1963 original notation score	R L R	kiss	R L R
current + 1981 videos	R L R	kiss	L R L
1992 rehearsals	L R L R	*no* kiss	L R L R

I attended 35 hours of rehearsal during the time I was engaged with the Royal Ballet and, in this particular example, the rehearsal presented yet another version to those I had already identified. Because my task was to write the current version, the 1992 rehearsal version became *the* version in the current notation score. Obviously, whether there are four, or only three, *bourrées* has timing implications. What did Ashton want done with the phrasing? Furthermore, did he specify a kiss or was he more flexible?

High lift

(Counts)	1 – 8	1 – 8	1 – 8
1960 archive video	lift on 7, facing upstage	(2 x 1 – 8) turn on place, leg extends when facing *en face* (only travels upstage when lowering girl from lift)	
1963 original score	lift on 7, facing upstage	turn once, leg extends when facing *en face*	travel upstage turning twice
1981 video	lift on 8, facing upstage right corner	travel upstage, 4 turns, leg extends by end of 1st turn, approximately count 6	
current video	lift on 7, facing upstage left corner	turn once, leg extends by end of first turn, approximately counts 7, 8	travel upstage turning twice
1992 rehearsal			extend leg as boy travels upstage

As illustrated above there are many variations with respect to the timing and direction of the lift, the timing of the girl's leg extension, the number of turns for the boy and when he begins to travel.

Picnic *Pas de Trois* – Act 1, Scene 2
Position of Alain's arm

Quoting from *Frederick Ashton and His Ballets* by David Vaughan:

The *pas de trois* of Lise, Colas and Alain, in which the latter is blissfully unaware of his rival's presence, is a little like a comic version of the *pas de trois* of the Sylphide, James and Effie in Gsovsky's production of *La Sylphide* for the Ballets des Champs-Elysées; Alain is terribly conscious of his function as partner, thrusting his arm stiffly up at not quite the right angle to complement the line of her *arabesque*.

current + 1981 videos	Alain's arm in line with *arabesque* leg
1960 archive video	Alain's arm way out of line

The humour intended by Ashton comes into question here. In recent Royal Ballet versions the humour seems to come from the way the corps de ballet turn their heads sharply to follow the direction Alain's hand points towards. The humour in the archive video seems to come simply from Alain's arm gesture reflecting his rather gauche movements (the corps' heads do not turn to follow the arm direction).

Clog Dance – Act 1, Scene 2
Last walk upstage

1981 video	all on pointe
current video	Simone on 'pointe' (on tips of clogs), 3 girls on flat with one on pointe
1992 rehearsals	Simone on pointe, all girls on flat
but	
1960 archive video	all on pointe with girls heads tilting from side to side with each step
1963 original score	all on pointe confirming girls heads tilting

1963 score

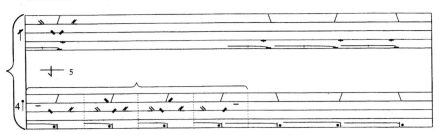

In addition to the question of whether the steps should be on pointe or flat, the humour intended here seems to have been lost with both the archive video and original score showing the heads tilting from side to side with each step upstage.

Spinning – Act 2
Pas de bourrée piqué section

Current video

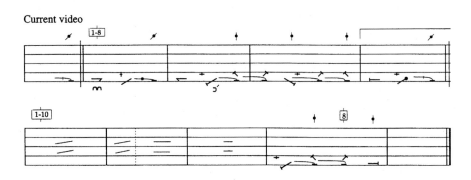

1984 Birmingham Royal Ballet

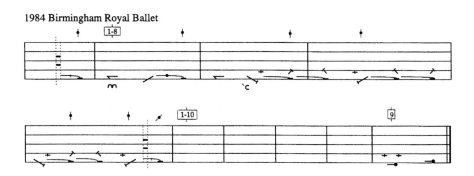

1984 Birmingham Royal Ballet alternative version

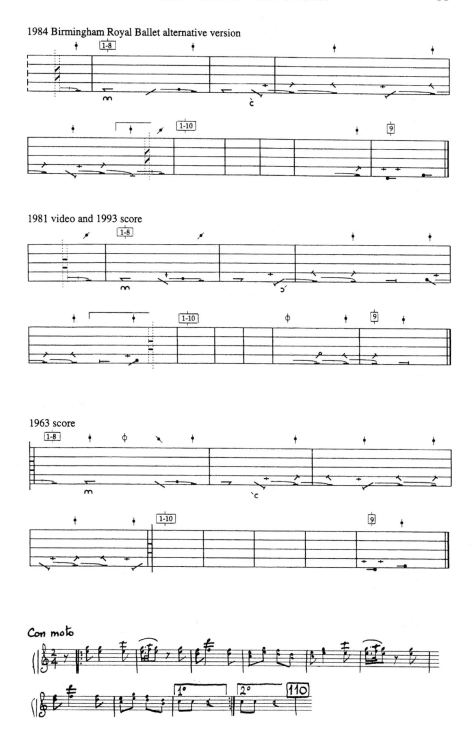

1981 video and 1993 score

1963 score

Con moto

	Step into 1st position	number of *bourrées*	final 5th position	repeat
current video	count & 1	2 then 3	count 8 &	opposite side
BRB 1984	count & 1	3 then 3	count 9, 10	same side
BRB 1984	count & 1	2$^{1/2}$ then 3	count 9, 10	opposite side
1981 video	count & 1	2 then 3	count 9 &	same side
1963 original score	count 1 &	3 then 3	count 9 &	same side
1960 archive video		4 then 4		

The above examples illustrate the extent to which each version differs with respect to the timing, the number of *pas de bourrée piqués* which in turn affects the phrasing, and whether the step is repeated on the same or opposite side. There is also a discrepancy as to whether the final position should be a closing into 5th on pointe or a *relevé* in 5th. On the presumption that Ashton intended to follow the musical phrasing, the step into 1st at the beginning of the phrase should perhaps be on 1 &, and the phrase should perhaps finish on 9 &, as recorded in the 1963 notation score.

Tambourine Dance – Act 2
Fly catching

(Counts)	2	&	3	&	4	5	6	7	&	8
1963 original score	let go	head	clap		watch	squash		point		look
1981 video			let go	head	clap	watch		squash	point	look
current video		let go	clap		watch		squash	point?		
1992 rehearsals			turn palm		let go	clap	watch	squash		stamp?

(1960 archive video – timing & movement unclear)

Again we see here many different versions for just one phrase of 8 counts. The timing of the clap should perhaps coincide with the musical accent on 3 as recorded in the original notation score. However, in the rehearsals attended for this section, it was 'clarified' as being on count 5.

The examples I have shown here are only an *indication* of the problems I faced with this project. For almost every sequence of movement in the ballet I was confronted with a variety of choices upon which I had to make a decision. It is clearly evident that video was not able to provide clear-cut solutions. Although some of my questions were answered through attending some rehearsals and by reference to the original notation score, many more remain unanswered.

It is for this reason that I question the validity of the score. Who can say that the choices I made were the right ones? I ask myself whether perhaps someone with more experience and knowledge of the Ashton style and his way of working would have been able to make more informed decisions than I was able. Putting this aside, I feel the best I can do is to state clearly at the beginning of the score the circumstances under which it was written so that other choreologists will be aware of the fact that it may not be the definitive version.

One of my main concerns throughout this project was the realisation that over 30 years of history seems to be have been lost. Many changes appear to have been made over the years but yet few of these changes have been added to the original score. I kept asking myself who made the changes, when were they made and for what reason. Allen commented in her letter :

> I do hope the Royal Ballet have not changed too many things in their recent productions as Ashton always wanted Fille to be taught in the original version even though he agreed to many variations for many different people.

This worried me throughout the project – what *was* the original version and what were the many variations which were agreed by Ashton? If he subsequently made changes over the years, as most choreographers tend to do, what were the circumstances behind the changes? Did he prefer the newer version or would he have preferred to retain the original movement if at all possible?

Although my task was to write the current version of *Fille,* I feel it was also my responsibility to retain as much of the original work and original intention of the choreographer as possible, but this was almost an impossible task after the event. I feel that the company for whom the work was made also has this responsibility to the choreographer to preserve the original work and, if the choreographer or others make changes to the work, then it is also their responsibility to keep a record of these. In turn the notator needs to be kept informed and it is our professional responsibility to note these changes accurately and to date them with reference to the circumstances. For instance, perhaps a change was made for one particular individual. This should therefore not become the new version for all casts. I am not suggesting that a dance work should be frozen in time. On the contrary, I believe dance should live and breathe, but surely we must be responsible for preserving the very essence of a choreographic work which makes that particular work the work of that particular choreographer.

If I had had the time I know that some of my questions concerning the work might perhaps have been answered through further research. I could have obtained further videos for reference, although perhaps this may not have been helpful as I may have ended up with yet more versions to add to the many I had to choose from already. I could have spoken to those involved with the production over the years, for instance, dancers, rehearsal staff, and perhaps the arranger of the music, John Lanchbery. However, the project had to be financially viable for the Royal Ballet and therefore time did not permit further research.

Returning to the title of this paper, 'Freeze Frame or Fast Forward', I have calculated that it has taken me eight and three quarter hours to master one minute of choreography compared to the Benesh Institute guidelines of six hours per minute. Therefore with respect to the time taken, I was well over target and yet had only produced a score of one version, the current version. I was constantly aware of the time factor and felt frustrated and concerned that decisions had to be made as quickly as possible but, should the project have taken longer to complete, the Royal Ballet may have been discouraged from undertaking similar projects in the future. Perhaps my only consolation has been the opportunity to share my experiences with a wider audience so as to encourage greater awareness of the complexities of documenting dance and the role all dance professionals can play in this process.

References

Vaughan, D. (1977), *Frederick Ashton and His Ballets*, London: A. & C. Black

10 bars from score of *La Fille mal gardée*, arr. Lanchbery, © Oxford University Press. Reproduced by permission.

Benesh Movement Notation examples – Choreography © Frederick Ashton, 1963

This paper was first presented to Benesh Institute members at the Institute's 1993 Congress.

The Preservation of the Ballets of Kurt Jooss

Clare Lidbury

This paper will examine the ways in which the works of Kurt Jooss are preserved and consider the effect of this preservation on contemporary performance.

At present Jooss's ballets are not revived or reconstructed or remade but 'staged' by Jooss's daughter, Anna Markard. She is a living document of the work: she uses Labanotation scores for reference together with her own notes, but, essentially, the ballets exist in her intellectual and physical memory waiting to be transferred to the dancers in front of her through physical demonstration and verbal descriptions of the movements and the emotional states of the characters. As Markard has said, 'I demonstrate, I talk, I sing, I scream ... I demonstrate every detail as well as I can so that a lot of the learning process is learning directly from me, learning rhythm, form and content' (1994: 67). In effect, the works are preserved both in her and by her.

The works are filtered through Markard's own dance experience, her understanding of the works and her many years' experience of staging them. Any discrepancies between her stagings and the early Labanotation scores or other people's memories of the works are accounted for by the work that Markard did with her father in the mid-1970s. Then the four extant works were defined and documented as Jooss wanted them preserved – thus they are not the works that he created in the 1930s but represent the subsequent revisions that Jooss made. Markard can now maintain that there are no versions of *The Green Table*, only *The Green Table* (and similarly that there are no versions of *The Big City, A Ball in Old Vienna* or *Pavane on the Death of an Infanta*).

There is much evidence to suggest that the works have changed considerably since the early Ballets Jooss days in costume and lighting design and in movement material, but not in music. Apart from the writing of a new score for *The Big City* by Alexandre Tansman in 1935, to take into account Jooss's specific requirements for the last scene (originally Jooss had used Tansman's *Sonatine Transatlantique*), and a brief flirtation with the orchestration of the piano scores in the 1940s (Hall, 1947: 205), the music for the extant ballets has remained unchanged since the mid-1930s.

Pictorial evidence shows changes in costume design reflecting, perhaps, developments in materials and dyes. If we look at *Pavane on the Death of an Infanta* (1929), we see that Leeder's costume designs capture the flavour of the period in which the ballet is set (late seventeenth century) and also a flavour of the time in which the ballet was created through the Schlemmer-influenced designs. The neck ruffs, hoops on the sleeves of the female courtiers and hooped pantaloons of the male courtiers, the wigs and hats and the plastic-like gores in the women's skirts remain. However, now the wigs are shorter, the hoops on the male costumes are much smaller, and the hats are a different shape. These changes are likely to have taken place over a period of time rather than as a single decision to change being made. (Changes in The Infanta's costume from its original, quite simple, three-coloured dress contrasting greatly with the courtiers' costumes, to one that is more striking in colour (greeny-yellow) and more formal, with its panniers similar to those of the female courtiers, were made consciously when the ballet was taken into the repertoire of the Ballets Jooss in 1932. The decision to increase the number of female courtiers from three to five was also made at that time.)

Similarly we may observe changes in the costumes of *The Big City*, particularly in the individual characters' costumes in the Street Scene and in the design and colour of the dresses of the workers and the Charlestoners in the final scene. The female workers now all wear dresses of the same design and colour, denying their individuality, while the dresses for the female Charlestoners are much glitzier than originally, thus providing a greater contrast with the simple white dress of The Young Girl. These revisions were made by Hermann Markard, with Jooss's permission. These perhaps small changes in costume design reflect minor revisions in the concepts of the works.

We know also that the lighting designs for each of the ballets have changed showing perhaps an awareness of developments in technology. Jooss designed his own lighting and was considered by many a master in this field but he worked happily with Hermann Markard on the lighting designs which exist today. The lighting effect which is most often talked about was the follow-spot on Death at the end of each scene of *The Green Table*. Hermann Markard has replaced this with 'a sort of floating light which doesn't touch the stage' (1994: 64). Obviously this creates a different effect from Jooss's original intention but was one with which Jooss agreed.

These changes to lighting and costume are relatively minor and may be seen to reflect a desire to keep the ballets alive without obvious alteration. At no point have the ballets been redesigned in the way that a *Sleeping Beauty* might be. This is because the original design concepts are essential aspects of the works. To change the design significantly would be to make another ballet, for the designs are an integral part of each work. Any company acquiring a Jooss work for their repertoire must recreate these specified designs without alteration or decoration, preserving Jooss's intention for each work

Changes in the dance material itself are revealed through an examination of the original Labanotation scores by Ann Hutchinson, herself a Jooss-Leeder trained dancer, and early film material, in comparison with later scores of the works. (It is important to note that in Hutchinson, a student at the Jooss-Leeder School in Dartington, we had a notator well-versed in the style and technique of the work being notated, thus giving the score a particular 'insider-knowledge', (Hutchinson, 1991.) Such an examination reveals that some of the Jooss-Leeder dance vocabulary has been lost and replaced by an increasing use of the classical ballet vocabulary – for example peripheral 'ballet' arms (that is, movements for the whole arm moving as one piece) replacing the use of central arms (that is, movement for the arms that begins with the shoulder and flows outward through the joints); for The Infanta (*Pavane*) this actually changes the meaning of the movement. Central movements may be personal, revealing and exposing one's inner thoughts and feelings, while peripheral movements are external, keeping at a distance from one's centre.

We may also see that developments in dance technique may have overshadowed some of the expressive qualities of the movements – take for example the 'tiger' movement (an unfolding of the torso, arms and gesture leg as if pouncing on one's prey) for The Partisan (*The Green Table*) where exaggerated extension distracts greatly from the intention of the unfolding leg – and that some movements have become more complex where the original statement was quite simple. We can see an example of this by comparing movements in the duet for The Libertine and The Young Girl in the Workers' Quarters (*The Big City*) in the early film with the recent score where the turning has become much more complex.

Most importantly, with these latest scores, the dance material is now fixed while, when Jooss was staging the works himself, he had a flexible approach, adjusting the material to suit the dancer or encouraging dancers to find their personal response to the situation. As Peter Wright remembers about learning the role of The Standard Bearer (*The Green Table*), 'it didn't matter that the actual arm movements were different at every performance or different from other interpreters, provided that you felt the power and strength being drawn out of you' (1994:54). Such freedom does not exist in the way these movements are recorded in the most recent score.

It is possible to give several explanations for such changes in the dance material. Firstly it seems essential to remember that the ballets were created on dancers with whom Jooss had worked for many years. Elsa Kahl, for example, on whom the role of The Partisan was created, had worked with Jooss and Leeder for some time. She knew Jooss's dance language – his physical and intellectual vocabulary – and his way of working, that is, drawing material out of the dancers from the starting points which he gave them. Thus, like most of the dancers with whom Jooss worked until the end of the Second World War, she had a practical, working knowledge of the Jooss-Leeder method.

After the Ballets Jooss were finally disbanded in 1947, Jooss never again worked with a company that had such an intimate knowledge and understanding of his style. He began to work with companies that were, in the main, trained in classical ballet (as Markard does now). It seems clear that although these companies were keen to learn the Jooss repertoire they had little if any knowledge of the Jooss-Leeder language, except as the ballets were taught to them. The dancers could not, of course, go through the creative processes of the original casts, nor did they have the background and experiences of those in the first cast or in subsequent companies directed by Jooss. The ballet companies with whom he worked did not have the time to learn the Jooss style, but were able to dance the ballets without necessarily understanding how they functioned. An example of this is seen in the opening phrase of The Infanta's solo in *Pavane*. It is as if Jooss's original movements were not demanding enough, so that as ballet-trained dancers have taken on the role they have (subconsciously) made the movements look more complex – for instance, where the original score shows a simple *behind, side, front* and later *step hops,* in the most recent score these movements have become *pas de bourées piquées* and *temps levés* in *arabesque.* But – and it is a crucial but – Jooss went along with this, apparently quite happy with what he saw.

Secondly we know that Jooss's view of classical ballet changed radically over the years. In 1927 he wrote that, 'conventional ballet' was 'wonderfully perfected but out-dated, dead from within and uninteresting', (Markard, 1985: 35). In 1976 he was to say, 'In time some of us found out ... that Classical Ballet was not as dead as we thought it was ... as an art in itself it was a magnificent thing' (Jooss, 1976). In that 50-year period Jooss saw the works of choreographers such as Ashton, Tudor and Balanchine. They all, in their own ways, developed the classical vocabulary and style for their own ends, perhaps in ways undreamt of by Jooss in the late 1920s when, in Germany, ballet had stagnated while modern dance flourished.

It is interesting that in Jooss's plan (drawn up in 1956) for a dance academy, classical dance (Cecchetti method) heads the list entitled 'overall training of the dance students'. Ballet was to be studied for correct basic posture, placement and alignment, and was to include pointe work. Modern dance was to be studied for 'dynamic technique', choreutics and eukinetics (Markard, 1985: 153). These two disciplines formed the core of the training. This suggests, even proves, that Jooss had accepted the importance of ballet in the training of dancers but only alongside key elements of his own work – that is, training in the choreutic and eukinetic aspects of modern dance. It is my observation of the stagings of Jooss's work nowadays that it is these two elements that need most emphasis. To use an example from The Infanta's solo again, compare the spatial and physical complexities of the diagonal body movements of Hutchinson's score with the diagonal facings of the later score.

This leads on to the third point, which is that Markard does not use the Jooss-Leeder language when staging the Jooss ballets. Although this would seem sensible in that she would be spending time teaching the dancers a new vocabulary when rehearsal time is limited, it means that the dancers are learning movements almost phonetically. If an actor were to play a part in an unfamiliar language (for instance, if the play were in French) the actor would spend as much time with a language coach as with the director. The dancer taking on Jooss's ballets works only with Markard and not with a 'movement coach' to learn the nuances and intonation of the language. Jooss's language was not and is not the language of ballet, although there are similarities. Perhaps then, it would be more correct to call Jooss's language a 'dialect'; the dancers still need a 'dialect coach'. If one reduces Jooss's movement language to, for example, 'a sort of *développé*', one has removed the dialect and placed it in standard ballet-speak. Interestingly, although Markard uses ballet vocabulary to convey what the movements are, she often demonstrates with Jooss's dialect – one sees a hint of a central movement or a subtlety of rhythm in the use of an impulse at the start of a movement. Particularly observant or sensitive dancers pick up on this, although too often dancers see the outer shell of the movement and translates it into a movement which is more familiar to them (in the way that one might read English-looking French words as they are spoken in English). Markard out of necessity must be both director and dialect coach because, at present, she is the only person to stage the Jooss ballets.

This takes us to the final point about how Jooss's works are being preserved. Markard has several projects under-way, including, most importantly, the training of an assistant who works with her. But, more importantly in terms of preservation of Jooss's works, various notation projects are in hand. In 1980 Gretchen Schumacher began work on notating *The Green Table* as part of a Dance Notation Bureau project. The ballet was reconstructed from that score by Odette Blum, the project manager, in 1985–6 for the repertory class in the department of dance at Ohio State University with subsequent revisions to the score made by Jane Marriett. Some ten years on, that score is now being prepared for publication. *Big City* was notated by Airi Hynninen while Jooss was staging the ballet in 1974. Hynninen then revised the score during several stagings of the ballet by Markard. This score was reconstructed on dancers at the University of Birmingham during 1998 and is also being prepared for publication. Thus Markard is trying hard to have the ballets preserved as Jooss wanted them preserved, that is, in their final revised form. As yet this is only a starting point, for none of the ballets have been reconstructed from the scores on professional companies for public performance without Markard's input.

Since Jooss's death Markard has always played a major role; indeed, until recently, she has been the only player, in the staging of his works. Until it can be shown that the works survive without her then there is no certainty that the works will be preserved, for in the processes of notation and reconstruction, all those nuances of style and intonation of dialect must be found. The outer shell of the ballets may exist in notation, but it is the inner understanding of Jooss's dance vocabulary that needs preserving too. For Jooss, each movement had a meaning and was intended to convey something to the audience; the dancer had to know the motivation for each action in order to communicate. These aspects are essential in the performance of his ballets, so it will be interesting to see whether non-Jooss-Leeder trained notators can give enough to the score for non-Jooss-Leeder trained reconstructors to make the ballets live on non-Jooss-Leeder trained dancers.

In conclusion, the works are preserved, they are seen and appreciated by audiences around the world and for this we must thank Anna Markard, for she has worked tirelessly to ensure that the works are both seen and preserved as her father wished. Nonetheless, even if it was with Jooss's sanction, the works would seem to have lost a richness and a certain quality which made them unique in their time and made them live in the memories of those who saw them performed in the heyday of the Ballets Jooss. Of course, dancers and audiences have changed, and what we see of Jooss's repertoire now has been filtered through the enormous political and social changes of the last 60 years, tremendous advances in dancers' training, and the challenges of American postmodern dance and British New Dance – perhaps about as far away from Jooss' work in Western dance culture as one could get. It is not possible for us to see Jooss's ballets as they were once, but it is possible that the ballets might have even more to offer to a contemporary audience if some of those nuances of style and intonation of dialect could be recaptured.

References

Hall, F. (1947), *Modern English Ballet*, London: Andrew Melrose

Hutchinson-Guest, A. (1991), *The Jooss Leeder School*, unpublished typescript in possession of the author.

Jooss, K. (1927), 'Mein bisheriger Lebenslauf', in *Jooss*, ed. A. Markard and H. Markard, Cologne: Ballett-Buhnen-Verlag Rolfe Garske, p. 35

Jooss, K. (1956), 'Proposal on the establishment of a German Dance Academy', in *Jooss*, ed. A. Markard and H. Markard, Cologne: Ballett-Buhnen-Verlag Rolfe Garske, pp. 151-155

Jooss, K. (1976), Interview with Tobi Tobias for the Oral History Project, The Dance Collection, New York Public Library, September 1976

Markard, A. (1994), 'Open Forum', in *Kurt Jooss: 60 Years of The Green Table*, ed. A. Adamson and C. Lidbury, Birmingham: The University of Birmingham, pp. 63-81

Markard, H. (1994), 'Open Forum', in *Kurt Jooss: 60 Years of The Green Table*, ed.

A. Adamson and C. Lidbury, Birmingham: The University of Birmingham, pp. 63-81

Wright, P. (1994), 'Wright on Jooss', in *Kurt Jooss: 60 Years of The Green Table*, ed. A. Adamson and C. Lidbury, Birmingham: The University of Birmingham, pp. 50-62

Reconstruction: Living or Dead? Authentic or Phony?

Muriel Topaz

What are the elements that make for an 'authentic' restaging? How do we capture 'style'? How slavishly must we follow the text? Does a reconstructor have the right to change the choreography? What can each new performer legitimately bring to a role? What is the performer's appropriate contribution to the reconstruction?

These are the pressing questions which face a reconstructor when taking on the terrifying responsibility of restaging a dance and presenting the fruits of that labour to an audience which by and large has not yet accepted the idea that faithful restaging of a dance is not the same as a 'Mickey Mouse' reproduction. These are the problems which I myself have faced as a dancer, a dance director and a notator. Over the years I have developed a plan of action which I would like to share, both hoping for some agreement and simultaneously seeking new ideas and strategies. From this plan of action there results, hopefully, a philosophic approach to the dance itself.

The plan attempts to address the following concerns:

1. The Cultural Context of the Dance
2. The Artist's Context
3. The Text
4. The Details of the Movement
5. The Communication of the Dance
6. The Dancers' Role: Interpretation Versus Changing the Steps
7. Coaching

Responsible restagers must begin the work of understanding the dance they are to remount long before they set foot in the studio. They must first examine what resources are available, and where they can be studied and internalised. In the best of all possible worlds there will be:

1. An opportunity to acquaint oneself with the cultural context in which the dance was created, what was going on in the world at that time.

2. Documentation of other works by the same choreographer.

3. A good, sufficiently detailed notation score of the dance which includes a marked music score and copious production information.

4. Access to the choreographer or someone who has worked closely with the choreographer.

5. A reasonably accurate, clear visual recording, either on videotape or film.

6. A group of dancers who are enthusiastic about learning the work and are willing to work until they get it right.

Should, by some miracle, all of these resources be available, the reconstructor is fortunate indeed. What is to be found in these various resources? Why are they important and what can or should be learned from each?

The Cultural Context

It is my conviction that every dance, in fact every work of art, is affected by the time and place in which it was created. In order to reproduce a dance authentically, the director needs to understand its cultural context, the *Zeitgeist* or atmosphere surrounding its creation. For example, if one were to remount Doris Humphrey's *With My Red Fires*, choreographed in 1936, it is important to understand that Martha Graham's *Panorama* was made in 1935, that Kurt Jooss's *The Green Table*, created in 1932, was first performed in the United States in 1936, that mass, sculptural movement was 'in the air.'

Ben Shawn was painting his pictures of the plight of the common man. Aaron Copland was composing music for the people. It was the era of the Great Depression and the WPA (Works Progress Administration, a United States governmental organisation that subsidised artists by commissioning work for the people. Murals were created in post offices, dance concerts were presented for Labor Union audiences and the like). The Nazis were becoming increasingly powerful and increasingly expert at manipulating crowd psychology. Social protest was the passionate concern of the arts.

These are the years in which Alexander Calder was experimenting with the idea of mobiles. Arnold Schoenberg's orchestral version of the *Chamber Symphony*, which premiered in 1935, spoke to the desire for development of new forms and new ways of expression. New ways of expression – that was the very spirit of innovation, the motivating force for what we now call Modern Dance.

That the group in *With My Red Fires* represents an evil societal force and that its jagged rhythms, unexpected silences and sharp distortions are highly original is, at least in part, made understandable by this cultural context. Humphrey and Graham, for all their differences of vocabulary, are similar in the forceful, phalanx-like use of the group in these works of the 1930s. Jooss certainly was involved with social protest just as were Humphrey and Ben Shawn. The movement experimentation and invention in *With My Red Fires* is akin to the experimentation taking place in music and sculpture.

It is not an accident that jazz's 'Birth of the Cool' appeared at the same time as the early work of Merce Cunningham. Nor would Antony Tudor's *Jardin aux lilas* (1936) or *Undertow* (1945), or Doris Humphrey's *Day On Earth* (1947) have taken the form they did if there had not been a widespread acceptance of and fascination with the work of Sigmund Freud.

Understanding the cultural context is very much a part of understanding any individual work. Knowledge of the *Zeitgeist*, the milieu of the times, helps the director underline what is of overall importance in the piece, what should be emphasised in shaping the performance, what is its deeper meaning.

The Artist's Context

We also need to understand what the artist was after when he or she made the particular work that we are thinking of remounting. Any artist of breadth has more than one message, although the messages and the way of expressing those messages may be similar or related from one work to the next. Both Doris Humphrey and her protégé José Limón dealt with at least two recurrent themes, one was about the human condition and the other a fascination with Apollonian formalism. Some examples of their concern with human affections are: Humphrey's *Quasi Waltz* (1929), *Two Ecstatic Themes* (1931), *With My Red Fires*, and *Day on Earth*; Limón's *The Visitation* (1953), *The Moor's Pavane* (1949), and *Missa Brevis* (1958). The formalistic works include: Humphrey's *Air for a G String* (1928), *Passacaglia in C Minor* (1938), and *Partita* (1942); Limón's *Chaconne* (1942), and *Vivaldi Concerto* (1945).

It would not do at all to have the coolness or formality of Humphrey's 'structural' dances such as *Partita* or *Passacaglia* creep into *With My Red Fires*, *Day On Earth*, or *Quasi Waltz*. In *With My Red Fires* if one does not understand that the soloists are archetypes, larger than life characters, the dance will not 'read' as Humphrey intended. It is important to understand exactly the function of each of the dancers in *Day On Earth*. If one does not, the work themes of planting and sowing in the opening man's solo become meaningless gesture and the role of the young girl, his first love, can be completely misinterpreted. In *Quasi Waltz*, the dance must be projected as the inner thoughts, perhaps the dreams, of a young woman or it will simply become a lyrical, formal study, not at all the choreographic intent.

It is essential to have an understanding of the overall concern of the choreographer in any particular work. As Selma Jeanne Cohen (1982: 13) stated when writing about Balanchine, 'The jagged thrusts of *Agon* would be inappropriate to the flowing lyricism of *Serenade*... Different kinds of dances should not be expected to have the same kind of constituent properties.'

The Text

While it would seem self evident that the 'text', the movement itself, the 'steps' are the basic building blocks of a dance, this view is hardly universally accepted in the dance world. Our oral tradition has led us to fantasise that the *argument*, the plot line or meaning of the dance, lies elsewhere. When I question people who subscribe to this point of view, I can never get a satisfactory answer concerning where exactly the dance lies if it is not in the movement itself. People like to talk about the dynamics or the motivation – certainly important factors – but unless the desired dynamics and/or motivation are expressed in the particular movement shapes which the choreographer chose, we certainly will not have the original dance in any recognisable form.

It is inconceivable that a strong restaging will radically depart from the actual sequences the choreographer invented or put together. These actual steps are the building blocks, the materials or text of the dance. While they alone may not be sufficient to produce a stylistically authentic rendition, any more than a score of a Beethoven symphony or the text of *Macbeth* guarantees a good performance of the work, the movements set by the choreographer are the first and most essential ingredient.

Almost every great choreographer has a movement profile, a vocabulary that is immediately recognisable. Movement sequences from *Swan Lake* could never be inserted into *Les Sylphides* (1909) without destroying the Fokine flavor. Could you imagine the 'Fred Step', Ashton's signature phrase, suddenly appearing in Tudor's *The Leaves Are Fading* (1975)? What a mess that would make!

I believe the misconception that the dance is different from the steps comes primarily from poor restagings which seem to consist of mechanical reproductions of sequences. In these inauthentic renditions, the steps are performed tentatively, without conviction, without the requisite energy, and *with no understanding of their function in the dance*. Thus, they no longer represent accurate performance and so do not embody the dance. The solution is to perform them better, more accurately, more dynamically, more sensitively or with more understanding of their motivation, their meaning in the dance; changing them is not the solution and should rarely if ever be an option. The reconstructor is not the choreographer and cannot think and feel as that choreographer did. The responsibility is to work for a better performance, not to change the material to make it comfortable.

The Details of the Movement

It is all very well to say that the performance must be better, but how can we go about improving it? It is my conviction that attention to the detail of the movement, that is, its exact performance including its dynamic phrasing, its motivation and its shape in space and time, is the key. What at first glance may seem to be small differences in sequence can often be critical to projection of the meaning.

In Tudor's *Jardin aux lilas*, Caroline, the heroine, has a series of *chassés pas de bourrée*, a quite standard sequence. She uses the arms, however, quite idiosyncratically. Only one arm moves, the other hangs down at her side, held naturally. Note: held naturally, *not held in fifth position en bas*. The other arm lifts forward, bent at a 90 degree angle with the elbow in and the palm up. Note: palm up, elbow in, *not fifth position en avant*. The entire meaning of the sequence is contained in these few details of the arm movement, totally distinguishing it from a purely classical *enchaînement*.

In *The Moor's Pavane*, in one of the duets, there is a 'question and answer' dialogue between the Iago figure and his consort Emilia. If the timing is not quite accurately reproduced, the sequence ceases to be a dialogue and simply becomes repetitive movement, not at all its purpose in the dance.

It is the responsibility of the reconstructor to dig into movement details to learn what they reveal about the meaning of a sequence. Approximate reproduction will not do.

The Communication of the Dance

Another important ingredient of a successful reconstruction has to do with the way the material is communicated to the dancers. Our oral tradition of mounting dances is inherently inefficient, so it is essential to waste as little of the dancers' time and concentration as possible. The restager's first responsibility is to know the dance very, very well and to be ready to pass it on as efficiently and as accurately as possible. Burying heads in the notation or fishing around on videotapes are simply not acceptable practices and give the reconstruction process a bad name. Although demonstrating the movement is the tried and true way in our field, I remain unconvinced that it is the only or even the best way of communicating. Nona Schurman, one of the early Humphrey/Weidman dancers and a highly respected teacher, coined the wonderful phrase 'mouth to foot dancing'; dancing which never detours through the brain or sensibilities of the performer. I have even had the experience more than once of having dancers watch a videotape and perform the movement from it in order for me to capture it in notation, since notating is so much more satisfactory from a live body than from tape. At the end of these demonstration sessions, I had captured the dance, but the dancers had not; I had to go back and teach it to them. It seems that it had never gone through the brain, nor was it imprinted on the kinesthetic memory.

My experience in restaging dances has led me to the conclusion that mere copying of demonstrated movement is not necessarily the most efficient way to a good performance. Rather some combination of physical indication of the movement combined with explanatory coaching and shaping of the movement on the bodies of the performers is more productive in the long run. When this method of communicating is used, the dancers are simultaneously making the movement their own while learning the sequences. It seems to result in better memorising, more internalising of the role, and a richer interpretation.

The Dancer's Role

It is an uphill battle to convince the dance world that an authentic reconstruction is not the same as a 'Mickey Mouse' reproduction. All too often we hear that a dance is not the same as it was originally. Of course not! No two dancers' bodies, breathing, artistic conscience, heart, soul, energy level, or inherent dynamic profiles are the same. And, even if they were, the eye of the beholder has changed. We have new standards for technical prowess, there are fabrics used for costuming which move in new ways, our expectations about lighting have changed, the kind of music we are used to hearing is different and so on.

Clearly, if a dancer merely copies what a previous performer did with a role, they will be missing a vital ingredient, that is, a point of view on the material. Every dancer needs to think about what the dance means, and what his or her role is in that meaning. This does not imply changing the steps; rather it has to do with the attitude towards those steps and a personal investment in them. To paraphrase the words of two dancers with whom I have worked: (Anthony Salatino about the farmer in *Day on Earth*:) I don't have to live in José's breath; (Anabelle Gamson about teaching the Duncan material:) Why should they perform it like I do? They don't have the same dreams and they didn't know my father.

What distinguishes the performing technician from the performing artist is an ability to absorb all the information provided by the director, the scores and/or individual investigation, and from it to conceive and project a viable interpretation of a role. The task includes an accurate, dynamically energised rendition of all of the steps, performed full-out and with the knowledge of their function and meaning in the dance as a whole, coloured by the understanding of the time and place of their invention.

In the theatre and the concert hall we accept the idea that a performer will bring a fresh, often exciting new interpretation to a role or a piece of music without departing from the original text or score. One can only hope that we will grow as an audience and our performing artists will mature enough to accept and fulfill these same expectations in dance.

Coaching

The importance of coaching cannot be overestimated. One is lucky indeed if there is access to the choreographer or someone who has worked closely with him or her for this vital step. There is no substitute for the authenticity that this can bring to a restaging. If such an informed coach is available, one need not do any second guessing. With an inexorable keenness their eagle eyes will root out personal or stylistic idiosyncrasies inappropriate for that particular dance.

Barring the good fortune of access to the horse's mouth, the responsibility for polishing, deepening and authenticating a performance falls inevitably to the restager, who must be a true artist. Sometimes it is helpful to have the aid of an outside eye. I can remember my awe when watching Ashton coach Gelsey Kirkland in the lead role in *Swan Lake*. Why should any of us settle for less?

In Conclusion

To sum up, the director must impart and the dancer portray the meaning of each gesture in relation to the whole if the dance is to remain true to the choreographer's vision.

Only through an exhaustive search for a philosophical approach to a dance, which evolves from an in-depth knowledge of the cultural context, the artist's context and the text of the dance, the details of the movement, efficient communication, an informed contribution from the interpretive artist and good coaching, can there be an authentic restaging.

References

Cohen, S.J. (1982), *Next Week Swan Lake*, Middletown, Connecticut: Wesleyan University Press

The Staging of Doris Humphrey's *Passacaglia*
A Director's Perspective

Lesley Main

The theme of this conference has acknowledged the resurgence in the staging of existing contemporary dance works and that such works can have a continuing validity. My own work in both production and research focuses on the processes through which the contemporary director can achieve that validity. My production work is located within a particular context: that of the repertoire of the American choreographer, Doris Humphrey. The issues covered in today's paper are therefore based on this specific experience, though undoubtedly, and hopefully, generalities exist.

The act of staging an existing dance work, and certainly the works I am concerned with, has commonly been referred to as 'reconstruction'. I find it interesting that no such term exists in the same way in relation to theatre and opera production, although the activity is essentially the same. It should be acknowledged also that there are different forms of production, and in contemporary dance I would suggest the following at the very least – reconstruction, re-creation, restaging, revival and directing. Clearly a directorial element exists within all these forms, but it is within directing that parallels exist most closely with theatre and opera, principally in relation to interpretation.

The role of director is by no means a new one. Ray Cook, formerly of the Dance Notation Bureau in New York was writing about the dance director as far back as 1977, in his book *The Dance Director* and in 1985, Judy Van Zile emphasised the need for a distinction to be made between the roles of the reconstructor and the director when a Labanotation score was part of the production process. She noted that the term reconstruction 'carries with it the connotations of one who reassembles an original object in much the same way an archaeologist digs and reassembles an original artefact. But the nature of dance is such that reassembling an original creation may not be a desirable objective' (Van Zile, 1985: 45). In 1992, at the 'Dance ReConstructed' conference at Rutgers University, leading figures from the Dance Notation Bureau, including Ilene Fox and

Stuart Hodes, emphasised that the score should be regarded as a 'part of' the process rather than the process itself. Fox commented that 'the score is just a starting place... the director has to provide the essential juices, make it live in the moment again' (Fox, 1993: 172). Whilst agreeing with her latter points, I would question the issue of the score being a starting point, as this need not necessarily be the case. As a director of Doris Humphrey's work, my personal route into a dance, and I would emphasise the personal here, is through the choreographer and her ideas. Therefore what may exist outside of those parameters is not relevant at this stage, particularly since a dance score is undoubtedly a secondary interpretation – as seen through the eyes of the notator as opposed to the mind of the choreographer. One illustration is the process used for my production of *Passacaglia* in 1995. The starting point for this encompassed Humphrey's documented thoughts on the work; her preference for a particular orchestration of the music, that by Leopold Stokowski, the occasion of her centenary and her renowned comment on 'the nobility of the human spirit and letting young dancers move harmoniously with each other' (Stodelle, 1978: frontispiece).

As director my intention was to create an interpretation of Humphrey's *Passacaglia* that had contemporary relevance, which could reach and engage today's audience beyond the sphere of historical interest. From the outset the staging was regarded as a 'new' production as opposed to a revival or reconstruction, because there is, I believe, a fundamental distinction between these positions. With reference to contemporary dance, the terms 'revival' and 'reconstruction' have a sense of the historical, of something 'of its time', that exists for reasons other than artistic; historical, scholarly and archival come to mind in this context. There is a validity for the continuing existence of such works for these purposes. There is also a validity in ensuring that there are works which retain a 'new-ness' and vitality, and can belong in the contemporary repertoire on artistic grounds alone. *Passacaglia*, I contend, is such a work.

Any production of an existing work, across the perfote (Benedetti, 1985: x). One interpretation of this is that whilst the essence of a work will remain, as it must if the work is to be recognised as belonging to the creator, the notion of extending this is key to the work living on, as opposed to just surviving as an unchanging relic. Each individual begins from the same place; the desire to stage a particular work. The director will have an idea of the work based on its theme(s) and its structure. This 'idea' is akin to Benedetti's reference to nature, the resulting production being the extension, which in turn will alter with each new production, but will always begin from that one source.

There has been much debate across the literary and performing arts on the issue of the author or artist's intention, and whether or not it can be located. My own view is that it cannot, because in my case the artist is dead so she can say no more about it other than what is already documented. There is, however, much to be said for searching for 'an' intention, as it is through the act of searching that the director can reach the essence or spirit of a work. A sense of Humphrey's intention can be determined through the range of literary evidence that exists, including programme notes she wrote for *Passacaglia* in 1938 and comments made by her directly about the work to close associates. One example is the following remark from American dance writer Margaret Lloyd, based on a conversation with the choreographer: 'she simply needed music of lofty serenity for what she wanted to express, and felt that no modern composer could give it to her' (Lloyd, 1949: 108). Whilst the context of this was a defence of Humphrey's use of Bach, which had caused some consternation at the time, the remark also contains a number of clues for the director.

The choice of musical recording was extremely significant, with the Lloyd reference having a relevance here too. For past productions I had had available only the organ recording. The 'lofty serenity' ascribed to the dance had, for me, been contained solely within the movement, as the sound created by the organ does not generate this state. In fact, if anything, it works against the spirit of the dance and could potentially alienate a contemporary audience, an observation I can make based on reactions by dancers and audience members to both the orchestral and organ recordings. Humphrey's preference for the orchestral version by Stokowski is well documented, as is the fact that she used this orchestration during her creative process. She was never ultimately to have the opportunity of performing the work with Stokowski, though they did discuss the possibilities at one time. The dynamics created by the orchestral version produce the 'lofty serenity' described by Lloyd and raise the impact of the dance to a different sphere. Humphrey does not simply match the music structurally, she has captured and further enhanced the dynamic and drama contained within Stokowski's interpretation. The 'sound' of the music therefore played a major role in my interpretation of the choreography. Whilst the dynamic aspect was a major factor, this orchestration was not without problems, significantly in its tempi changes at climactic points, which created both technical and timing challenges for the dancers.

The occasion of Humphrey's centenary in 1995 was instrumental in two ways; in the actual choice of *Passacaglia* and in the decision to give prominence to the female lead role. *Passacaglia* was chosen because of all the works available, this dance, I contend, epitomises Humphrey's artistic credo. In the autobiography, *Doris Humphrey: An Artist First*, Selma Jeanne Cohen notes the following:

> For Doris, the fall and recovery, climaxed by the suspension, spoke the nobility of the human spirit. This was her faith... all of her works (*with the exception of Corybantic*) are resolved on a positive assertion, an affirmation that man can and will live in peace with himself and in harmony with his fellow man. (Cohen, 1972: 231)

These sentiments could equally apply to *Passacaglia* itself.

With regard to the staging of the dance, the lead female role was given greater prominence than is indicated in the Labanotation score and other documentation. There are two leading soloists, one male and one female, with the male role taking a clear lead at certain climactic points in the dance. Adjustments between the two roles were made to redress the balance. One reason for the shift of emphasis was to create an embodiment of the spirit of Doris Humphrey within the dance itself, as the work is being performed. This evolved primarily as an 'honorary' aspect for the centenary celebrations, although there is also a parallel with her basic philosophy – of working from within and moving from the inside out. The creation of this 'spirit of Humphrey' may not have been specifically evident from the audience perspective, and this was not essential as its existence had relevance 'within' the work for the director and the performers. The audience would perhaps have been aware that the female lead had a greater share, though not exclusively, of the soloist material.

Existing documentation, in which I include the Labanotation score written by Lucy Venable in 1955, a film of the dance reconstructed by Venable in 1965 and various literary references, all depict the male lead as the prominent role. Based on this evidence one could assume this to be Humphrey's intention regarding the relationship between the lead roles. What then is the justification for making a change? There are two principal reasons, in addition to those previously discussed. The Labanotation score indicates that the roles can be reversed and that one of the principal variations in the *Passacaglia* section, the turning solo, can be danced by either of the leads. In addition to this, the film version by Venable has the soloists dancing it together. This evidence suggests a certain latitude for the director, which I in turn applied to two further variations in addition to the turning solo – the first solo in the *Passacaglia*, and the final solo in the *Fugue*. These are arguably the two pivotal variations in the work through which the leadership emerges from within the democratised community of the ensemble in *Passacaglia* variation 7, and is emphatically affirmed in *Fugue* variation 10. To ensure some balance within the partnership, the male soloist retained his lead in the *Passacaglia* duet; variation 10, and the assigned solos; variations 5 and 7 in the *Fugue*.

A second reason relates to my original intention of creating a 'new' contemporary production. I believe that had the work been staged as it has been written and filmed, with the man leading throughout, the production could have looked too traditional. A complete role reversal, on the other hand, would have left the male role somewhat emasculated, in that *his* role would then have consisted of following the female lead throughout, and that was not my intention either. The adjustments described above created a balance which, whilst not being completely equitable, did allow for the establishment of both leads as individuals alongside the partnership.

With regard to casting, 'balance' was a key factor. To me the dance is in part about a community of individuals moving with and through each other through life. To this end, I sought a range of body types who would collectively create a balance as an ensemble and within the smaller groups which emerge throughout the dance. The structure of the dance essentially follows the phrase structure of the music. The phrases, or 'variations', range from solo and duet up to full ensemble. According to the score, there is a clear hierarchical structure in how the dance is cast. To a certain extent this has to be adhered to, because of basic positioning throughout the dance. There is scope for adjustment, however, and this allowed me to realise further the balance within the ensemble, with each member of the 'community' having a role of some substance. The other essential element in casting was youthfulness. I wanted the dance to look young and fresh, to capture the abandonment of youth that Humphrey herself emphasised.

It is twenty years now since Cook wrote *The Dance Director*, yet the role itself still seems to be emerging within the art form, which could in part be due to the irregular opportunities for presenting existing work in mainstream theatre. This being the case, and given that the role of the theatre director is now an established one, it is useful to acknowledge parallels in the staging of certain playwrights. The work of William Shakespeare, for example, can be used as a reference point due to the extensive history of the staging of his plays, particularly since the 1960s, and because of the distinct style in relation to language, which arguably equates with dancing in a particular choreographic style.

Sir Peter Hall commented, 'in a sense we are all making new art objects out of old plays, almost as if we are writers. A dangerous activity' (Benedetti, 1985: x). He is right about the 'new-ness' aspect, he is right to imply the process is creative, and he is particularly correct to point out the dangers, because the creativity involved has to be within parameters otherwise the production could cease to belong to the author and become instead an original creation. Contemporary dance is more open to this danger because of the ephemerality of movement generally, along with the nature of the dance score and the fact that there is no great depth of history or tradition to draw upon. Whereas the words and therefore the ideas of a play can be contained in the relatively concrete form of a text which can be universally read, the dance score does not have this same accessibility. The director therefore has added responsibility in communicating clearly the ideas and essence of the work. This is one reason why those who direct from a score have to be working from an informed position regarding the choreographer's style, or work with someone who is. Style is significant because it encapsulates the choreographer's 'signature', and is what makes the work recognisable as belonging to that particular artist. In 1996 the American writer and critic Marcia Siegel commented that 'Labanotation has to be retranslated back to the bodies by someone who not only can read it but can teach the movement effectively' (Siegel, 1996: 6), which I concur with, and I would further define 'effectively' as being fluent in the particular choreographic style.

This is by no means an exclusive issue for dance. In reference to the speaking of Shakespearean text, Robert Benedetti states that 'style is the medium through which the "message" of action is conveyed, it endows that action with its specific quality and meaning' (Benedetti, 1985: 22), which is equally pertinent in a movement context. He comments further that the 'aim in production is to manifest the particular reality of the play not only by telling the story... but also by capturing the precise tone, texture, and meaning of the action as communicated by the play's style. Only then will we have produced an authentic manifestation of the essential life of the play' (Benedetti, 1985: 23), which could also be interpreted as capturing the essence of the work. Peter Hall is noted for the significance he places on the speaking of the text (Berry, 1989: 209). For him, the style, which encompasses understanding of the verse structure, the phrase rhythm and intonation, is central. Kristin Linklater, former voice coach and colleague at the RSC explains why, 'if the plays are spoken and performed... and if the sounds of the words and rhythms of the language are felt, Shakespeare's voice will call to the voices of eloquence that live in everyone...' (Bennett, 1996: 4), which suggests that for the playwright's message to be understood, it needs to be conveyed in a specific way. Other Shakespearean directors, I am sure, would debate this particular point, but for dance it is right. For the choreographer's work to be understood, the language must be clear. And it can be. We still have first generation dancers who are handing down the respective philosophies, and across the art form there are exponents who are fluent in specific styles.

Contemporary dance as a genre has a limited history, made more so because the dances that could comprise this history are not regularly seen and therefore recognised. In 1993 Marcia Siegel warned of this very state, that the art form was in danger of losing completely its distinctive works and artists, and becoming an ever-evolving form without concrete foundations (Siegel, 1993: 15). This could indeed come about, but it need not. Since Siegel made these remarks there have been admittedly small but significant and systematic developments in both the Humphrey and Graham traditions, with the Humphrey centenary and resulting performances in 1995 both here and in the US, the Graham retrospective likewise in 1996 and both choreographers being represented recently in 'The Singular Voice of Women' production at The Place Theatre in London (September, 1997).

It is important, and perhaps vital, that dances are made relevant and accessible for a contemporary audience. However, because our history is still emerging, the director's creative licence should perhaps have limitations. A director can approach Humphrey's *Passacaglia* or *With My Red Fires* as one might *Macbeth* or *A Midsummer Night's Dream*, and create a contemporary, imaginative production, but the crucial question here is the extent to which the creative imagination should be employed. If one thinks of some of the more fantastical productions of Shakespeare, like Peter Brook's *A Midsummer Night's Dream*, and Ninangawa's *Macbeth*, one question is whether imaginative creativity to this extent could ever be appropriate for contemporary dance. Another is whether dance directors would want to go to those lengths. Robert Lepage, for example, turned a full ensemble piece into a solo work in his production based on *Hamlet* (*Elsinore*) at the Royal National Theatre in 1997. There are no straightforward answers to such questions, and it may well be that these will only emerge over an extended period of time, as the art form moves beyond its first generation.

I have just referred to *Passacaglia* and *With My Red Fires* in a similar context in terms of directorial approach, but despite similarities, in style for example, there are also fundamental differences which must be acknowledged. *Passacaglia* has a certain universality. *With My Red Fires* however is far more specific – with its characters, clear narrative and reference to the William Blake poem – and is perhaps even more in keeping with the staging of a Shakespeare play. *Water Study*, on the other hand, is different again, as is *The Shakers*. All of these works, and others, I believe can be made 'new' – although I am still in the process of discovering how with some of them, but this is what is so exciting. Because these works can 'speak' today, they can influence today, and thus our history and tradition will continue to have living roots, which for an ephemeral art form is no bad thing.

References

Benedetti, R. (1985), *The Director at Work*, Eaglewood Cliffs: Prentice Hall

Bennett, S. (1996), *Performing Nostalgia*, London/New York: Routledge

Berry, R. (1989), *On Directing Shakespeare*, London: Hamish Hamilton

Cohen, S.J. (1972), *Doris Humphrey – An Artist First*, Connecticut: Wesleyan University Press

Cook, R. (1977), *The Dance Director*, New York: Ray Cook

Fox, I. (1993) 'Strategies for Documentation and Retrieval' in Palfy, B. Gitelman, C. & Mayer, P. eds. *Dance ReConstructed*, Rutgers University: New Jersey, p.169-172

Lloyd, M. (1987) *The Borzoi Book of Modern Dance*, Dance Horizons: Princeton, New Jersey. First published 1949, Aldfred Knopf: New York

Siegel, M. (1993), 'Perspectives in Reconstruction' in Palfy, B. Gitelman, C. & Mayer, P. eds. *Dance ReConstructed*, Rutgers University: New Jersey, p.14-15

Siegel, M. (1996), 'Humphrey's Legacy – Loss and Recall', *Dance Research Journal* Vol. 28 No. 2, pp. 4-9

Stodelle, E. (1978), *The Dance Technique of Doris Humphrey and its Creative Potential*, London: Dance Books

Van Zile, J. (1985), 'What is the dance? Implication for Notation', *Dance Research Journal* Vol. 17 No. 2, pp. 41-47

Venable, L. (1955), Labanotation score for Doris Humphrey's *Passacaglia*, Dance Notation Bureau: New York

Passacaglia, film, (1965), The Four Pioneers, directed by John Mueller

Interpreting or Remaking the Text?
A Cross-Arts Panel

Scribe: Henrietta Bannerman

The Cross-Arts Panel comprised Theatre and Opera directors Tim Albery and Phyllida Lloyd and Ann Thompson, Professor of English, University of Surrey Roehampton, London. After introducing the members of the panel to the audience, Neil Taylor, Dean of the Faculty of Arts and Humanities, University of Surrey Roehampton gave an overview of the issues to be addressed. Neil Taylor explained that the major theme running through the panellists' papers concerned the nature of the text and its status in the 1990s: what is the text? Does the name or identity of the author matter?

Report based on notes provided by Tim Albery

Tim Albery began by reading an extract from *Attempts On Her Life* (1997) by Martin Crimp directed by Albery earlier in the year at the Royal Court Theatre, London. Albery explained that the dialogue he quoted concerned a woman who had never finished any text that she had set out to read or study. The tendency to skim through or half read something suggests that, regardless of what an author sets out to do, the text is unlikely to be received according to his or her intentions.

Attempts On Her Life was a new, untried text. Nobody apart from the author, Albery and 'a few people running the theatre' had had any exposure to it. There were no previous productions or associated texts on which Albery, as the director, could draw. Moreover, there was a marked lack of guidance from the author as to how the play should be set be set. Albery explained that the play does not have any characters but only speakers and, although the various speeches are indicated by hyphens at the beginning of lines, there is no specification as to how many speakers should be involved. For example, Albery remarked that 'section seventeen could have two speakers or four hundred.'

The text on which Albery was working, then, was very open and there was no indication from the author as to the order of the sections or how they should be performed. Albery remarked that he had 'massive choice' and that the challenge for the director of this play was to imagine and create a complete world in which the audience could believe. When asked, the author refused to comment on matters even as basic as to how many actors there should be in the cast. Finance, however, settled this problem and it was decided that there should be a cast of four male and four female actors.

When rehearsals started, Albery confronted a series of unseen problems that arose from the fact that 'our text was everything and nothing.' There is only one character in the play but she has no fixed identity or stable characteristics and, moreover, she never actually appears, she is only talked about by others. As there are no specific protagonists and supporting roles, the lines in the play are not ascribed to any particular speaker.

Albery decided to work on the final section of the play at the first rehearsal and asked the cast to work on the principle that whoever felt like speaking the lines should do so. Such a way of working resulted in one actor not speaking at all until near the end of the scene. Although Albery arranged for the stage manager to make a note of who said which lines, there were eventually problems with the random nature of the creative process. By the time the scene came to be staged, several of the actors felt that some of the lines they had picked by chance at the first rehearsal were no longer appropriate for the characters they had created. Albery found himself in the midst of heated debates and arguments. Faced with the necessity of having to make decisions about who should speak which lines, he decided that all the actors should keep to their original choices. Eventually, the actors became used to the inconsistencies and contradictions that were thrown up in connection with their characters and the lines they had to say. They came to feel that they were reflecting real life situations where one might, at a dinner party for example, contradict oneself to avoid hurting someone or in order not to seem socially inadequate. Ironically - the text that gave no information except 'the words on the page' became sacrosanct in a way that other texts do not.

Albery found himself in a very different situation when involved in opera productions. Here it is a matter of confronting multiple texts because an opera, in the first instance, is often based on an original text which is adapted by someone, usually other than the composer, and becomes, therefore, a libretto. If the opera is sung in English, there is the version of the libretto in translation to contend with and, of course, there is the music. In addition to the concrete fact of the various texts and their intermingling is the more ephemeral history of the opera, the slippery issue of 'how it goes.' As far as operas by Verdi are concerned, for example there are detailed records of original productions. The design element constitutes another text and the designs and plans for the decor are completed often a year ahead of rehearsal. The costumes are also designed ahead of time and each of these several layers has validity. Problems with casting also abound and Albery pointed out that the quality of a singer's voice did not always match with her/his physical suitability to interpret particular roles. The primary necessity of finding a performer with the right vocal skills limits the director's choice in casting when it comes to staging operas. There are, then, several texts to contend with, often of equal validity.

The third kind of creative process that Albery discussed involved working with the text 'that doesn't exist.' During his collaboration with Ian Spink and Second Stride, Albery helped to create *New Tactics* (1983). He explained that the starting point for the project was little more than the idea of the search for rest or calm. There was no music as text to begin with; the composer was present during the early stages of development and came up with material later. The text as movement or words evolved through improvisation in the early days of rehearsal. These elements were shaped and edited to create the performance text. Issues that arose from this process included some performers feeling protective about and personally attached to the material that they improvised. They were reluctant to let it go into the shared domain of their fellow performers. Another version of this problem occurs when one performer's role is taken by another in a revival (see Pina Bausch) who ends up acting the original person s private memories and emotions.

In the case of a play like *Attempts On Her Life*, the text is the single, crucial, source. In opera, there is a multiplicity of texts of ever-changing importance. In devised pieces an original idea or concept generates a web of interconnected and imprecise texts that are honed down to a final spectacle or performance text of words, movements, sound, light, set and costumes.

Notes provided by Phyllida Lloyd

I'm a theatre director who has slightly lost her moorings. Opportunities to work in prestigious theatres, in large spaces and on classical texts that would have electrified me five years, are no longer appealing. Preservation of literature, music, dance sets up a canon and tries to make a fixed entity of what is essentially improvisatory by nature, thus challenging the notion of theatre as fundamentally live and unrepeatable. Our canon of dramatic literature in English is substantial and our freedom to play within and explore its philosophy gladdening. But improvisation has a low status in our culture and the supremacy of the spoken text in the theatre over other forms of performance expression such as song, music and dance, is remarkable. The work I have been doing recently with dancers and actors, however, has begun to open up new areas of possibility.

Every choice one makes as a director declares a new text and what was complete becomes utterly incomplete. The production struggles to be born with a certain identity for a specific audience in a particular space and on a particular night in history. The director's textual intervention into classic works provokes outrage that exceeds the damage he/she seems to be causing. This is particularly evident if the notion of the authentic experience of Shakespeare is challenged as, for example, when Matthew Warchus cut the political plot in his 1997 production of *Hamlet* at Stratford.

The manner in which a play is cast makes a new text but it can provoke hostility as, for example, when Fiona Shaw played Richard II[1]. Unless it makes nonsense of the social context, I have always cast as many women in a production as I can. I want the women in the audience to feel part of an experience in a way that, in the past maybe, they could not. There is also a conventional attitude to the shape of performers for certain roles. A fat man rarely plays Hamlet and fat women are never seen in Shakespearean roles such as Viola, Ophelia or Lady Macbeth. Actors from different regional backgrounds, races and nationalities are rarely seen in this country in certain roles. When I directed *Pericles* at the National Theatre in 1994 there was critical disapproval of the 'fruit salad of nationalities' in the production with a reference to the 'ugly Ulster accent' of the leading lady and the observation: 'of the French-accented dancer chosen to speak, the less said the better'. These remarks concern a play set not in a world of domestic realism but in a fabulous dream world of multiple nations. It was as though the histories of these voices from Spain, South Africa, France, Ireland, Greece could not but release at least some new meaning whatever might be lost in terms of fine classical speaking. In this production, I wanted also to use dance and music to convey parts of the story. I was excited at the possibility of working with dancers and felt that Shakespeare's best writing would be thrown into relief by movement. The reaction to the inclusion of dance and music was mixed with one critical comment being that 'there is dance but not as much as advance publicity had led us to fear'.

There are preservation orders on more modern dramatic texts. Translations are restricted, productions are blocked, stage directions must be adhered to, casting must be approved. By placing a preservation order on a certain way of producing a work it may atrophy and refuse to speak to the audience of the moment. When it was announced that playwrights would remain in the control of their estates for seventy rather than for fifty years, there were few theatre directors who did not sigh wearily. Such restrictions mean that I will be eighty-six before I can fulfil my ambition to direct Noel Coward's *Private Lives* (1930).

Panel discussion

Neil Taylor led the way for the audience's questions to the panel by asking each member of the panel whether they noted, respected or revered the text? Phyllida Lloyd expressed the view that no text which had withstood the test of time and was still held in high regard would be likely to suffer irreparable damage from a director's interpretation of it. The other panellists agreed with this and felt that, for example, Shakespeare's Hamlet could not be destroyed as a result of the various treatments it received through time. Ann Thompson talked about her feminist edition of *The Taming of the Shrew*[2] and how, despite the controversy it inspired, the actress Fiona Shaw had wanted to use it when she played the part of Kate in Jonathan Miller's production of *The Taming of the Shrew* for the RSC in 1987. Thompson also pointed out that editions of Shakespeare are usually updated or changed every ten years whilst editions of the plays of authors such as Thomas Middleton would be unlikely to be replaced within the century, so more lasting damage could be wreaked on Middleton's plays from individual editions than on Shake-speare's.

The panel lists were concerned that Estates or Trusts prevented the production of plays unless the authors' instructions were respected and adhered to. They felt that, in order for plays that were written in other eras to have contemporary relevance, a fresh approach might help these works to live for today's audiences. On the other hand, both Albery and Lloyd described how they go to considerable lengths to obtain permission if they want to make changes in a text. When, for example, Lloyd wanted to commission songs with colloquial, guttural lyrics for her production in 1995 of Kurt Weill's *The Threepenny Opera* at the Donmar Warehouse Theatre, she carried out lengthy negotiations with the play's custodians. Albery made the point that the plays of Schiller are as sacred in Germany as Shakespeare is in Britain and that when he directed Schiller here (rather than in Germany) people did not notice massive cuts or reorder-ing as they would with Shakespeare. The text, therefore, has just as much importance to audiences as it does to interpreters. Ann Thompson felt that the Americans were more 'purist' with regard to Shakespeare than were the English.

Albery observed that when he works with young opera singers who have just left music college, they often sing the words of recitatives in a traditional manner as passed on to them by their teachers. This way of delivering the words was only one way. They need to be shown the many possible ways that need to be pursued before choices are made.

The panel were asked how they regarded treatment of their own texts or productions when they saw revivals of them. Albery replied that he was usually invited to revive his own productions and was able to main-tain control over them. He pointed out that a well-rehearsed production grows and changes naturally during performance although from time to time actors are satisfied with performances that in fact need more work. In the case of the foreign, international companies, the director has less control once the production has opened. Here, there is a tendency to recast with inappropriate performers and not to provide sufficient re-hearsal for them.

Both Lloyd and Albery agreed that productions inevitably change over time and there was discussion regarding the role of the director and whether or not the performer was secondary to the director. Lloyd com-mented that when she directs opera, she has to contend with certain limitations with regard to choice of performers. For her production in

1997 of *Carmen* for Opera North, she cast a black singer as Carmen but the dearth of non-white singers in this country meant that she could not surround Carmen with a multi-racial band of smugglers as she would have chosen to do.

Lloyd commented that there is an atmosphere where the performance product is more highly considered than is the artistic process used to create it. It is no easy matter, therefore, for the director to search for and to release new meaning, thereby allowing the audience to hear the text afresh or to hear it unforgettably for the first time.

Notes

[1] This production directed by Deborah Warner took place at the National Theatre (Cottesloe Theatre) in *1995.*
[2] Cambridge University Press, Shakespeare Series (1987)

Shakespeare: Preservation and/or Reinvention?

Ann Thompson

Unlikely as it might seem from the perspective of the 1990s, it is conceivable that Shakespeare the dramatist might not have been preserved. Shakespeare the poet, on the other hand, probably would have lasted: he took some care over publishing texts of his narrative poems, *Venus and Adonis* and *The Rape of Lucrece*, and his *Sonnets* are frequently concerned with the promise of immortality bestowed by verse. When he died in 1616, less than half of his plays had been published, many of them in versions which were corrupt, abbreviated and apparently unauthorised – versions we used to call 'bad' quartos but which it is now politically correct to call 'short' or 'textually challenged' quartos.

In 1623, seven years after Shakespeare's death, fellow members of his acting company, the King's Men, took a considerable financial risk by bringing out a big collected edition of his works – the volume we now call the First Folio, which contained 35 of his plays including 18 which had not previously been published. They were able to do this because Shakespeare, to his and our good fortune, worked for the same company for most of his life; other contemporary dramatists, such as Thomas Middleton, who wrote for a number of different companies, had much less chance of their work being collected or even identified. Without the First Folio we would have had a Shakespearean canon consisting of only 17 plays, some of them in a very garbled condition; it is questionable whether this apparently uneven body of work would have achieved lasting fame. The First Folio was a success and it was reprinted in 1632 (the Second Folio), but 10 years later in 1642 the theatres were closed and they remained closed for nearly 20 years during the Civil War and Commonwealth period, potentially jeopardising the chances of Shakespeare or indeed any other dramatist achieving lasting fame.

With the Restoration of the monarchy in 1660 however, the theatres reopened and Shakespeare's plays came back into the repertory, albeit in truncated and altered versions, and during the eighteenth century his reputation was consolidated by the publication of a number of scholarly editions and monographs, the erection of a monument in Westminster Abbey (1741) and the promotion of Stratford-upon-Avon as his birthplace and the site of David Garrick's festival or 'Jubilee' (1769). While the plays were usually being rewritten wholesale for the contemporary stage, their texts were simultaneously being 'restored' with great care (and even more ingenuity) by editors who contributed largely to the 'canonisation' of the author. This has essentially been the story of Shakespeare's survival ever since: we still (in the total absence of manuscripts) pursue the chimera of 'what Shakespeare really wrote', while, on the other hand, we treat his plays as endlessly adaptable, available for reproducing, rewriting, rereading and reinterpreting by each generation. Thus 'preservation' has always been going on simultaneously with 'reinvention'.

In our own time we have witnessed the literal reconstruction of 'Shakespeare's Globe' and the accompanying debate about 'achievable authenticity'. This is an obvious area of 'preservation politics' which I shall be happy to discuss later, although I am not going to focus on it now. I shall concentrate instead, as an editor on a panel with two theatre practitioners, on one quite specific issue where both editors and performers are faced with decisions about whether the earliest texts of *Hamlet* have indeed preserved its original staging, and if so, what use we can make of this information.

Unfortunately, Shakespeare's *Hamlet* does not exist as a single cultural object that can be recovered and preserved like a painting or a building. As a work realised in performance it must even in its first run (c.1600) have been slightly different every night. It was published in two very different forms during Shakespeare's lifetime: the First Quarto (Q1) of 1603 and the Second Quarto (Q2) of 1604, then again in yet a third version in the First Folio (F) of 1623 after his death. The orthodox position on these variant texts at the moment is (briefly) that the First Quarto is a 'bad', 'short', or 'textually challenged' text, put together by actors or auditors with no reference to an authentic manuscript; the Second Quarto (which is twice as long) is thought to be based on a Shakespearean manuscript, and the First Folio is thought to be based on a Shakespearean revision of that manuscript – but this is mainly conjecture based on internal evidence.

I propose to consider just two stage directions. Most texts from this period are very deficient in stage directions. The dialogue is preserved reasonably well, but what the actors did while they spoke, how they were dressed and how they moved is often a matter of conjecture. Star actors from the seventeenth century onwards have invented particular pieces of 'stage business' and this has given rise to a stage tradition whereby the 'business' created by one actor can be copied from generation to generation and can itself become preserved or canonised until another actor changes it. Meanwhile editors choose either to preserve or to alter stage directions, accepting or rejecting those of the early texts, and adding their own in the interests of clarifying the action for readers.

While most editors dismiss the First Quarto of *Hamlet* as a hopelessly corrupt text in most respects, they are prepared, sometimes grudgingly, to admit that it could preserve some aspects of the original staging. For example, in Act 3, Scene 4, the 'closet scene' in which Hamlet kills the concealed Polonius and upbraids his mother with her choice of a second husband, the Ghost of his father reappears. The First Quarto has a very specific stage direction: *Enter the ghost in his nightgown*; the other two (more 'authentic') texts simply read *Enter ghost*. Two recent editions of the play indicate the range of choices for editors, readers and performers: Harold Jenkins (1982:325) puts the simpler *Enter ghost* in his text but includes a footnote which reads 'How the Ghost now appeared, in contrast with the armoured figure of 1.1, is indicated by Q1 '*in his night gown*', i.e. robe of undress. It is not perhaps what we should expect from l.137 below [where Hamlet claims he has just seen "My father, in his habit as he lived"] but not incompatible with it.' George Hibbard (1987:282) actually prints *Enter the Ghost in his night-gown* in his text and comments, 'It seems right to preserve this direction from Q1 for several reasons. It is the only indication we have of how the Ghost appeared in this scene in Shakespeare's day. Moreover, its precision leaves little doubt that it represents what the reporter recalled. Nor is there anything incongruous about the *night-gown*, so long as one remembers that what it signifies is a *dressing-gown* and, it can be assumed, a very splendid one at that .... Above all, however, the *night-gown* has two functions: it reminds the audience that it is night on stage [though it would be daylight in the theatre]; and, in its domesticity, it suggests that old Hamlet is about to play a rather different role from that of the martial figure of the first act. In fact, our last glimpse of "the majesty of buried Denmark", showing him "in his habit as he lived", modifies our previous impression of him greatly by bringing out his humanity.' Here, Hibbard builds a whole theory of interpretation of character on the costume.

A similarly controversial stage direction occurs in 4.5 where Q2 reads

Enter Ophelia, F reads *Enter Ophelia distracted* and Q1 reads *Enter Ofelia playing on a lute, and her haire down singing*. Jenkins opts for the simple *Enter Ophelia* and records his disapproval of the more elaborate version in a note, 'Q1 no doubt records some contemporary staging. The hair down is conventional for madness, but the lute, uncalled for in the text and incongruous with the ballad snatches Ophelia spontaneously breaks into, looks like an actors' embellishment' (ibid:348). Hibbard again prints the Q1 stage direction in his text and supports it with a note, 'This full and explicit direction in Q1 probably reflects the manner in which the part was played when a boy who could play on the lute – the Lucius of *Julius Caesar*, for example, – was available. [Boys of course played women's parts.] Jenkins' objection that the lute is incongruous with Ophelia's songs is, in fact, an argument for her using it, since only a mad woman would think of doing so' (ibid:298). Both editors assume that an Elizabethan audience would have noticed the incongruity between the instrument and the music, whereas today we might not (in part, ironically, because this very scene has become so familiar) and directors may have to invent a modern equivalent.

Obviously editors can disagree: both Jenkins and Hibbard think that Q1 does record 'some contemporary staging', but Jenkins is much less happy about giving that staging any great authority by incorporating its stage directions into his text, especially if they record what he calls 'actors' embellishments' – as opposed, presumably, to authorial instructions. Even Jenkins however draws our attention to these possibilities by taking the time and space explicitly to question them, so readers of his edition, including potential performers, can consider the following questions which I take to be central to 'preservation politics':

1. On what grounds and to what extent can one argue that these directions preserve the original staging?

2. If they do, is it a reason for a modern director to obey them?

3. Might not a modern director choose rather to reinterpret *Hamlet* for a modern audience to whom ghosts (whether in armour or in nightgowns) and lutes are impossibly archaic?

4. So, in the case of Shakespeare, does 'preservation politics' represent a reasonable area of interest for editors who have an obligation to attempt to reconstruct the conditions of the original production, but the dead hand of antiquarianism for performers who must reinvent Shakespeare rather than preserve him in order to keep him alive?

References

Hamlet, Arden 2 Shakespeare (1982), ed. Jenkins, H., London: Routledge

Hamlet, Oxford Shakespeare (1987), ed. Hibbard, G., Oxford: Oxford University Press

Reproducing the Dance
In Search of the Aura?

Helen Thomas

This paper draws on participant observation and interviews from a case
study of a modern dance reconstruction. This is part of a larger ongoing
project which addresses issues surrounding dance reconstruction and
body techniques in relation to notions of cultural reproduction.[1] Thus the
paper needs to be treated, much like the body in dance, as an incomplete
entity that is in the process of being fashioned and turned as it moves
through space and time. Part of my interest in the topic of dance reconstruction, reinvention, revision, or whatever term you might prefer to call
it, stems from a related concern to explore the ways in which shifts in
dance techniques and/or training can contribute to shifts in the aesthetics of given genres, and alter the physicality of the dancing bodies and
vice versa. Consider, for example, the extended rib cage and long torso
that is clearly visible in the Cunningham dancer, or the soft shoulder line
that marked the Ashton dancer of the 1950s and early 1960s, or the use of
speed, flexibility and the long line which has become the marker of the
female Balanchine dancer. Melissa Hayden seems to confirm the transfor-
mational qualities of the female body under the tutelage of the master
when she states, 'You make yourself a Balanchine ballerina by dancing
his ballets... Your legs change, your body changes, you become a *filly*'
(cited in Jowitt, 1988: 265). Shifts in training and/or dance techniques
over the years can alter or modify the look and the experience of dancing
bodies so that contemporary dancers may find it difficult (or impossible)
to get particular movements into their bodies that were important and/or
routine in the bodily techniques of an earlier period, leading us to ask if
we can indeed speak of a dance entity such as Martha Graham's *Frontier*
(1935). In order to explore this further, I want to turn my attention
towards my reconstruction case study of the 'classic' early modern dance
Water Study, choreographed by Doris Humphrey in 1928.

Water Study is a group dance for fourteen dancers that uses breath
rhythm to create 'a collection of images of moving water' (Siegel, 1979:

29). The dance is non-representational, rather the rhythm and the pulse of the movement in each individual dancer accords with, although not necessarily corresponds to, that of the group, to create 'the ebb and flow of energy' (ibid.) of the water, through expanding or shrinking the body, or by travelling across the space at speed to a different location. Humphrey's starting point for *Water Study*, according to Margaret Lloyd (1974: 87) was 'human feeling ... with body movement and its momentum in relation to the psyche and to gravity, and as it developed the movements took on the form and the tempo of moving water.' Lloyd goes on to point out that, even at this early phase of her career, Humphrey's 'desire to get to the living source' led her to focus her attention towards natural rhythms and natural movement. In a programme note for *Water Study*, Humphrey states that the elimination of the measured beat of musical rhythm in favour of breath rhythm in the dance enables the rhythm to flow in natural phrases as opposed to what she calls 'cerebral measures'. 'There is no count to hold the dancers together in the very slow opening rhythm, only the feel of the wave lengths that curve the backs of the groups' (Humphrey, 1972: 85).

I have been observing Lesley Main teach *Water Study* (1928) to two groups of third year dance undergraduates.[2] Lesley also has a company which is devoted to bringing the works of Humphrey back into contemporary performance spaces. What interested me in the sessions I observed and in the discussions with the students was how they managed, or not in a number of cases, to get the feel of the Humphrey movement style into their bodies, particularly the successive movements that, here, seem to start in the knees and ripple all the way through the body to the head and the arms, sometimes with the spine curving the body inwards, and at others with the back arching the body outwards and hurtling the dancers across the floor.

Two groups of dancers were learning the dance in the same session and each in turn watched the other group rehearse what they had learnt. Initially, none of them appeared to be able to get the successive movement into their bodies. The dancers' movement looked stilted and comic at the same time; they did not quite know how to control the movement flow. At times the movement flow through the arms seemed to be halted too abruptly and then to go in to a slight recovery, giving a kind of bouncing appearance. This was particularly evident at the beginning of the dance where the dancers are on their knees curled up in a tight ball and one by one they unfold from the centre of the body to create the image of a small ripple across the floor. At other moments in the dance the successive flow, given impetus with the intake of breath, seemed to stream out of the dancers' fingertips into the space beyond, when it should have been hovering on the tips of the fingers so that with the expulsion of breath their bodies would surge of necessity to a different point in the dance space.

The students' bodies generally seemed much softer and fleshier than I usually associate with modern or contemporary dancing bodies, particularly around the area of the abdomen. Moreover it was evident that a number of them did not seem to possess the flexibility in the spine which is so necessary for this dance, but that this improved measurably when they managed to listen to their breath rhythm. Towards the end of the first session, one particular student, who was beginning to stand out in terms of her ability to get the rhythmic movement flow into her body and her commitment to the work, commented with visible pleasure to another member of her group, 'I can feel it now when I get it wrong'. This is a rather interesting comment. She is implying that she does not feel when it is right, her body now knows that in its bones. Rather, her awareness is raised when she moves in an inappropriate way, when she is out of style. This brings the taken for granted bodily knowledge of the Humphrey style, in other words, the rules or codes, into bodily consciousness, and this can then be drawn on reflexively for the purposes of corrective action. I want to suggest that that dancer has acquired what we might call, following Pierre Bourdieu (1993), the bodily 'habitus' or 'hexis' of the movement style which this dance requires to be recognisable for both the dancer and the informed viewer as a successful revision of a dance from this choreographic position in the modern dance 'field'.

The body, for Bourdieu, is an incomplete substance. It is a carrier of symbolic value which develops in consort with other social forces and it is important to the preservation and reproduction of social inequalities. As the body comes to be formed, it bears the unmistakable marks of class and, we might add, gender and race. The idea of the bodily habitus or hexis refers to a disposition towards a habitual or standard condition, appearance, posture, gesture and so on. The concept of habitus, however, entails more than simply habit or bodily techniques and dispositions that are merely reproduced on a mechanical and or automatic basis:

> The habitus, as the word implies, is that which one has acquired,
> but which has durably become incorporated into the body in the

form of permanent dispositions. So the term constantly reminds us
that it refers to something historical, linked to individual history,
and that it belongs to a genetic mode of thought, as opposed to an
essentialist mode of thought (like the notion of competence which
is part of the Chomskian lexis). (Bourdieu, 1993: 86)

Bourdieu, then, does not treat the body as if it were simply a blank
sheet that is written on by extrinsic social forces. The social construction
of the body is bound up with individual history, which means that there
is a relationship between the represented body and the embodied subject. The bodily habitus is conceived as being productive as well as
reproductive. Although by and large it remains out of consciousness, the
habitus can be awakened in the bodily consciousness under certain conditions, supplying the potential for generating strategies for constructive
action and/or change. What Bourdieu is pointing to is that individual
bodies have histories, but that these histories are not entirely of their own
construction. Although I am using this complex construct in a rather
liberal manner in relation to the artistic field of dance, I think it provides
potential for a discussion of the transmission and embodiment of dance
techniques and styles in a way that other more discursive or representa-
tional models such as that of Foucault, do not (see Csordas, 1994). Other
writers such as Ann Daly (1995) and Jane Desmond (1998) have applied
aspects of Bourdieu's theory of practice (1977) to the analysis of modern
dance.

Over the following session of the reconstruction process, a number of
the members of the group of which this student was part also managed to
get some of the required movement qualities into their bodies, and their
version of the dance was transformed, as was their experience of it. It
was clear from the discussions I had with them that the dance had
become more meaningful to them as performers and it was also evident
that this had affected their group experience, as it had affected my experience of their performance of this work.

These observations, in turn, led me to think about the problems of
passing down modern or contemporary dance forms, which do not have
a standardised vocabulary like ballet, from generation to generation, and
in what sense, if any, we can we speak of this passing down or, indeed, if
they *should* be resurrected or reconstructed on other bodies. When Balanchine's moves break with the conventions of ballet, he is not doing so

from outside the system, rather his iconoclastic moves invoke and sustain the tradition. As Deborah Jowitt (1988: 254) has noted:

> [in] … Balanchine's ballets to contemporary music … classical tradition may seem to be subverted, but a turned in leg is understood in terms of the turnout that follows, a flexed foot in relation to a pointed one; a swing out of a centred posture imprints its in-balance counterpart in our brains.

But does this follow for modern dance? American modern dance, as John Martin (1965) indicated, did not constitute a system, but was founded on the creative interests and practices of particular individuals and it may be argued that any reconstruction or restaging of modern dance works refers back to its creator, not the tradition. Thus it could be argued that in modern dance reconstructions, it is the 'aura' of the individual creator that is invoked, as opposed to the tradition. In 'The Work of Art in the Age of Mechanical Reproduction' Walter Benjamin (1973: 244) defines the concept of the aura as follows, 'The aura is a unique phenomenon of difference, however close it may be.'

The aura is distant, unapproachable, the very opposite of closeness, its unapproachability constitutes a 'major quality of the cult image. True to its nature, "it remains distant, however close it may be"' (ibid.).

'The presence of the original', for Benjamin (ibid.: 222), 'is the prerequisite to the concept of authenticity'. Developments in mechanical reproduction in writing, photography and film in particular however have reaped havoc on the sanctity and authority of the work of art. Technical reproduction, according to Benjamin, displaces the authority of the original because it is largely independent of it. Mechanical reproduction detaches the reproduced object from its domain of authority. By making many objects from the one, mechanical reproduction substitutes plurality for uniqueness and by bringing things closer, it encompasses a democratising spirit capable of shattering the sanctity of the aura. The work of art becomes, in contemporary life, a work that is capable of being reproduced. We can, for example, make any number of prints from a negative and it becomes pointless to ask which is the *original*.

The extended use of film or notated scores of modern dance could also contain a democratising spirit, insofar as their usage offers the possibility of transmitting a sense of tradition for future generations, which is necessary for cultural reproduction. The students who worked on *Water Study* were in fact recipients of this process. But the strength of this democratising spirit is largely dependent upon the concept of reproduction that is being invoked. The idea of producing an exact copy along the lines of mechanical reproduction, as Raymond Williams (1981) has pointed out, can lead to the ossification of a *lived* tradition and the reinforcement of what Lincoln Kirstein named the 'apostolic succession' (Garafola, 1993) and Mark Franko (1995), following Lyotard, called the 'master narrative of modern dance'. In this case, rather than the aura being jeopardised by reproduction, it becomes sanctified. This leaves little room for the emergence of different possible readings of choreographic voices of the past to be viewed from the standpoint of the history of the present. The idea of 'genetic reproduction' that Williams (1981) favours as a metaphor for the transmission of culture is more hopeful. It offers the possibility of conjoining tradition and innovation, of making anew, rather like the idea of reproduction and production contained within the concept of the habitus discussed above. Having said this, it is arguable that dance's difference and power lies in its non-reproducability (see Phelan, 1993) and to a large extent Benjamin would agree with this. In a footnote he states that the 'poorest provincial staging of Faust is superior to a Faust film in that, ideally, it competes with the first performance at Weimar' (1973: 245). However even here there is a sense that the first performance constitutes the basis for measuring all other performances and thus the 'aura' of the work is left intact, while subsequent performances remain mere shadows of the original.

Notes

1. This will form a part of *The Body, Dance and Cultural Theory* (Palgrave) which is due to be completed by the spring of 2001.
2. I would like to thank Lesley and the students for allowing me to observe the classes and interview them afterwards.

References

Benjamin, W. (1973), *Illuminations*, Glasgow: Fontana/Collins
Bourdieu, P. (1977), *Outline of a Theory of Practice*, Cambridge: Cambridge University Press
Bourdieu, P. (1993), *Sociology in Question*, transl. Richard Nice, London: Sage

Csordas, T.J., 'Introduction: The body as representation and being-in-the-world' in Csordas, T.J. (ed.) (1994) *Embodiment and Experience: The Existential Ground of Culture and Self*, Cambridge: Cambridge University Press

Daly, A. (1995), *Done into Dance: Isadora Duncan in America*, Bloomington: Indiana University Press

Desmond, J.C. (1998), 'Embodying Differences: Dance and Cultural Studies', in *The Routledge Dance Studies Reader*, ed. A. Carter, London: Routledge

Franko, M. (1995), *Dancing Modernism/Performing Politics*, Bloomington: Indiana University Press

Garafola, L. (1993, Spring) 'Book Review: Martha: The Life and Work of Martha Graham' by Agnes de Mille, New York

Humphrey, D. (1972), *Doris Humphrey, an Artist First: An Autobiography*, ed. and completed S.J. Cohen, Pennington: Princeton Book Company

Jowitt, D. (1988), *Time and the Dancing Image*, New York: William Morrow and Co. Inc.

Lloyd, M. (1974), *The Borzoi Book of Modern Dance, 1949*, New York: Dance Horizons

Martin, J. (1965), *The Modern Dance*, (1933) New York, Dance Horizons

Phelan, P. (1993), *Unmarked: The Politics of Performance*, London: Routledge

Siegel, M. (1979), *The Shapes of Change: Images of American Dance*, Boston: Houghton Mifflin Co.

Williams, R. (1981), *Culture*, London: Fontana

More than an Expert Scribe?
The Human Dimension

Ann Whitley

At the heart of my presentation is someone else's conclusion, one belonging to Norman Morrice when co-director of the Ballet Rambert where I once worked. 'In conclusion it must always be remembered that a notator is also a human being...' (Morrice, 1971: 19). These typically sensitive words conclude an article we wrote in 1971 describing the many advantages and possibilities for the company employing a choreologist.

It is the human dimension of preservation politics which now deserves some thoughtful attention. I will speak of some contemporary attitudes to notators. I shall also refer to a challenge to my authority during a revival production, and will try to illustrate how the human touch can add an extra dimension to the use and value of the choreographic score.

In my experience, people outside the world of dance are always interested in the concept and potential of movement notations such as Laban and Benesh. To satisfy the genuine curiosity of the public, I carry in my wallet two visual aids – an illustration of a gavotte written in longhand and three notation systems, and a published extract of some contemporary choreography.

Within the dance world, though, many people still treat movement notation as just a good idea, like double-glazing. They suppose that a choreologist's work is limited to stick-figure shorthand taught by semaphore from a sitting position. In the course of my freelance work in dance, opera and music theatre, I still meet people who say, 'Hasn't your work been superseded by video-technology?' or 'Oh, do you actually *move around* at rehearsals?' or 'The work you do isn't really *ballet*, is it? Do you, sort of, invent your own notations?' or, with money in mind, 'Tell me, why do you have to be at *all* the rehearsals?' and, typically, 'Surely, this work must *fossilise* the movement – dance is an ephemeral art...' – the implication being that the transference of movement to a notation must, surely, devalue the choreography, making the choreographic score a mathematical, lifeless document incapable of growth.

Clearly, both notation and notator have to be extraordinarily versatile to cope with current trends in dance production. But, in Britain, it seems that any recognition of a dance notator's or reconstructor's work is seldom associated with any artistic or intellectual involvement. The work is not accorded the media attention devoted to reconstruction or restoration in the fields of music, painting, furnishing, architecture or archaeology, for example. Our professional dance experience, our rigorous notation training, our temperament, artistic and practical capabilities as rehearsal directors and collaborators, are deeply valued by choreographers, managers and dancers in some companies, but many choreologists are left with an unjustifiably undynamic public image.

If I revealed that a choreographer had made provision in his will for the ownership of one of his works to pass to me, expressions of confidence and delight would come from relatively few people. Many figures of influence in the dance world would remain uneasy about this revelation, reluctant to concede that the bequest to a choreologist *could* be founded on a certain subtlety and vision... could it not?

Perhaps the sheer weight of responsibility and attention to detail so encumbers and consumes the choreologist that any 'profile' we might aspire to will never emerge. Our position as amanuensis, guardian or all-purpose intermediary gives us a certain authority yet seems to leave us vulnerable. We are 'uncategorisable', as the Arts Council once described me, and therefore marginalised.

As we know, some choreologists have become the respected guardians and teachers of certain productions in their country of origin and world-wide. Yet my research confirms that the knowledge and experience of these quiet ambassadors is seldom investigated by dance specialists for their or the public's enlightenment. Have productions by, say, Ashton, Bruce, Cranko, Darrell, MacMillan or Tetley successfully spread across the world by magic in recent decades? How could a busy choreographer stage his works in America, Sweden and Germany within a three-month period, during which he is also choreographing a new work in Holland and directing his own company in Britain? .. even if he could remember the choreography and had the patience to do this.

In 1984 I was invited by the Royal Opera at Covent Garden to work with choreographer Kate Flatt on a new production of the opera *Turandot* by Puccini. Since its premiere this successful production has been revived 11 times, including a tour to the Far East and an adaptation for the Wembley Arena. Increasing responsibility for the revivals and aftercare has been given to me by Kate Flatt and the opera company. It has been a huge challenge and I am fortunate to have been part of this production's 13-year life from its first rehearsal, through many cast changes, and on towards its forthcoming premiere in Spain.

I cannot adequately describe in a short paper the style of a powerful three-act drama, nor the skills of the production team. With a cast of over a hundred performers, the action is dominated by the principal singers and ten masked dancers. The movement style is rooted in the discipline of *T'ai Chi* and in the traditions of oriental theatre. Armed with daggers, the dancers whip up the excitement and blood lust of the screaming population of Peking with death-mocking savagery. They ride on or manipulate huge oriental carts, and are participants in much ritual and entertainment.

My focus is on the contents of the choreographic score. I want to confirm that both notator and score are capable of life, growth and adaptation. I shall try to indicate how the score shows respect for the choreographer's mind and work, and I shall claim that this sensitive form of 'evidence' contributes to efficient, detailed and lively restagings without compromise to the quality of the original production.

The master score took 400 hours to compile from the notation and diagrams recorded during rehearsals and subsequent performances. Throughout the 81 pages, I have adopted a documentation scheme in which the choreography is written on the right-hand manuscript. On the left are my production notes with diagrams of furniture and stage settings, plus the choreographer's comments on imagery and style, and sections of her alternative choreography. Any alterations made to the rehearsal copy are dated and added to the master score.

My production notes now even include detailed instructions for the dancers' quick changes of costume to ensure that nothing is left to the speculation of new costume staff who may be unfamiliar with the sheer speed of the dancers' transformations. You will also find in the score the details of copyright and score ownership, and extensive production acknowledgements. There is notation analysis of hands, fingers and walking technique, of the use of the neck and masked face, and of the choreographed movement language of the daggers manipulated by both male and female dancers.

When there is illness in an already depleted cast and some dancers are

Turandot, Royal Opera House, 1984
Photographer: Zoë Dominic

to combine their own roles with those of absent performers, the transitions must be efficient and seamless. The choreographic score provides the most comprehensive source of reference with which I can devise strategies for coping with such emergencies.

A regularly updated record of dancers, understudies and their roles has proved an important resource for the stage management team's cueing records and prop lists. I have sometimes found that the opera management's documentation has been incomplete, so my lists have proved to be the reliable record for 1984–1997.

I have tried to make the score accessible to those involved with the production who cannot read the notation. When anything is extracted and adapted as a memory-aid, it is important to ensure that although welcome, like photographs in all their glorious ambiguity, the information is used in conjunction with all the musical and physical refinement of the full choreographic score.

At production meetings prior to a revival, the availability of one particular page, which describes the dancers' presence in 17 scenes, is evidence which clearly reminds everyone that the choreography is extensive and integrated with the roles of the principal singers. Often deputising for the choreographer, and constantly alert to the threat of cuts in rehearsal time or to the dancers' working conditions, I try to ensure that the integrity of the choreography for dancers and singers is fully respected.

Most significant of all, perhaps, is the booklet which now influences all revivals entitled *Revisions and Notes to Accompany the 1984 Score.* This has grown season by season to include more than a hundred additional notes. This companion to the score has been crucial to the life and quality of the revival productions and to the confidence and happiness of the choreographer, dancers and singers. Far from being a fossil, it has sustained my authority and credibility and contributed to the savings of tens of thousands of pounds on rehearsal time and facilities.

I would now like to look at how choreologists tend to be treated in print. This quotation by Noa Eshkol, co-inventor of the Eshkol-Wachman system of notation, appeals to me. She refers to notators as 'resembling the scribes of ancient times... kind of expert menials in the service of an inspired elite of artists and creators...' (Eshkol, 1979).

In my experience, most notators have a heightened sense of serving. A truly effective 'service' though, as choreographers will endorse, is one which is creative, discerning, dynamic, diplomatic. This is expertise with which we scribes are not publicly credited. Only in American and Canadian companies have I encountered genuine interest in, and respect for, the skills I bring with a production when deputising for a choreographer. This curiosity and subsequent co-operation is demonstrated by casual visits to my rehearsals by company staff who, elsewhere in the world, do not bother. I have welcomed administrators, conductors, chorus masters, finance and press officers and secretarial staff, to name a few. This is so encouraging.

Unfortunately, with the evidence of countless reviews from newspapers and specialist dance journals, I am tempted to suggest that when some British and European reviewers discover that a revival production will be staged by a choreologist, this foreshadows, at best, a 'stiffly-obedient restaging'. No matter how skilled or respected the choreologist is, the restaging is judged to have less power, detail and less 'humanity'. This judgement is often in complete contrast to the view of the audience, performers, their management and the choreographer or director.

Dare I allow my spirits to rise in response to praise? On one occasion an opera deputy-director and I were applauded in a press notice with giving an opera revival 'the kiss of life'. 'A revival, not an exhumation,' it said (Seckerson, 1994). Is the reviewer's insight the result of pre-revival research? I have been complimented upon the improvement and reinvigoration of the movement content of an opera during a revival season. Would the absent living choreographer have felt affronted or confident had he known?

I once suggested to a dance journalist that he might be interested to meet informally the choreologist responsible for the British staging of a production from Germany. The writer, who was looking forward to this event, burst into an explosive mixture of laughter and derision, 'Don't you see, that would totally *spoil* it!'

The subject of printed acknowledgement is not insignificant. I have noticed in the printed programmes of a few dance companies a more imaginative and generous acknowledgement of the choreologist's work. I wish other companies would follow this initiative when it is appropriate. I have been mystified by a factual confusion in press notices following some dance revivals. I believe that, if there had been an explanatory programme note placed close to the names of the principal revivers, the press comment might have reflected the true facts about the historical background to the revival *and* the survival of the choreography.

The Rambert Dance Company's 1996 *Dark Elegies* revival programme properly acknowledged that their production was not the version authorised by the Tudor Estate, but it did not include among the biographies one for the reconstructor, Sally Martin, without whom this restaging could not have begun. This additional information might have helped press and public alike to appreciate the choreological importance of her engagement and her professional links with previous performers and caretakers of *Dark Elegies*.

Within my profession, I sense that most notators are reluctant to respond in print to inaccurate or unfavourable press or book comment. It is time-consuming and, sadly, viewed as not ultimately constructive. With a few exceptions, notators generate very little literature beyond their scores. Some even dispute the need for greater exposure of their work. Few belong to dance research bodies and many are geographically isolated and overworked. They and their artistic directors seem oblivious of what I see as an unfavourable press. It may be a minority view, but I feel that our professional silence leaves our image, legacy and the truth at the mercy of a handful of writers.

Currently on the bookstalls is John Drummond's book *Speaking of*

Diaghilev published in 1997. In the chapter 'Preserving the Text' we find the following, 'We need choreologists with modesty about what notation leaves out...' (1997: 335), and 'Yet dance notation even at its most subtle can never tell you what to feel' (1997: 330). Here are challenging statements which take no account of the real achievements of Benesh and Laban choreologists *and* their scores in recent decades. The point is that various references to notation in this recent book place the profession in poor light and in need of defence.

Consider this from *The Dancing Times* in December 1995: 'A producer of the work of a dead choreographer must approach the assignment with absolute commitment...' – I am sure we would all agree. 'If the slog is just a chore taken on by a choreologist or ballet master whose main interest in the work is the fee involved, the result would have been better forgotten in the first place...' (Sinclair and Kersley, 1995: 247). How do other choreologists react to this? Perhaps any who are present and 'in it' for the money, would like to reveal the key to lucrative negotiations!

How should we remedy the slur? Push more volubly among the figures of influence in the dance world? Remain silent? Avoid problematic terminology such as 'notator' and 'choreologist'? Conceal the name of the notation system employed and just say 'I'm so-and-so's assistant'? Russianise our names, perhaps, for instant pedigree, mystery and credibility – certainly in the eyes of the press!

Of particular importance to a revival is the skill with which choreologists plan exactly how best to teach the choreography in all its complexity, especially if we are working in the partial or total absence of the choreographer. If one's authority in rehearsal is unexpectedly challenged, there is a predicament to resolve. I would like to bring to light an episode which links authority-in-revival with the current concern to preserve the style of Sir Frederick Ashton's choreography. More important than personal identities in this abbreviated report are the issues which left me wiser but distinctly uneasy.

Twenty years ago I was engaged to notate a new *pas de deux* by Ashton. I am not aware that any creative rehearsals took place without my presence. Twelve years later, while preparing the choreography for its fifth revival, I wanted to know whether the new casts would change partners at all due to the demands of their repertoire. I telephoned the company office. In the background I heard, 'What's the girl worrying about, she's only got to teach the steps.' I was tempted to ask the voice to define 'only' and 'the steps' as I had not thought of my work for the now-deceased choreographer as the recitation of a choreographic shopping list.

In attendance at my third rehearsal was a principal male dancer from the company. He had been formally asked to 'keep an eye on' the *pas de deux*. A company memorandum had informed me of this arrangement and I had queried it, primarily because the dancer was not a company *répétiteur* and had no previous connection with the infrequently-performed *pas de deux*. It crossed my mind that perhaps it was I, the guest, who would be watched. I was abruptly removed from my position as rehearsal director and realised that my growing relationship with the dancers had been interrupted.

The new rehearsal director began by questioning the extent of the choreographic floor-patterns. The dancers and I had already agreed that any adjustments should wait until stage rehearsals with the scenery in place. The interrelationship of music and movement was 'adjusted', including three places in the music score marked 'poco ritardando'. These delightful and tricky choreographic 'cliffhangers' should, I felt, have been left for each pair of dancers and me to discuss with the conductor, as on previous occasions. With his enthusiasm to see the new casts looking perfect immediately, the rehearsal director tended to suggest alterations to the choreography to cover the dancers' temporary inadequacies. Unprotected from alteration were the carriage and style of the upper torso and arms – features I had so carefully demonstrated and guarded lest the form dilute or exaggerate, thereby blurring a hallmark of Ashton's style. I was unhappy about an inclination to suggest more than an already finely-judged degree of interplay between the dancers, and alarmed by what I felt was an inappropriate exhortation to 'camp it up a bit'. That was not how I had described the choreography and the dancers knew that.

I felt it would be unproductive to devote precious rehearsal time to a discussion with the new rehearsal director in which we might clarify our responsibilities, so I tried to do this later. However, it was clear to me that he had little regard for my knowledge or concerns. The *pas de deux* now contained unauthorised alterations and a change of quality. If I sound inflexible, pedantic and defensive, I had sufficient experience to recognise the difference between a change in quality due to inappropriate physical emphases, and a change in quality attributable to the innate differences between different dancers performing the same 'steps'.

I had watched these changes take place. Some people might comment, before learning all the details, that I had allowed them to happen.

I found a discreet way in which to temper the rehearsal director's more radical changes. On visits to the dancers' dressing-rooms, I re-affirmed the choreographer's wishes and the substance of my first rehearsals rather than simply contradicting the rehearsal director's observations. This did not appear to create any confusion. I expressed my concerns to the management and to the copyright owner of the *pas de deux*. In due course I received a brief apology from the company. Nine months later, the copyright owner asked me to take the *pas de deux* to another company where I taught four casts for an all-Ashton programme. Naturally, I was relieved to find continuing confidence in me and an understanding of my previous predicament, but I would have welcomed that personal contact and support nine months earlier.

Two years later while rehearsing two new casts I again found myself protecting the *pas de deux* from someone else's attention. The remaining influence of that intervention is evident on the video of a gala perform-ance, a recording which everyone will want to treat as definitive. I can speak in detail about these episodes because I recorded the choreo-graphic changes as they occurred.

My aim has been to draw attention to some aspects of the human response behind experienced notators' skills. Clearly, there is a need for deeper understanding of our professional role, and real *respect* for the variety of functions within it, especially with regard to revival produc-tions at home and abroad.

We choreologists should, I suggest, be both vigilant and as flexible as possible in our approach, while cultivating a more vocal and articulate presence in the world outside the rehearsal studio.

References

Drummond, J. (1997), *Speaking of Diaghilev*, London: Faber and Faber, pp. 330–35

Eshkol, N. (1979), exact origin not known. Quotation appeared in advance public-ity for the First International Conference on Movement Notation, Israel, 1984

Morrice, N. (1971), 'Movement Notation and the Ballet Rambert', *Arts Bulletin, Ballet*, No. 4, Spring, Arts Council of Great Britain, pp. 16-19

Seckerson, E. (1994), press notice for *Turandot*, *The Independent*, 14 September

Sinclair, J. and Kersley, L. (1995), 'Remembrances of Ballets Past', *The Dancing Times*, December, p. 247

The Present Past
Towards an Archaeology of Dance

Alessandra Iyer

Reconstruction is a most familiar concept in archaeology. Many people would say that this is what archaeology is about: through digging and piecing things together, the past is reconstructed. But how does this reconstruction take place? Post-processual theory has highlighted the ambiguous nature of a notion of reconstruction based on concepts of absolute objectivity, re-evaluating subjectivity and multiplicity of inter-pretation.

To a post-processual archaeologist the data is a 'network of resistance' against which the act of interpretation is measured (Barrett, 1996: 577–8). The relationship between the interpretation (and interpreter) and the 'network of resistance' is defined by the refinement and contextual sensitivity or appropriateness of the methodology adopted. This will also determine authenticity which, when it is thus conceived, no longer has an absolute value. Interpretation, by definition, is a never-ending process.

Recreation and reconstruction:
the politics of Indian classical dance

The International Council for Traditional Music (ICTM) has two subcommittees dealing with dance and iconography. This in itself is indicative of the fact that acknowledgement is given to the relationship that exists between the two. But when one asks whether a dance technique can be reconstructed from iconographic evidence, it becomes clear that the interpretation of iconographic representations of dance as documentation of dance forms which may no longer be in use, is not universally accepted as a valid methodology, either in the context of Western or in that of non-Western dance research. Questions have been asked about how accurate static visual representations can be in recording dance movements and also whether these movements can authentically be recreated from a practical point of view (Fermor, 1987; Brakel, 1976).

Reliability of the dance image as record is moreover questioned because it is thought that its narrative, devotional or symbolic function would automatically exclude a relationship with reality. This is clearly only an assumption. There is no reason why these images would not have taken their cue from forms known to the artists and craftsmen through living performance practices while also having a function other than realistic representation of dance.

In India, dance forms such as Bharata Natyam and Odissi have been re-created in the twentieth century by referring to iconographic representations of dance movements, interpreted as static poses and postures. I use the word re-created rather than reconstructed, drawing a distinction between the two. The distinction is one of degree. Both reconstruction and re-creation translate and interpret existing data but this is done in different ways. A re-creation can completely ignore 'the network of resistance'. The work can be entirely fictional.

In the case of Bharata Natyam and Odissi there was much that had been irretrievably lost in terms of repertoire and formal structure of both dance genres. In Bharata Natyam, existing *adavu-s* (dance steps) were further developed in order to allow for the transition from a court or temple setting to the modern urban stage. Poses inspired by those seen on the walls of Indian temples were introduced as an embellishment, perhaps following the model of Western classical ballet in which poses are used a great deal.[1] The fiction of a 2000-year-old unbroken continuity was invented in order to project the image of a glorious past as part of a postcolonial nation-building programme, following the struggle for independence.

The re-creation of Bharata Natyam and other styles gave impetus to dance reconstruction as a form of scholarly enquiry. Dance reconstruction tried to make sense of the data found in very old Sanskrit texts dealing with dance and drama, especially the *Natyasastra*, in which a dance technique based on dance movement units called *karana-s* was described in detail. Different models of *karana* reconstruction have been proposed over the past three decades, notably by Vatsyayan (1968) and Subrahmanyam (1978). This work of reconstruction has established multiple relationships with the living dance practices, sometimes providing, through manipulation, a justification for the claims to antiquity of the specific dances made by different exponents of South Asian classical dance genres. Occasionally the work of reconstruction (see below) provided a disclaimer for such antiquity, as seen for example in the textual research carried out by Bose (1970).

When the reconstruction work was taken further than merely translating Sanskrit textual material, a conflictual situation arose in which the question of authenticity, interpretation and heritage became a hot issue. Subrahmanyam proposed a plausible model based on a correlated study of textual material and sculptural evidence from all over the subcontinent's Hindu (and Buddhist) temples and immediately found herself at the centre of a raging controversy.

The textual material consisted of the *Natyasastra* and its variant manuscripts and the tenth to eleventh-century commentary on this text written by Abhinavagupta (deemed by all scholars who have worked on the *Natyasastra* to be the essential tool for an understanding of the work), as well as a number of other texts, written in post-*Natyasastra* times. The reconstruction of the *karana-s* was not taken by Subrahmanyam as an end in itself. As a dancer her aim was to inscribe her reconstructed *karana-s* in her Bharata Natyam practice. This was frowned upon, because the re-created dance genre of Bharata Natyam had by then established itself as national tradition and heritage. Any change was suspiciously viewed as a deviation from the norm and from tradition. Eventually the hybrid form created by Subrahmanyam was crystallised into yet another dance genre, based on both the Bharata Natyam idiom and the *karana-s*. The new dance genre was named Bharata Nrityam. This whole episode is symptomatic of a complex state of affairs. It was not Subrahmanyam's initial intention to create a new dance genre. She was prompted to do so by circumstances. These reveal the extreme politicisation of dance discourses in contemporary India, through the use of dance heritage as a means to define national identity.

Towards an Archaeology of Dance

The creation of Bharata Nrityam fully partakes of the problems of authenticity and heritage as they are at present debated in the Indian context, with questions such as 'how truly authentic?', 'how nationally relevant?', 'how old?', as well as 'whose tradition?' and 'whose heritage?'. However the reconstruction of the *karana-s* takes on a life of its own, turning into a relatively neutral tool for historical and archaeological enquiry.

Vena Ramphal dancing Bharata Nrityam at 'Art in Action',
1996, Oxford

It is more or less accepted that *karana-s* can be plausibly reconstructed using the methodology presented by Subrahmanyam (textual/ iconographic correlation).[2] Following this it is possible to use the reconstruction as an analytical tool in the context of archaeological investigations in connection with dance images and representations found on Hindu and Buddhist temples, not just in India, but also in other regions such as Southeast Asia, where we know that both religions were practised. This is because *karana-s* are linked with the Hindu god Siva and, through a process of absorption, they also play an important role in dances associated with Buddhist worship.

An example of the pairing of archaeology and dance in reconstructing the past is my own research on the ninth century AD Prambanan temple

Vena Ramphal performing a Bharata Nrityam action at 'Art in Action', 1996, Oxford

complex in Central Java (1998). The research was entirely based on a study of the dance movements shown in the reliefs found along the outer balustrade of the main temple. Through movement analysis and comparison with Subrahmanyam's reconstruction model, I identified the movements shown in the reliefs and concluded that they were nothing other than representations of *karana-s*. Errors in the restoration of the temple could be highlighted, and it was also possible to focus on long-drawn controversies, especially the one relating to the nature of the relationship between the Indian subcontinent and island Southeast Asia until about the fourteenth century AD, providing a different historical perspective on the question of Indianisation (or localisation of Indian culture) and its dynamics.

I am referring to the above example to highlight the different but not mutually exclusive uses of dance reconstruction. There is room for developing an archaeology of dance, through a study of iconography and/or textual evidence, in which dance reconstruction is a means of historical enquiry. At the same time, dance reconstruction enters into a dynamic relationship with the present, through practice. It is an ideological matter whether dance reconstruction is construed as having an absolute value in terms of heritage and authenticity, or whether a relative one is assigned to it, through acknowledging the interpretive encounter as being characterised by plausibility. This, of course, is not peculiar to dance reconstruction alone, it is simply the way the past is reconstructed.

Negotiating Heritage and Contemporary Practice: the Case of Bharata Nrityam

To highlight the negotiation with heritage, my conference presentation included a Bharata Nrityam dance demonstration by dancer Vena Gheerawo. Vena initially trained in Bharata Natyam and was then drawn to the *karana* technique which she felt had much scope and great potential to be developed into a contemporary form. She went to Madras at the age of 17 to train with Dr Padma Subrahmanyam and has been dancing Bharata Nrityam for the past seven years. Her demonstration began with her showing the difference between an *adavu* and a *karana*. She then went on to show a dance phrase made up of *karana-s*. The phrase is known as *angahara-s*. There are altogether 32 fixed *angahara-s* listed in the *Natyasastra*. Vena danced *angahara* no. 4.

Vena then took a segment of a Bharata Natyam composition originally choreographed by Prakash Yadagudde of the Bharatiya Vidya Bhavan, London and using the same rhythmic pattern, known as *jati*, she rechoreographed it interweaving *angahara* no. 4 and a group of *adavus*. The resulting piece was a beautiful segment of abstract dance with no specific meaning, but enriched by the fluid language of the *karana* technique intermingled with the sharp and precise Bharata Natyam idiom.

Conclusion

Bharata Nrityam is an excellent example of how the dance past can be differently reconstructed and interpreted. Within an absolutist ideological framework the genre could be presented as the most truly traditional form of Indian classical dance, the only one which emphasises continuity and authenticity of tradition and heritage, advocating the revival of an ancient, long-lost dance technique. This is not however the only possible approach. Through Bharata Nrityam one can, in fact, question the notion of a conflict-free heritage in constant need of preservation. Dance reconstruction cannot function only as revival of a petrified heritage in the name of antiquity and for the preservation of authenticity of tradition. Rather, as a form of intellectual enquiry inscribed in the present, dance reconstruction, through acknowledging its dependence on interpretation, can distance itself from one-sided, absolute views of tradition and heritage. Thus our Bharata Nrityam becomes an empowering way to choreograph, but does not give any guarantee of a better and more authentically traditional way to do so.

Notes

1. I am grateful to Dr Andrée Grau for mentioning Ohtani's PhD thesis examined by her in 1994 in which Ohtani reveals that Rukmini Devi, founder of the Kalakshetra style of Bharata Natyam studied ballet for a while with Cleo Nordi.
2. There are still minor disputes on technical interpretations, but few people reject altogether the possibility of *karana* reconstruction.

References

Barrett, J.C. (1996), 'Post-processual theory', in *The Oxford Companion to Archaeology*, ed. B.M. Fagan, Oxford: OUP

Brakel, C. (1976), 'The Court Dances of Central Java', *Archipel* 11: 165-167 (Paris) pp. 165-167

Bose (Basu), M. (1970), *Classical Indian Dancing: a Glossary*, Calcutta: General Printers and Publishers

Fermor, S. (1987), 'On the Question of Pictorial "Evidence" for Fifteenth-Century Dance Technique', *Dance Research* Vol. 5 No. 2, pp. 18-32

Iyer, A. (1988) *Prambanan: Sculpture and Dance in Ancient Java. A Study in Dance Iconography*, Bangkok: White Lotus Press

Subrahmanyam, P. (1978), 'Karana in Indian Sculpture', unpublished PhD thesis, Annamalai University

Tilley, C. (1993), *Interpretative Archaeology*, Oxford: Berg Publishers

Bringing the Past to the Present
An Experiment in Reviving Eighteenth-Century Theatre Dances

Madeleine Inglehearn

In the seventeenth century Western Europe was both fascinated by and fearful of the Ottoman Empire. In 1600 its influence ranged from the shores of the Black Sea through to the Persian Gulf and along the coast of Africa, Egypt and the Red Sea, as well as northwards into the Balkan states. Thirty kingdoms acknowledged Turkish supremacy. Its success, however, led to its downfall. The multiplicity of nationalities with their differing languages and cultures weakened its borders and it is surprising that the Ottoman Empire continued to have so much power for so long. By 1683, however, Turkey had extended its influence to the very gates of Vienna and the situation could not be allowed to continue. The siege of Vienna was finally broken by the army of Duke Charles of Lorraine and the Turks were driven back at the Battle of Kahlenburg. From this date onwards, the Turks were less an object of fear for Western Europe and more an inspiration for masquerades, fancy dress diversions and comedy.

In 1670 when Molière and Lully produced their comédie-ballet *Le Bourgeois Gentilhomme* in which the foolish M. Jourdan believes he is to be ennobled by a Turkish lord, the make-believe Muphti and his Turkish followers sang in a bastardised version of Italian. By 1697 Lully's successor, Campra, was composing a more serious Turkish scene in his opera-ballet *L'Europe galante* (Campra, 1697), and it is interesting that Turkey now comprised one of the four countries represented in Gallant Europe, the others being France, Spain and Italy.

This Turkish scene is set in the gardens of the seraglio and although the principal characters sing in perfect French, the seraglio guards or Bostangis, use a similar bastardised Italian. These Bostangis have three entries, a march and two airs, and it is this music which was used by the dancer/choreographer Anthony L'Abbé for his *Turkish Dance*, notated in the early 1720s by F. le Roussau (L'Abbé, c.1725).

Anthony L'Abbé was a French dancer brought to England in 1698 by the theatre manager Thomas Betterton to perform at Lincoln's Inn Fields

Theatre. In that same year he danced at Kensington Palace before King William, performing a Spanish entry and a saraband, both to music from *L'Europe galante.* He returned to Lincoln's Inn Fields in 1700 and appears to have remained in England more or less permanently, as a teacher and choreographer. He was eventually appointed dancing master to the court of George I, teaching the young princesses, and composing several dances in honour of members of the royal family.

Of le Roussau very little is known, except that he was a Frenchman who had established a dancing school in London. In 1723 some of his pupils danced at the Little Theatre in Haymarket, and on 9 March 1724, Roussau himself danced there in the role of The Drunken Pierro of *Pierro Courting a Bottle.* The Little Theatre was home to several visiting French companies between 1723 and 1725, so much so that it became known as the French Theatre, which may explain Roussau's link with it.

L'Abbé's *Turkish Dance* is described as being performed by M. Desnoyer and Mrs Younger. Desnoyer first came to London in 1721 to dance at Drury Lane Theatre and danced with Mrs Younger for the first time on 18 January that year. Elizabeth Younger had followed her elder sister Mrs Bicknell to Drury Lane as an actress at a very early age and the first record of her as a dancer does not appear until 1714 when she is recorded as dancing a saraband and jig. She continued her acting career, only occasionally dancing, until 1720 when she began to appear more frequently as a dancer. It may be significant that John Thurmond had become ballet-master at Drury Lane by this time and perhaps he encouraged her to develop a dancing career. Certainly from September 1720 to the summer of 1724, she was dancing very much more than before, and with the arrival of Desnoyer she seems to have become his most frequent partner. Unfortunately, however, we are never told what they danced apart from one reference on 10 March 1722 to them performing 'new comic dancing'. On 2 May 1722, after a benefit performance in his honour, Desnoyer left London and did not return until 1732 by which time Younger had given up dancing and returned to her acting career. The *Turkish Dance* must, therefore, have been danced by them at some time between 1721 and 1722.

After the departure of Desnoyer, Younger continued to dance with various other partners. In 1723 she appeared in Thurmond's very popular 'after piece' *Harlequin Doctor Faustus* which concluded with a 'grand Masque of the Heathen Deities' in which Thurmond himself danced Mars and Younger danced Ceres. In March 1724 she is recorded as dancing a

'Turks Dance' with Thurmond. Unfortunately most theatre reviews at this time simply record that dancing took place, so that, although it is quite probable that they repeated this *Turks Dance* on several occasions, there is no record of it. Nor is there any way of knowing whether this *Turks Dance* was the one Younger had originally danced with Desnoyer.

It is a fact that London audiences were more used to seeing short *entr'acte* dances rather than full-length ballets or opera/ballets in which dance was an integral part of the action, as in France. They also seem to have preferred comedy or character dances. Harlequins, Peasants and Dutch Skippers were favourite characters. It may be significant that many English dancers at this time had started their careers as actors and would, therefore, have been happiest in character roles.

How then does one set about re-creating L'Abbé's *Turkish Dance?* Roussau gives us the steps and floor pattern, but this is a mere skeleton. How do we bring it to life? The dance begins with a solo for the male dancer. This is followed by a woman's solo, towards the end of which she draws her partner in and they finish with a *danse á deux*. From a total of 149 steps there are only 14 *fleurets*, 10 *contretemps* and 8 *coupés* or variants of these three most common baroque dance steps, together with a small handful of such steps as *ballonnés*, *pirouettes*, *pas graves* and so on, leaving nearly 100 non-standard steps. The man's solo is extremely virtuosic, and although the woman's solo is not quite as flamboyant as her partner's, she does have to match him beat for beat in the duo.

Examples of two of the more curious steps are firstly three hops backwards on one foot, and secondly a cut with one foot over the other turning first in one direction and then the other. These two steps are repeated by both dancers.

With so much unusual footwork, the normal baroque arms and up-right carriage of the body seem far too genteel and formal. The steps demand a much greater freedom of movement in the torso and for the hands and arms. For this reconstruction of the dances, I tried to look at the dances of Turkey and Eastern Europe, in particular those countries that had been under Turkish rule in the seventeenth century and whose traditions retain some Turkish influence; countries such as Armenia, Serbia and Bosnia. It seems appropriate to borrow gestures and hand movements from these where possible, whilst retaining as far as possible the opposition of the arms which would have been so automatic to dancers of the period. For example, I used stretched arms and broken wrists rather than the elegantly rounded arm and hand recommended by

Rameau and Tomlinson (Rameau, 1725:194-255, Tomlinson, 1735:152-156). Clenched fists give a greater impression of strength and dominance to the man, while the woman uses softer arm movements with the palms turned outwards and the hand raised in front of the face. In his *Treatise on the Art of Dancing,* Gallini, speaking of Turkish women's dancing, says that 'nothing can be imagined more graceful nor more expressive than the gestures and attitudes of these dancing-girls, which may properly be called the eloquences of the body' (Gallini, 1762:197). Lady Mary Wortley Montagu, being entertained by dancing girls in a Turkish harem in 1716, echoed Gallini, adding that 'Nothing could be more artful, or more proper to raise *certain ideas*' (Montagu, 1716).

The suite of dances as a whole is also unusual. Why are both dancers present on the stage throughout even though each is to dance alone? If these were to be simply exhibitions of virtuosity, surely each would appear on stage alone, as happens in romantic ballet, but here they stand and watch each other before dancing together. Could there be an explanation for this? A look at the shape of the dances suggests one possible answer.

The man's solo moves forwards and backwards in front of the woman, although he constantly turns sideways to face her, as though to keep her attention. At one point, he actually dances around her before beginning an even more showy and complex sequence of steps, ending his solo with an *assemblé*, slightly in front and to one side of her, but with his back to her. Does he make some signal to her at this point, to indicate that she should start her solo? By contrast, the woman dances towards the audience, never really turning towards him until the end of her solo when she turns to face him and takes his hand. Once she has invited him to join her, they dance turning towards and away from each other. The woman seems to be enticing the man to dance with her. Later, after circling around each other, they make a slow quarter turn towards each other as though hesitating, then with a final spring, they swoop towards the back of the stage and step closer, side by side, to begin their final duet with two decisive walking steps forward.

From now onwards the couple are dancing with and for each other. They pass and re-pass, move towards each other and away, take hands and circle. On two occasions, the man performs a *capriole* which his partner echoes, and together they repeat the cut steps and three hops on one foot which have appeared in the solos. The dance ends with the couple springing sideways towards each other, then taking hands and moving to the left, suddenly freezing with the right foot in the air as the music ends abruptly. Such a sudden ending suggests that perhaps the dance was violently interrupted. Was it originally part of a longer masquerade in which other characters rush in to break up the scene?

Finally, how would such a piece have been costumed? Western ideas of Turkish costume appear to have been eclectic. Anything vaguely Eastern would do. As far as the male dancer was concerned, the one thing which denoted the East was the turban, and this, together with baggy breeches, formed the basis for Eastern dress. We have two illustrations of dancing Turks, one from Lambranzi's *New and Curious School of Theatrical Dancing* published in 1716, (Part II, plate 38) and the other from a painting by Watteau of *Les Fêtes Vénitiennes.* The nature of the woman's costume is more difficult to ascertain. Turkish women did not travel widely abroad. Most Londoners had seen Eastern diplomats visiting their city. Indeed a special performance was put on at Drury Lane in 1724 for the Moroccan ambassador. They had almost certainly never seen the diplomats' wives, however, and a good deal of guesswork resulted. In Gillot's *Masquerade with Oriental Personages* the women are all wearing what looks like normal female dress of the time, but one or two seem to be wearing turbans. On the other hand, in the illustration of the ballet *Le Turc généreux* (1758), the women have skirts just above the ankle in the fashion of Camargo and Sallé, as well as some kind of head-dress with a short veil.

To conclude then, what was the background to this unusual and beautiful little miniature ballet? It does seem to be telling a story, but sadly neither L'Abbé, Roussau nor any contemporary report tells us what this story is. Could it be yet another representation of the seraglio theme which so fascinated Western composers and choreographers? The Turkish prince demonstrates his strength and virtuosity to the onlookers (perhaps in fact the stage was peopled with Bostangis, eunuchs and slaves). He then orders the dancing girl to dance for him, but she, like Princess Scheherazade in the *Arabian Nights*, is clever enough to know that he must be kept amused, although in this case it is by dancing with him rather than by storytelling. This may seem fanciful, but I suggest that it does give a purpose for the dances. No doubt others may have a different interpretation and, as we are given no information, any reading of the dances is equally relevant, but I would submit that these are not merely dances for the sake of dancing, and any reconstruction must set them in a viable context.

References

L'Abbé, A. (c.1725), *A New Collection of Dances,* notated by F. le Roussau(1991), Facsimile and Notes by Carol G. Marsh, Stainer & Bell, London 1991

Campra, A. (1697), *L'Europe Galante,* Copy of score arranged for piano and voice by Théodore de Lajarte for the Chefs d'Ouvres Classiques de l'Opéra Français, Paris, Facsimile score Broude Brothers Ltd. N.Y. 1971

Gallini, G. A. (1762), *A Treatise on the Art of Dancing,* (1967) Facsimile Broude Brothers N.Y.

Lambranzi, G. (1716), *New and Curious School of Theatrical Dancing,* translated Derra de Moroda, Imperial Society of Teachers of Dancing 1928

Montagu, Lady M. Wortley (1716), *LETTERS Of the Right Honourable Lady M-y W-y M-u: Written during her Travels in EUROPE, ASIA and AFRICA, To Persons of Distinction, Men of Letters etc. in different Parts of Europe',* Vol. 1, (1956) ed. Halsband, Clarendon Press, London

Rameau, P. (1725), *Le Maître á Danser,* (1967) Facsimile Broude Brothers N.Y.

Imitating the Passions
Reconstructing the Meanings within the *Passagalia of Venüs & Adonis*

Moira Goff

In 1712 John Weaver published *An Essay towards an History of Dancing*, which he concluded with a final chapter on the dancing of his own time. Here he divided '*Theatrical* or *Opera Dancing*' into 'three Parts, *viz. Serious*, *Grotesque*, and *Scenical*' and set down a complex and deeply considered definition:

> Stage-Dancing was at first design'd for *Imitation*; to explain Things conceiv'd in the Mind, by the *Gestures* and *Motions* of the Body, and plainly and intelligibly representing *Actions*, *Manners*, and *Passions*; so that the Spectator might perfectly understand the Performer by these his Motions, tho' he say not a Word. (Weaver, 1712: 160)[1]

Weaver put his definition to the test in 1717 when *The Loves of Mars and Venus* was produced at the Theatre Royal in Drury Lane with Hester Santlow as Venus and Weaver himself as Vulcan.

During this period Beauchamp-Feuillet notation was widely used to record and publish dances. Weaver himself was closely involved in the introduction of the notation to England and Hester Santlow was one of those whose dance repertoire was partly preserved. It is surprising therefore that so few attempts have been made to investigate these dances, to see what they might tell us about 'Stage-Dancing' at the time that Weaver was producing his experimental works.

One reason for this neglect is clear. A significant problem for those researching dance in the early eighteenth century is the difficulty of access to performances of reconstructions of the notated dances by dancers specialising in the style and technique of the period. Dance performances are an important source for dance historians, whatever period they are dealing with. For those researching periods before 1800 the original performances are now even beyond the reach of oral tradition, so recon-structions of those dances which were written down are particularly important. Such reconstructions must be based on extensive knowledge of contemporary dance manuals, treatises and other sources, as well as an understanding of the context within which the dances were created and performed.

My research into the life and career of Hester Santlow has included the reconstruction of all seven of the dances from her repertoire which were notated and published while she was still appearing on the stage. One of these dances, the *Passagalia of Venüs & Adonis* choreographed by Anthony L'Abbé, posed particular problems, but the process of recon-struction (combined with traditional academic research methods) yielded unexpected insights into the multiple meanings the dance might have had when it was first performed. In this paper I would like to explore some of these meanings, which I believe make this dance one of the most important to survive from the early 1700s.

The Context

The *Passagalia of Venüs & Adonis* was published in London between about 1722 and 1725 in *A New Collection of Dances*, which contains 13 dances by Anthony L'Abbé notated by F. le Rousseau, all of which were apparently performed on the London stage (L'Abbé, c.1725). It is one of four dances in the collection performed by Hester Santlow, and circum-stantial evidence indicates that it was probably created between 1714 and 1721 (Goff, 1996: 11).

The choreographer Anthony L'Abbé was trained and spent his early career at the Paris Opéra. He came to London for the first time in 1698, and returned in 1700 for a stay of nearly 40 years. His own repertoire of dances was mainly in the 'serious' style but also encompassed the 'gro-tesque'; although he retired from the stage in 1706, he continued to create choreographies for leading dancers in the London theatres into the 1730s. L'Abbé's career coincided with that of John Weaver, who wrote of him as 'that great Master in every Branch of this Art', referring to L'Abbé's mastery of all the genres of dancing (Weaver, 1721: ix–x). Hester Santlow was a leading dancer and actress at the Drury Lane Theatre between 1706 and her retirement from the stage in 1733. She was trained by the French dancing-master René Cherrier, and worked with both French and English dancers during her years on the stage. She enjoyed a varied and extremely successful career, with acting roles in both comedy and tragedy and a wide ranging dance repertoire which encompassed all three of Weaver's genres. She is now best known for her work with Weaver, who described her as 'the most graceful, most agreeable, and most correct Performer in the World' (Weaver, 1721: x).

Hester Santlow first worked with L'Abbé in 1706 when he created the *Passacaille of Armide* for her and Mrs Elford (another English dancer), and she began her collaboration with Weaver at much the same time, when he notated Mr Isaac's dance *The Union* (performed by Hester Santlow and the French dancer Desbarques) in 1707. Weaver and L'Abbé undoubtedly knew one another, for they shared an interest in dance notation and they subscribed to one another's works. I suggest that they also shared an interest in dancing 'representing *Actions*, *Manners*, and *Passions*', and that they each experimented with expressive dancing through Hester Santlow.

The decade between 1710 and 1720 saw a number of experiments in expressive dancing, in France as well as in England. One of the earliest seems to have been in 1714 at the Château de Sceaux, where Claude Balon and Françoise Prévost performed a 'danse caracterisée de Camille et d'Horace' (Jullien, 1876: 42). One of the most famous was *Les Caractères de la danse* created by Françoise Prévost in 1715 or soon after (Aubry and Dacier, 1905: 12-14). Prévost's dance, performed at the Paris Opéra, represented a variety of 'characters' who imitated different 'passions' according to their fortunes in love, each associated with a particular dance type. No choreography survives for *Les Caractères de la danse*, but an anonymous verse *parodie* published in 1721 indicates that Prévost used the vocabulary of the *belle dance* and accompanied the steps with appropriate gestures in order to convey its meanings to her audience (Parodie, 1721).[2]

I suggest that L'Abbé's *Passagalia of Venüs & Adonis* for Hester Santlow was another such experiment. She probably performed the dance during the *entr'actes* at Drury Lane, a small and intimate theatre with a regular audience well acquainted with the dancers and their repertoires. As she danced Santlow would have been virtually surrounded by her audience (some of whom sat on the stage) and the nuances of her style and technique as well as her gestures and facial expressions would have been clearly visible. L'Abbé created the steps and was undoubtedly responsible for many of the 'Characters' and 'Passions' they represented, but the close relationship between the dancer and her audience added to the *Passagalia*'s rich array of meanings in performance.

Reconstructing the *Passagalia of Venüs & Adonis*

The music for the *Passagalia of Venüs & Adonis* is from the opera *Venus et Adonis* by Henri Desmarets which was first performed at the Paris Opéra in 1697 (Michel, 1965: 192). The top line of the music on the notation is virtually identical to that in the score published in 1697 and is unusual for a *passacaille* since its 209 bars of music are in three sections: section A, bars 1–64, is in triple time; section B, bars 65-144, is in duple time; section C, bars 145–209, returns to triple time.

It is possible that Anthony L'Abbé danced in *Venus et Adonis* in 1697 and brought the score with him when he came to London, so his choreography may have been partly influenced by the original production. The *passacaille* ends Act V, Scene 5, in which the people of Amathonte rejoice over their deliverance from a monster killed by Adonis, unaware that he has been mortally wounded in the combat; in Scene 6, Venus (unaware of Adonis's death) sings of her sorrow at his absence and anticipates the joy of their reunion (Rousseau, 1697: 48–50). However, although L'Abbé may have associated Hester Santlow with the role of Venus, the dance he created for the woman who was a leading dancer-actress on the London stage was a complex and sophisticated choreography with a wider range of 'Characters' and 'Passions' than the original context could have suggested. L'Abbé made full use of both the affective range of the music and the expressive talents of his dancer.

When I first looked at the notation for this dance, I was struck not only by its length and complexity but also by the number of *pas composés* which did not seem to belong to the 'serious' style, which Weaver described as having 'a *graceful and regulated Motion* of all *Parts*' (Weaver, 1712: 163). The range of the step vocabulary highlighted several questions. What was this dance about? What did it mean to the dancer and her audience? How was the dance performed? Was the *Passagalia* a 'Serious' dance? An important part of the search for answers was the reconstruction of the entire dance for performance.

The reconstruction of individual baroque dances can be a lengthy and complicated process. Although Beauchamp-Feuillet notation provides detailed information about the path traced by the dancer and the steps (including their timing), it contains ambiguities and it does not usually record movements of the head, arms, or upper body. This is a particular problem given Weaver's declaration that 'it is by the *Motion* of the Body and Arms, that he [i.e. the dancer] must express the *Design*, and form the *Imitation*' (Weaver, 1712: 161). It is necessary to turn to several contemporary dance manuals and treatises, as well as Weaver's own works, in order to re-create rather than reconstruct the contribution of the upper body to the dance.

As I began to learn the dance, many features of its structure emerged. Here, I will look at only three sequences from the *Passagalia of Venüs & Adonis*:

- the first plate (p. 46), the beginning of section A.
- the fifth plate (p. 50), the beginning of section B.
- the ninth plate (p. 54), the beginning of section C.

These three plates are shown in the accompanying illustrations.

At the very beginning of the *Passagalia* the dancer, surprisingly, turns her back on the audience (Ill. 1). This feature is repeated at the beginning of sections B and C, although with different *pas composés* each time. It is also used within sections, but only at transitions between one musical variation and the next. I suggest that each appearance of this choreographic device marks a change from one 'Character' or 'Passion' to another. This idea is supported by the step vocabulary used in the *Passagalia*: each musical variation is characterised by its own steps and sequences of steps, none of the sequences is exactly repeated in other variations, and many of the *pas composés* are specific to their own variation. L'Abbé seems to have been following Weaver's description of 'Grotesque' dancing in *An Essay towards an History of Dancing*:

> 'the Master must take peculiar Care to contrive his Steps, and adapt his *Actions*, and *Humour*, to the *Characters* or *Sentiments* he would represent or express, so as to resemble the Person he would imitate, or Passion he would excite: (Weaver, 1712: 165–6)

After its unconventional first *pas composé*, section A continues with a sequence of steps which travel from upstage centre directly downstage. Many 'Serious' dances begin in this way, but this opening sequence is composed of steps which move alternately forwards and backwards, imparting a teasing air to the dancer's movements. If the *Passagalia* was created after *The Loves of Mars and Venus*, this sequence could perhaps

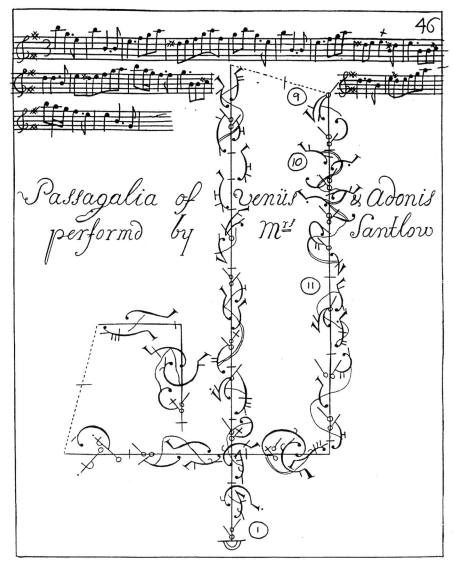

The three illustrations are plates from the Beauchamp-Feuillet notation for the *Passagalia of Venüs & Adonis* by Anthony L'Abbé, pp. 46-56 in *A New Collection of Dances* (L'Abbé, c.1725).

1. The first plate of the dance (p. 46), the opening of section A, bars 1, 9, 10, and 11 indicated.

All plates from British Library, Music Library K.11.c.5. Reproduced by permission of the British Library Board.

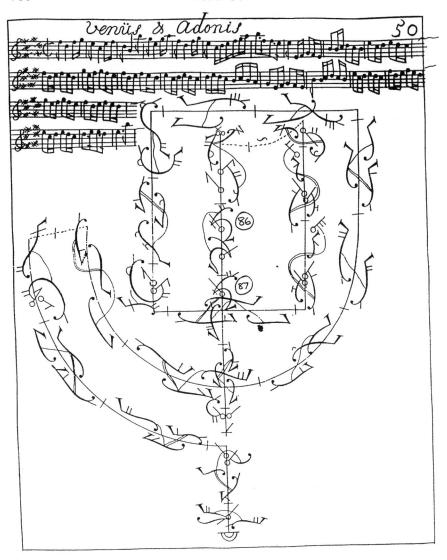

2. The fifth plate of the dance (p. 50), the opening of section B, bars 86 and 87
   indicated.

3. The ninth plate of the dance (p. 54), the opening of section C, bars 154 and 177 indicated.

recall the 'Coquetry' of Venus 'seen in affected Airs' to which Weaver referred in the published description of his dramatic entertainment of dancing (Weaver, 1717: 20, 22).

The sequence of steps which follows is markedly unconventional in the context of a 'Serious' dance. Bar 10 contains a very complex *pas composé* which includes two steps onto the heel (marked by a dot) and is followed by another in bar 11 which incorporates both a *pas tortillé* (indicated by the wavy line along the length of the step) and a placing of the heel.[3] Could these steps have been intended to remind Hester Santlow's audience of another of her dances, this time one in the 'Grotesque' genre, perhaps the 'Harlequin Dance' or the 'French Peasant'? Steps onto the heel feature in some of the notated dances for Harlequin, as well as in the engravings of peasant dances in Lambranzi's *Neue und curieuse theatralisches Tantz-Schul* published in Nuremberg in 1716.[4]

Section B opens with a change of affect and a sequence of steps moving from side to side, as if the dancer were introducing herself afresh in a new 'Character' or 'Passion' (Ill. 2). Among the variations of section B, there are more steps which are surprising in the context of a 'Serious' dance. In bar 86, a *contre-temps* is embellished with two pas battus, and in bar 87, a contretemps with a bound is similarly ornamented with a single *pas battu*.[5] It is interesting that very similar steps can be found in a number of the surviving notated dances intended for peasant characters. Was L'Abbé here deliberately using steps from a dance currently popular on the London stage (which was also a dance from Hester Santlow's own repertoire) in order to represent that 'Character'?

The final section of the *Passagalia* contrasts strongly with the two earlier sections. In the opening variations (bars 154–177), the step vocabulary is simple, but enriched by numerous turns of the body as the dancer faces first one side of the stage and then the other, and moves upstage, downstage and then upstage again (Ill. 3). The musical variations are sombre in feeling and I suggest that this sequence might be intended to depict 'Passions' such as grief or entreaty. The gestures described by Weaver for these 'Passions' can very easily be integrated into the flow of steps, for example 'Entreaty':

'The stretching out the Hands downward toward the Knees, is an Action of *Entreaty*, and *suing for Mercy* (Weaver, 1717: 28).

Later musical variations within this section seem to imitate other 'Passions' which are similarly characterised by a specific step vocabulary and could also be accompanied by gestures as described by Weaver. Was L'Abbé responding to the affect of the music, or perhaps trying to express 'Passions' derived from the original operatic context?

Imitating the Passions

The reconstruction of dances recorded in Beauchamp-Feuillet notation involves many subjective choices, blurring the distinction between reconstruction and re-creation. I contend that this does not invalidate reconstruction as a research tool, provided that it is undertaken alongside the more objective scrutiny of traditional academic research methods. On the contrary, reconstruction not only generates a wider range of possible interpretations but also contributes to a valuable iterative process whereby theories about dancing in the early eighteenth century developed through a study of the written sources can be tested by practical reconstruction of the dances surviving in notation, and the resulting reconstructions can then be themselves revised in the light of further academic study of the sources, and so on.

My reconstruction of the *Passagalia of Venüs & Adonis* led me to the conclusion that it was not simply a 'Serious' dance, but that, according to Weaver's definition in *An Essay towards an History of Dancing*, it had many elements belonging to the 'Grotesque' genre. It was intended by L'Abbé and his dancer Hester Santlow to represent 'Characters' and imitate the 'Passions' by the use of characteristic steps and specific gestures. Such an interpretation is supported by the wider context within which the dance was created, which included a number of experiments in expressive dancing. The notation for the *Passagalia of Venüs & Adonis* therefore provides a basis for exploring how the vocabulary of both 'Serious' and 'Grotesque' dance might be used to represent '*Actions, Manners,* and *Passions*'. It also allows us to come closer to an understanding of the dancing in both Françoise Prévost's *Les Caractères de la danse* and John Weaver's *The Loves of Mars and Venus*.[6]

Notes

1. The italics in these and subsequent quotations are Weaver's own.
2. *Belle dance* is the late seventeenth-century French term (also used in the early

eighteenth century) for the style and technique later referred to by Weaver as 'Serious Dancing'.

3. The *pas tortillé* is a step in which the working leg turns in and then out as the step is taken.

4. The titles of works published in the early 1700s are given as they appear on the original title pages. In the early eighteenth century, neither spelling nor accents had been regularised, and often differ from those in modern usage.

5. Terminology for the step vocabulary of baroque dance is principally taken from the second edition of Feuillet's treatise *Choregraphie* (Feuillet, 1701) and John Weaver's translation *Orchesographie* (Weaver, 1706). The baroque steps are performed quite differently to their modern namesakes.

6. The paper concluded with the author's demonstration of her reconstruction of the *Passagalia of Venüs & Adonis* created by Anthony L'Abbé for Hester Santlow. The steps were reconstructed directly from the notation; the arm and upper body movements were re-created using descriptions in early eighteenth-century dance treatises as well as some of the gestures prescribed by John Weaver for *The Loves of Mars and Venus* (Weaver, 1717: 21–3, 28). The music for the reconstruction was recorded by Evelyn Nallen (recorder) and David Gordon (harpsichord).

References

Aubry, P. and Dacier, E. (1905), *Les Caractères de la Danse*, Paris: Honoré Champion

Feuillet, R. A. (2nd edn, 1701), *Choregraphie ou l'art de décrire la dance*, Paris: l'Auteur, Michel Brunet

Goff, M. (1996), 'Serious, Grotesque, or Scenical? The *Passagalia of Venüs & Adonis* and Dancing on the London Stage 1700-1740', in *On Common Ground: Proceedings of the Dolmetsch Historical Dance Society Conference 24th February 1996*, Bedford: Dolmetsch Historical Dance Society, pp.8-26

Jullien, A. (1876), *Les grandes nuits de Sceaux*, Paris: J. Baur

L'Abbé, A. (c.1725), 'Passagalia of Venüs and Adonis', in *A New Collection of Dances*, London: Mr. Barreau and Mr. Roussau, ff. 46-56

Michel, A. (1965), *Henry Desmarest (1661-1714)*, Paris, Éditions A. & J. Picard

Parodie (1721), 'Parodie sur les Caracteres de la Danse', *Le Mercure*, June and July 1721, pp. 64-72

Rousseau, J. B. (1697), *Venus et Adonis, tragedie en musique*, Paris: Christophe Ballard

Weaver, J. (1706), *Orchesography. Or, the Art of Dancing by Characters and Demonstrative Figures*, London: H. Meere for the Author, P. Valliant

Weaver, J. (1712), *An Essay towards an History of Dancing*, London: Jacob Tonson, Chapter VII

Weaver, J. (1717), *The Loves of Mars and Venus*, London: W. Mears & J. Browne

Weaver, J. (1721), *Anatomical and Mechanical Lectures upon Dancing*, London: J. Brotherton, W. Meadows, J. Graves, and W. Chetwood, Preface

Pierre Lacotte and the Romantic Ballet
An Account of the Work of the French Choreographer and Director

Nadine Meisner

Pierre Lacotte was born in France in 1932 and has built a considerable reputation as an excavator of nineteenth-century ballets. He travels all over the world mounting his productions; but he has also directed a number of companies, most recently the Ballet de Nancy in northern France.

Obviously Lacotte did not wake up one morning as a boy and decide he was going to be a reconstructor of old ballets. Rather, he wanted to be a dancer and entered the Paris Opera Ballet School; from there he was taken into the company where he won quick promotion and at 19 became *premier danseur* (the rank just below *étoile*). He also wanted to be a choreographer and it was this which pushed him to leave the company, aged 22.

Lacotte started off wanting to choreograph his own, original pieces – and this he still does. At the same time, his formative years in the Paris Opera Ballet shaped him as a nineteenth-century specialist. He came into contact with teachers, ancient enough and with memories stretching far back, who could hand down knowledge in the apostolic succession that keeps ballet alive. Gustave Ricaux, who had partnered Spessivtseva, made his pupils work on variations from the old French repertoire of Louis Mérante and Jules Perrot. Lubov Egorova, a former ballerina of the Imperial Russian Ballet, had worked with Marius Petipa and been a pupil of Christian Johansson, one of Marie Taglioni's partners. She could remember what Johansson had told her about the dances of Taglioni, Elssler, Grisi and Cerrito; and she had noted down sequences he showed. She taught Lacotte different roles and sections from old works, including some that had disappeared even in Russia.

And there was Carlotta Zambelli who had trained in Blasis's methods at La Scala, Milan. She had become prima ballerina at the Paris Opera and had also danced with the Russian Imperial Ballet. Before going to dance *Giselle* in Russia she had learnt the original Coralli and Perrot version from old Paris dancers, even though *Giselle* was not performed in

France any more. (In fact, when she arrived in Russia, she knew the Act I vendanges *pas de deux* in all its former entirety; but Marius Petipa, who had abbreviated it, said, 'No, no, it's wonderful that you know it, but I prefer you bring a variation of your own as do all ballerinas now.')

Another component in the making of Lacotte is that, like all dancers, he was thoroughly trained to rely on memory, and he perhaps had more memory than most. His staging of Saint-Léon's *Coppélia* for the Paris Opera Ballet in 1973, after it had disappeared for a while from the repertoire, relied much on his own memory of growing up with it, as a *petit rat* and a company dancer. He also remembered watching Carlotta Zambelli, a former Swanilda, coach other ballerinas in the role.

But I do not want to dwell too long on *Coppélia* since my focus is the Romantic ballet, whose time span stretches from 1831 to around 1850. *Coppélia*, premiered in 1870, does not properly belong here. I shall just say that Lacotte's *Coppélia* was mostly revival and partly recreation. The first two acts, he says, are entirely Saint-Léon; but he completely re-created the third – which after the 1870 premiere had been shortened and soon altogether dropped – trying to be as faithful as possible to Saint-Léon's style. To that end, he studied the class notebook of Saint-Léon's father and teacher Michel Léon to find the sources of his son's technique.

Coppélia was Lacotte's second work as a historian-choreographer, Filippo Taglioni's *La Sylphide* (1832) was his first – and I propose later on to look in detail at this ballet, which is largely a reconstruction. Here, though, let me give you a brief overview of Lacotte's revivals, of which there are more than a dozen. These apart, many of the other ballets he tried to reconstruct by Filippo Taglioni, Joseph Mazilier and others, became re-creations because of lack of documentation. For example, with Taglioni's *L'Ombre* (1839), which he staged a few years ago, he was able to reconstruct the structure and mime, but could find only small fragments of choreography. So he had to rely on his knowledge of the style of the choreographer and the period, examining whatever records exist of Taglioni's work and his other ballets.

However, Lacotte has made some reconstructions from very precise and reliable sources. Using Saint-Léon's notation system, *la steno-chorégraphie*, he decoded the *pas de six* from *La Vivandière* (1844), and that is the version the Kirov performed here. (Sadler's Wells Royal Ballet also performed this *pas*, in Ann Hutchinson Guest's production.) He has reconstructed two Fanny Elssler solos: the *Cachucha* (after Coralli in *Le Diable boîteux*, 1836) from the notation system by Friedrich Zorn; and *La*

Cracovienne (after Mazilier in *La Gypsy*, 1839) from notes by August Bournonville.

In *Giselle*, which he has mounted for several companies, he made a compromise between the 1841 Perrot-Coralli original and Petipa's modifications. Lacotte restored the full vendanges *pas de deux* in Act I (learnt from Carlotta Zambelli), thus returning to Albrecht the dancing of which he had been robbed. But elsewhere he feels that Petipa's changes – which are mostly cuts – have become an integral part of the ballet. One excision he tried to restore was Bathilde's return on horseback at the ballet's end, to help Albrecht away; but he had to delete her again because audiences protested. People were simply not used to this.

Before going on to *La Sylphide*, here are some general points. I asked Lacotte a series of questions starting with a rather obvious one: why search for the past? Like many of us, he believes that we need to know and respect our past, for the past is the departure point for everything. But he also says, 'The search for the past in ballet is also a search for oneself. It allows us to realise that we have a family, that others tried to make an art evolve. And it allows us to be more humble, because we can understand that if ballet exists today, it is because it has already been thought out with great talent. Others made works and those works should not be forgotten.'

He says: 'A lot of dancers are ignorant about what happened before them and it's a great pity. They say, oh, before people didn't have strong techniques. But that is false. When you see the *pas de six* from *La Vivandière* the difficulty of the technique is clear. It was a time when there were great virtuosi, the technique was actually very hard, very advanced. Of course they lifted their legs less high and pointework was not so developed, but the vocabulary was richer and more varied than today. Only it was done with such art that it did not seem difficult. Now we put more emphasis on pirouettes, on extensions, on big lifts: in short, on what is spectacular. But our female dancers today jump and beat a lot less; they are not comfortable in the extremely fast allegro which demanded great virtuosity.'

'And it makes sense, when you consider that the nineteenth century was an era of great technical virtuosity in all the arts – think of the speed and complexity of Czerny's piano exercises. It was a period preoccupied by *tours de force*. And when you think that great artists were allowed two, three or four benefit galas a year which brought together musicians, actors and dancers of very high calibre, you can imagine that dancers could not allow themselves to create an inferior impression next to Liszt or Paganini.'

'And these reconstructions allow us also to see that, contrary to what is often supposed, men – at least those of the first half of the nineteenth century – danced a great deal and danced very well. Be it Perrot, Saint-Léon, Louis Mérante, Joseph Mazilier, they were very great dancers, repeatedly invited, for example, to London.' Théophile Gautier may have written in 1838 that 'it alarms our sense of decency to see these big creatures frantically jigging about', but like many men of the time he was biased in favour of pretty ballerinas. 'The fashion,' says Lacotte 'was for the woman and she was given pride of place. But a romantic drama needs a man and a woman and the men did not stand immobile on stage. When you read the musical scores and the various documents, you find that the technique for the male dancer was as important as that for the ballerina. It is simply that the male dancer was not written about extensively in the reviews of the time.' It was later in the century that the male dancer did suffer, so that by the time of *Coppélia* in 1870 Saint-Léon reluctantly had to bow to public taste and allow the role of Franz to be performed *en travestie* by Eugène Fiocre.

Another question I asked Lacotte was what criteria he used in choosing ballets for revival. 'I work on the principle,' he said, 'that if a ballet was talked about – and not only in France, but in London, Germany, St Petersburg, Vienna – then it must have had quality. And I think that if it later disappeared it was because of fashion. This happened a lot in France where many new ballets were created and there was a snobbish taste for novelty. Hence we owe it to the Russians that we have *Giselle* today.' In his time, Filippo Taglioni was an international choreographer of immense repute. His career was the antithesis of Bournonville's, who in his day was not so well known and owes his fame to posterity. Bournonville's *Sylphide*, created in 1836, was not performed outside Denmark until this century. (Lacotte was actually the first non-Dane to dance the role of James outside Denmark, partnering Toni Lander in a televised extract in 1952). By contrast Taglioni's earlier version appeared all over Europe and in America soon after its premiere. Yet if Taglioni was a big celebrity when he was alive, now he is largely forgotten. 'But,' Lacotte believes, 'the fact that he was so much in demand means that he must have had talent. Some who were jealous of him said that he owed his success to his daughter. But he continued mounting ballets into the 1860s, long after his daughter had stopped dancing.'

Fanny Gaida and Manuel Legris in Lacotte's *La Sylphide* in Paris.
Photograph by Jacques Moatti

Lacotte mounted Taglioni's *Sylphide* for French television, then for the
Paris Opera Ballet, in 1972. Since then, like the original, it has gone to
companies all round the world. Lacotte approached the task of collecting
information for this ballet in the same way as for all his subsequent
revivals. Some material he already had from his teachers. Egorova had
demonstrated for him the scene where the sylphide appears at the window in Act I; she had got that from Christian Johansson, who at Petipa's
request had revived the ballet in St Petersburg in 1852. Similarly, Carlotta
Zambelli had taught him *enchaînements* for Effie and some of the ensemble Scottish dances of Act I.

He studied the violin score used by Taglioni and embellished with
Taglioni's writings about the steps and action. (The music was composed
by Jean-Madeleine Schneitzhoeffer and it is, I have to say, undistin-
guished.) For the principal roles he examined notes made by Antoine
Titus of a performance in Paris; Titus, as chief ballet-master of the Russian Imperial Ballet, had mounted the first Russian production of *La
Sylphide* in 1835. (Or is it 1937? I have seen both dates.) He derived
inspiration from the sketches Taglioni's son Paul made for the groupings

in Paul's 1847 ballet *Théa ou la fée aux fleurs*, after he discovered a review of it criticising Paul for copying the ensembles from *La Sylphide.*

Lacotte also looked at drawings and prints of the ballet. And in the Bibliothèque de l'Opéra de Paris and in the French National Archives, he looked at the sketches Ciceri made of his designs, the detailed inventory for the costumes by Lami, the plans for the stage machinery. He read the biographies, of course, of Marie Taglioni. He sifted through museums and private collections. He ferreted out old newspapers and letters. But, I asked him, are not the reviews often very nebulous? For instance, we get precious little precision in Gautier's rhapsodic description of Marie Taglioni as resembling 'a happy spirit whose pink toes hardly bend the tips of heavenly flowers'. 'Yes,' Lacotte says, 'Gautier is rather woolly. But he does communicate images, impressions and metaphors which are helpful.'

At the same time, some reviews are actually very precise, especially those in England; Lacotte thinks they were probably written by ex-dancers. 'They explain variations in *La Sylphide*,' he says. 'They specify *enchaînements* of steps using the vocabulary of classical ballet.' He found an English review of the ballet's British premiere on 26 July 1832, listing the steps in one of Marie Taglioni's solos – *ronds de jambe avec glissades jetés, pas de basque en tournant* – which he discovered fitted with absolute accuracy on to the music. Letters and accounts by dancers are similarly specific.

But holes remained in the choreography. He treated them as a restorer would a damaged painting. 'It's like,' he says, 'when certain patches of paint are missing. You need to consider what is on the other side of the gap, why there is this here and that there. And if you have a real understanding of the style, then you can make the link.' He used Taglioni's teaching notebooks as material, on the principle that Taglioni made his dancers work hard in class at steps he used in his ballets.

Finally, when even that failed, he used his ultimate tool, the one he has found to be a lifeline, even though he knows it is not scientific: intuition. It was this that allowed him to solve the problem of how the sylphide entered in the second act. He looked at the decor and worked out that she might have appeared on the rock on the left and James would have held her hand. And later, when the Paris Opera Ballet took *La Sylphide* to St Petersburg, he found in the Theatre Museum a drawing showing exactly this. He was very struck by it.

If we take intuition as a leap of imagination, though, inspired by knowledge and experience, then maybe it is not so strange. And this brings us to the essential accoutrement of the restorer, which is the need to have a deep understanding of the context. Without studying the sensibility of the period, you cannot add the correct accents and perfume. 'You have to know how people lived,' Lacotte says, 'how they went to the theatre, how they thought, how they idealised women. You have to know the style and the technique in the other arts, the way painters treated light, for example. So when you recreate a decor, you think of the paintings of the time. It's an interesting process because you become simultaneously the reader of the book and the one who opens the book for others.'

Filippo Taglioni's *La Sylphide*, premiered in 1832, certainly fits Lacotte's stipulation about choosing ballets that had a big impact in their day. With *La Sylphide* Taglioni and his pupil and daughter Marie caused the renaissance of ballet.

Its genre was actually anticipated a year earlier thanks to Meyerbeer's opera *Robert le diable*. In it was Taglioni's *Ballet of the Nuns* which featured Marie and made a big impression. So strictly it is from the Ballet of the Nuns that we can date the beginning of the Romantic ballet. But *La Sylphide* became the emblem of Romanticism, causing ripples in the public at large. Women took to wearing white and light silk stoles called sylphides, a flower was given this name, so were a fashion magazine and even a type of barouche.

La Sylphide brought ballet into step with what was happening elsewhere in the arts, with Géricault, Goethe, Byron, Victor Hugo. Romanticism represented a break with rigid convention and a freer form of expression. Romantics were fascinated by the mysterious dark corners of the mind and as a result revelled in the metaphysical and supernatural. The Romantic ballet became obsessed by the theme of man's pursuit of the unattainable, the ideal, the infinite, as exemplified in *La Sylphide* by a mortal's hopeless love for a fairy.

La Sylphide, in Ivor Guest's words, was 'the prototype of the *ballet blanc* ... The vision of Taglioni as the Sylphide has haunted choreographers ever since' (1966: 5). The draped Grecian tunics imposed at the Paris Opera at the time of the Empire were replaced by Taglioni's vaporous corolla of white tulle, invented by Eugène Lami. As André Levinson wrote in his monograph on Marie Taglioni, this costume allied itself to the cult of drift and evanescence, as well as to the idea of a poetic, chaste simplicity (Levinson, 1930: 49). The dancer ornamented it with only a few flowers at her bosom and on her head, supplemented with a three-rowed pearl necklace and pearl bracelets. The wide skirt also facilitated jumps and travelling and broad *degagés*.

So what was the Romantic style in dancing? What did Lacotte expect from *his* dancers? Romanticism put technique at the service of dance, allowing it to flower as an expressive art. The divertissements of before, the easy effects and professional smiles to win applause disappeared; from now on dance was not just for the eyes but for the soul. Yet, this was not a break with the past; it was an evolution which surged into its most developed and heightened form with the Taglionis. The Romantic style aimed for rounded lines, softness and flow; adagios stressed large *développés* and *arabesques* and *penchées*. Dancers were forbidden to show effort; instead they had to have a graceful ease and *ballon*. Anything which lacked dignity or decency was proscribed. Filippo said to his daughter: 'Women and young girls must be able to see you dance without blushing; your dance must be full of austerity, delicacy and tastefulness.' Accordingly, he invented gentle positions of the arms, such as the arms crossed in front of the chest, as in Fra Angelico's *Annunciation.*

Taglioni held, as Saint-Léon wrote (p. 16), her torso slightly forward; this affectation gave an impression of fragility, the dress following behind. It extended the movement of her arms, so that her *arabesques* became enriched with a wonderful lyricism. To erase any brusqueness, she slowed down her pirouette and finished softly by descending in slow motion from pointe, her hands delicately marking an accent by opening very slightly after the music. She was the first dancer to hold a balance on one foot, on demi-pointe, and she is recorded as describing how in class she would train herself by holding the particularly difficult poses to the count of one hundred. In performance, balances were not a mere trick, but a way of punctuating her dance. And she was the first to show how pointes could be used as a poetic device, lengthening the line and giving it an ascending, ethereal quality.

According to Lacotte, the ballerinas of the time did far more to harden the pointes of their shoes than we had imagined. 'When,' says Lacotte, 'I first held one of Taglioni's shoes in my hands, I thought, how can she go up on pointe? There was no hard sole, nothing. But then when I looked at the inventories of the costumes I saw that they gave so many pairs of shoes and so many sheets of cardboard. And actually on some of the shoes, if you look closely, there are traces of an inner sole, and of varnish and cotton padding. So Taglioni, Grisi and all the dancers would cut a sole out of this tough cardboard to put inside the shoe, right to the tip,

Pierre Lacotte in rehearsal, 1997. Photograph by Ifan Pierce

which allowed them to go up on pointe as you would with an espadrille. They used the varnish to glue the cardboard and cotton padding together. And when they gave their shoes away they removed all that. So everybody said, what a miracle!' Even so, pointe technique was not as strong as today, the shoes not as protective, and balances on pointe tended to be performed as the final note of a phrase; but in Paris there were jumps on pointe, and a lot of steps, such as pirouettes, were done on pointe, not just for the soloists but for the corps de ballet too. Choreographers often specified in their notes whether a movement was on demi-pointe or pointe.

People danced much faster, and sometimes much slower than today. In other words, there was a greater contrast of speed. In fitting the steps to Schneitzhoeffer's score Lacotte realised just how far tempi have been slowed down in this century and how much *petite batterie* has been neglected. He had a lot of trouble persuading the Paris Opera Ballet that they needed to apply such rapidity to a multitude of small steps. He managed by getting the rehearsal pianists to quicken the tempi gradually over the weeks. He also eventually succeeded in convincing the dancers of the necessity of a forward-leaning posture and in persuading them for rehearsal to wear whalebone corsets, as romantic dancers would have done, which contributed to this stance – although at one point the Paris Opera Ballet dancers did threaten to strike. They found the *pas de deux difficult*, with extremely slow lifts, alongside exhausting variations and codas.

I asked Lacotte about the mime in *La Sylphide* which surprised me by its sketchiness and artifice. 'The mime has to fit in with the style of the dance,' he said. 'We know that people danced softly, like the tulle they wore, and they also attenuated the mime. The mime could not be realistic and emphasised, the contrast would have jarred. The sylph has to maintain her fragility in not just her dance, but her mime. And it fits in with the characters. When James says to the sylph "don't go", he does it with great restraint because he is afraid the gesture might frighten her. She is an apparition and he is afraid this apparition might disappear.' I put it to him that the style in Bournonville is nonetheless more realistic. 'Bournonville's version is wonderful, but it is far removed from Taglioni's. Bournonville was Vestris's pupil and Vestris was a realist; he had nothing to do with poetic romanticism. Bournonville never saw Marie Taglioni dance *La Sylphide*. He saw the ballet only once or twice in Paris, with others in the role. He choreographed his own version because his company couldn't afford the Taglionis' fees. The Royal Danish Ballet at that time was not one of the leading companies. So although I admire Bournonville enormously, he is not one of the main examples of what happened in the nineteenth century.'

Lacotte keeps the later *pas de trois*, called *L'Ombre*, which Filippo Taglioni added to the first act in 1839: this is a dance for Effie, James and the sylphide in which only James can see the sylphide. Lacotte has also made his own adaptations. For reasons of safety, he simplified the flying effects. 'Throughout the second act waltz,' he says, 'there were a dozen suspended dancers rotating at different heights, which required many counterweights. Moreover, these dancers were made to disappear for a while, effectively meaning they had to remain suspended 20 metres. up in the flies – which at the very least is dangerous.' In fact, there were anxieties in 1832. The director of the Opera, Dr Véron, banned *premières danseuses* from being suspended, stipulating supernumeries instead – obviously they were more disposable – and before each performance he personally checked all the apparatus. This did not prevent two sylphs from getting stuck one evening: they could not be moved up or down, so a stage hand, suspended from a rope, had to extricate them; and Marie Taglioni then walked to the footlights and reassured the audience that no one had been hurt (Pastori, 1987:50-1).

In the dancing, Lacotte allows *déboulés* – he disapproves of the term *chaînés* – to be performed on pointe, whereas in Taglioni's day they would have been on demi-pointe. Lacotte says that he did not want to jar the expectations of today's audience. But this decision surprised some experts, who were also dubious about seeing the corps de ballet on pointe, given that in Bournonville's ballets there was a great deal of demi-pointe. (I remember seeing early film of the Royal Danish Ballet confirming this.) 'Yes,' says Lacotte, 'but that was in Bournonville. It was not the custom in big dance cities like Paris, London, Vienna, Berlin or Russia. The Royal Danish Ballet was a more provincial company and the overall standard of technique was less sophisticated when Bournonville arrived. So he choreographed accordingly and the corps de ballet was probably not on pointe.'

Throughout we have seen Lacotte making a compromise between authenticity and today's expectations. He retained some of the cuts in *Giselle*; he likewise excised part of *La Sylphide*, because people nowadays have shorter attention spans. He asked his dancers to wear corsets, to acquire the correct posture; he made them learn to move faster. Yet he allows them to perform *déboulés* on pointe; he allows extensions that are certainly higher than they were in the 1830s. 'Because,' he says, 'nowadays we are used to high extensions or *déboulés* on pointe. If instead you perform them exactly as Marie Taglioni would have done, it runs the risk of looking like caricature. And that is the difficulty. You have to use your fine judgement to achieve a delicate balance –neither demanding legs too low or accepting them too high.'

He says, 'Either you make a completely authentic reconstruction, out of pure intellectual interest, as a museum piece. Or you make a reconstruction to be performed and to please a public. So you have to compromise, in order not to alienate.'

And that, surely, is a consideration that will remain in the future, even if restorers will increasingly consult video recordings and notation scores, instead of dusty files and old memories. 'On the one hand,' says Lacotte, 'I have to feel as though I am somebody else, thinking differently, living in another time. On the other, I have to affect the spectators, make them suddenly forget where they are and watch with such attention that they will receive the message completely. And that is very difficult in our era. Believe me, it's not easy at all.'

Notes

1. All Pierre Lacotte's quotations are taken from an interview with the writer in September 1997.

References

Guest, I. (1966), *The Romantic Ballet in Paris*, London: Pitman (new edn 1980, London: Dance Books)

Levinson, A. (1930), *Marie Taglioni*, trans. C. Beaumont, London: Imperial Society of Teachers of Dancing (new edn 1977, London: Dance Books)

Pastori, J-P. (1987), *Pierre Lacotte, Tradition*, Paris: Favre.

Saint-Léon, Arthur (1856), *De l'Etat actual de la danse*, Lisbon

Vaillat, L. (1942), *La Taglioni, ou la vie d'une danseuse*, Paris

'Bien écoute ...'
A Study of Nineteenth-Century Ballet Mime

Giannandrea Poesio and Marian Smith

While it could be safely affirmed that primary sources on nineteenth-century ballet technique are not scarce, nineteenth-century technical manuals focusing on the vocabulary, the syntax and the dynamics of what is generally referred to as 'ballet mime' are non-existent. Apart from some theoretical pamphlets and a few sporadic references to be found in dance treatises of the first half of the nineteenth century, the only publication that focuses on the art of mime applied to theatre dance is Carlo Blasis' *Saggi e Prospetto di un Trattato di Pantomima Naturale e di Pantomima Teatrale* (*Essays on and Proiect of a Treatise on Natural and Theatrical Pantomime*).

Nevertheless this work, published in 1841, was intended to be the introduction to a more 'technical' subsequent manual, that 'Trattato' – or treatise – mentioned in the title which, as a matter of fact, was never published. Even the technical principles of the Italian ballet mime that became so popular at the turn of the century – mainly thanks to artists such as Enrico Cecchetti, Malvina Cavallazzi and Francesca Zanfretta – were codified only between 1910 and 1930, namely when that art was already declining because of the innovative approaches to narrative theatre dance expounded by choreographers such as Mikhail Fokine. It is not surprising therefore that the lack of technical sources casting some light on the lost language of ballet mime has affected the way mime scenes are regarded today. With few exceptions, dancers and dance repetiteurs look at those scenes as merely ornamental components of the choreographic layout that can be easily edited or overlooked, regardless of their actual function within the dramatic development of the plot. Another problem that affects both those people responsible for the various restagings and dance scholars is the common, yet erroneous, belief that ballet mime remained the same throughout the nineteenth century and across Europe.

It is worth mentioning here that an eminent theorist such as Carlo

Blasis discussed the differences between French and Italian ballet mime in his *Code of Terpsichore* as early as 1828. Further distinctions can be made however when this particular language of gesture is considered in relation either to diverse choreographic styles or to different cultural and artistic contexts. The aim of this paper is, on the one hand, to reassess the significance of ballet mime, particularly within the context of the Romantic ballet and, on the other, to suggest the possible existence of other forms and uses of ballet mime than the ones we know today.

To this end we have worked on a case study; the practical realisation of an annotated rehearsal score for *Giselle*, which is housed in the Theatre Museum in St Petersburg. This rare score has long been known to exist but has not yet been thoroughly analysed. The Russian dance historian Yuri Slonimski suggested that it was annotated in Paris and then brought to St Petersburg to assist in the production of *Giselle* there. Though even the date of this manuscript has yet to be ascertained (it has been said to date from as early as 1842 and as late as the 1850s), it is plain (because it is lacking Petipa's addition to the Act 2 *pas de deux*) that this manuscript does reflect an early, pre-Petipa production of *Giselle*.

It is also clear that this manuscript was designed to transmit a key aspect of this ballet; its story. The manuscript captions, which are in French prose and are to be found on nearly every page except in the *danced* segments of the ballet, lay out explicitly and in great detail the substance of the mime and action scenes and even, in many scenes, include the words the characters are miming in the first person. Examples of these characters' words in the mime scenes include these: 'listen well'; 'finally he is gone, nobody sees me'; 'it's all the same to me'; 'what are you doing there? You have thrown your staff there?'; 'no, no, you will not die; I love only you'.

This rare document reveals a *Giselle* that in many ways would seem surprising to today's audiences. Firstly, it shows that in the old *Giselle*, 54 minutes were devoted to mime and action scenes, while 60 minutes were devoted to dance. Unaccustomed as we are to the idea of a near-even ratio like this, it does fittingly recall the term 'ballet-pantomime', the official designation at the Paris Opéra in the age of *Giselle* for the genre we now call simply 'ballet'.

A second feature of the old *Giselle* that would perhaps be even more jarring to the late twentieth-century audience is the extremely close relationship between music and gesture that is carried out throughout the work. As Parisian writers from the 1820s, '30s and '40s tell us, music did play a crucial role in imparting the ballet-pantomime plot, a point Ivor Guest has made and one that bears repeating (1980: 10-13). The words of contemporary observers reflect the high expectations that were held for ballet music:

> Ballet music has particular character; it is more accented, more *parlante*, more expressive than opera music, because it is not destined only to accompany and enhance the words of the librettist, but to be itself the entire libretto. (Baron, 1824: 296)

> Generally, one does not expect music from a ballet-pantomime composer, but an orchestra that is the translation, the commentary of the text which one would not otherwise be able to understand. (Anon., *Le Moniteur Universel*, 21 September 1827)

> . . . if music doesn't express the feelings of players, what else is there to express them? Arm movements are a poor language. (Anon., *La Siècle*, 23 September 1836)

> The composer is practically charged with telling the action... (Anon., *Le Constitutionnel*, 11 August 1845)

> ... the music has a *mission* to explain or translate [the scenes] (Anon., *La Sylphide*, 26 September 1840)

One way in which composers helped fulfil this *mission* of 'explaining or translating' the scenes was to write music that carefully matched the stage actions and gestures moment to moment, not simply accompanying them with background music or bland musical wallpaper, but actually helping to give them meaning. Composers also occasionally supplied the sound of the human voice, sometimes even matching the speech rhythm of the 'text' that the performers were miming. (For example, the text 'on verra' is matched by Adolphe Adam with a dotted rhythm that perfectly fits the words.) The close relationship of music to action is evident in *Giselle*. However it is not simply the captions in this *Giselle* score which have led us to the conclusion that music and action were carefully matched in Romantic ballet-pantomimes. Indeed other annotated scores of the 1820s and 1830s show an even less subtle approach than *Giselle* to the co-ordination of gesture with music. In any case it must be realised that the characters in mime scenes of ballet-pantomimes imparted certain information that was crucial to the plot, engaged in heated exchanges and underwent radical emotional ups and downs – just as opera characters did in *recitativo* scenes. Such scenes are not glossed over in latter-day performances of nineteenth-century opera, for it is here that so much of the plot is imparted. But in *Giselle* many of the details and nuances of such scenes have been lost in modern-day performances.

What would happen if *Giselle* were performed with the tight matching-up of music and gesture that this manuscript rehearsal score calls for and, in a way, that identified as such the voices existing in this music? It would surely seem quite melodramatic. Audiences would certainly also be surprised by the sheer amount of detail of the mime, for there are many more gestures per musical phrase than we are accustomed to. Also if *Giselle* were performed in a way that brought out the voices as such – physically *showing* the talking and singing quality of the mime music – audiences might view it as inappropriate. For it might seem more like an unsubtle melodrama or an opera than a ballet.

The interaction between the *musique parlante* and the accompanying gestures conferred a more 'realistic' quality onto the mime *recitativos*, thus contributing considerably to the narrative of the dance work. The 'singing' quality of the mime passages, in fact, allowed and still allows, in theory, a more complete rendition of the silently acted section than those schematic fixed gestures on which the Italian ballet mime of the late nineteenth century relied. At the same time an analysis of the captions to be found in the score reveals a more complex and richer vocabulary than that of the Italian ballet mime. Still one might wonder whether this richer vocabulary existed as such – passed orally from one generation of dancers on to another – or whether it was constantly re-created and reinvented by each artist.

It is worth remembering that since the publication of the early manuals dealing with conventional movements, most mime theorists reiterated that, apart from some set rules of symmetry and aesthetic, the expressive/narrative gestures had to be 'invented' every time by the performer. It was, in other words, up to his or her artistic skills to be able to 'act without words' and to render the 'silent speech' intelligible. As the same concepts were reiterated by dance theorists of both the end of the eighteenth century and the early nineteenth century, one might wonder if it was because of this 'creative and interpretative freedom' which stemmed directly from the impromptu actions of the Commedia Dell'Arte that constraining sets of rules were never written or published. Finally the singing quality of the mime gestures would suggest that both the dynamics and the musicality of each gesture differed considerably from that which is known today as ballet mime, which follows a more restraining system of balletic counts.

Our case study realisation of the rehearsal score for *Giselle* is not exactly a reconstruction, rather a practical way to provide supporting evidence to what has been said so far. The mime movements that we used throughout the passage are, as a matter of fact, a hybrid, namely those set signs that eventually became the core of the Italian ballet mime, referred to by Carlo Blasis as 'conventional' gestures, and more 'natural' ones, to use Blasis' words again, that do not have a set meaning. The chosen combination however is not arbitrary, for it draws from the precepts to be found in those theoretical pamphlets and dissertations mentioned earlier on. Blasis, for instance, recommended a combined use of both 'conventional' and 'natural' movement (1830:118). Some of the gestures used are very familiar and can be seen in the well-known Mother's scene taught by Tamara Karsavina included in both the Royal Ballet and the Birmingham Royal Ballet's productions of *Giselle*. Some other movements have been derived from another manuscript, the *Trattato di Arte Scenica*, by Serafino Torelli, acting master in Milan (Torelli, 1862?). This work, written between 1860 and 1882, was intended as a reference text for actors and singers. Yet dancers also used it, for Torelli taught at the celebrated academy attached to La Scala theatre. Although the manuscript is enriched with illustrations, the work does not prescribe a set of conventional movements, but simply offers some guidelines for the execution of appropriate and meaningful gestures.

The passage realised is from Act 1, scene 6. The following is the text from the St Petersburg manuscript, translated into English: [1]

[Berthe's music]
Berthe to Giselle: What are you doing there, you over there? You should be cutting grapes, and you mesdemoiselles, what are you doing there? You have thrown down your staff here? The young women while dancing say that it is Giselle. Berthe goes to her daughter and tries to grab her by the apron. She touches her heart and says to her: you poor thing, you will exhaust yourself.

[Snippet of the Giselle Waltz]
Berthe:
You with the dance, you are not thinking that this way you will die.
Giselle: Yes it is true that my dancing and him [pointing to Al-
brecht] and you that is all that I love. [Tense music] Berthe to her
daughter: You on your back, there will grow wings. [Giselle] The
wings I will not notice. [Berthe] You won't notice them, yes, and
listen well ['bien écout']

[Storytelling music]
Loys, Giselle and the 12 women gather around Berthe. Berthe calls
them and says: over there, over there in the dark night, young girls
like you and like you, the earth will open up and phantoms will
come out, covered in shrouds. On their backs they have wings
[tremolo forte as she mimes 'wings']. They surround those whom
they meet and force them to dance until they die [seductive oboe
melody].

[Nonchalant, bouncy music]
Giselle says: I do not believe all that. She crosses the stage dancing.

[Melancholy music]
Her mother expresses fears for her health. Loys reassures her.
Giselle and Loys go upstage saying that they will return. Berthe to
her daughter: come with me. Giselle: no, no.

A philological reconstruction of those mime scenes is out of the question, for we do not have enough primary source material and we can only
come up with hybrids as the one demonstrated.

Nevertheless, by referring to the few existing theoretical sources, it is
possible to 're-create' those mime sequences, bearing also in mind that
they should be the natural outcome of the creative and interpretative
skills of each performer. To reinstate those mime passages within their
original contexts could also prompt a sudden rediscovery of the dramatic
quality of nineteenth-century narrative works in an era when gratuitous
technical displays are far more important than interpretation and ballet
has become everything but a theatre art.

Notes

1. At the conference Marian Smith read the text as accompaniment to miming by Giannandrea Poesio.

References

Blasis, C. (1830), *The Code of Terpsichore*, London: Bull

Blasis, C. (1841), *Saggi e Prospetto del Trattato Generale di Pantomima Teatrale e di Pantomima Naturale sui Principi della Fisica e della Geometria e dedotto dagli Elementi del Disegno e del Bello Ideale*, Milano: Guglielmini e Redaelli

Baron, A. (1824), *Lettres et Entretiens sur la Danse*, Paris

Giselle, (n.d.), annotated rehearsal score, St Petersburg: Theatre Museum

Guest, I. (1980), *The Romantic Ballet in Paris*, London: Dance Books

Torelli, S. (1862?), *Trattato di Arte Scenica*, manuscript, Milano: Biblioteca Teatrale della Scala, CR. Q. 122

A la recherche des pas perdus
In search of lost steps

Alastair Macaulay

It astonishes me that, in the new age of dance scholarship that we have entered in recent years, so little work has been done on the most internationally influential of all choreographers, Marius Petipa. I must explain that, by 'Petipa', I mean a very catholic term. I mean the dancer and ballet-master from Western Europe who, during the mid-nineteenth century, came to work in Russia; the ballet-master and choreographer who, in Russia, revised several of the Romantic ballets that had first been staged in Western Europe, some of which already existed in Russia in earlier stagings; the patenter of a genre of post-Romantic choreographic ballet classicism whom we recognise as the spiritual father of George Balanchine and Frederick Ashton; the canopy or umbrella under whose shade worked such other ballet-masters and choreographers as Lev Ivanov and Enrico Cecchetti; the fragmented corpus of extant choreography which is still performed, in his name, on stages from Vancouver to Tokyo.

At first, the reason for the shortage of Petipa research seems simple: the answers lie in Russia, which until recently has been more or less inaccessible and whose language poses a problem for most dance scholars. However, not all the answers do lie in Russia. Many of the dance people who worked with Petipa (and Ivanov) came to the West (Mathilde Kschessinskaya, Olga Preobrajhenskaya, Nicholas Legat, Anna Pavlova and many more). Both his and Ivanov's ballets were recorded, several of them during his lifetime, in volumes of Stepanov notation that were brought to the West by the *régisseur* Nicholas Sergueyev, and some of which were used by Sergueyev as the main basis of his seminal revivals of these ballets in London and elsewhere. I love to think of Sergueyev leaving St Petersburg with his books of notation like Aeneas fleeing from the fall of Troy, bearing the household treasures with which he would in due course rebuild Troy on Italian soil; for Sergueyev would play an important role in rebuilding the repertory of the Russian Imperial Ballet in London. Therefore some of the answers to our enquiries into Petipa (and Ivanov) lie here, in London.

Nicholas Sergueyev (also spelt Sergueeff, Sergeyev, Sergejev): how very little research has been done into him. And yet he was the most important dance reconstructor in history – staging *The Sleeping Princess* for Diaghilev in London in 1921, restaging it for the Vic-Wells Ballet in 1939 as the crowning achievement of several major stagings for that company, and staging it and other ballets again in the 1940s for the International Ballet (the latter stagings were, he claimed, the most correct of all). Soviet scholars used to say that his understanding of the old ballets was thoroughly impure. However, some envy may, naturally, have prejudiced their views; and in recent years I have met Russian scholars who, as is only to be expected, are extremely interested to study the Stepanov notation that he brought to the West. André Levinson, Broni-slava Nijinska and Ninette de Valois all found serious fault with various aspects of his work – even, in Levinson's case, with the work that he was doing as *régisseur* while still in Russia (Wiley, 1997: 143; de Valois, 1977 and 1959: 106-7). We should therefore proceed into Sergueyev research with some scepticism. Nonetheless, he was a complex figure.

He fussed over non-dance details of stagings that were not notated – and indeed there is virtually no notation anyway for the first scene of *Casse-Noisette* (*The Nutcracker*), which he first staged here in 1934 (Wiley, 1985: 206–20, 387–400). He also fussed over steps as a teacher in class to the young British dancers. Pamela May has recently recalled how he incorporated steps from the classics into his classes, so that, for example, the female Vic-Wells dancers all learnt to do the ballerina's three *ronds de jambe*, at the start of Odette's variation in *Le Lac des cygnes*, each one larger and higher than the one before it – and that Sergueyev drummed this into all the female dancers by making them do it in class, coming forward from the back of the room to the front (Macaulay, 1997a).

This evidence of Sergueyev's fuss over detail tells us of his passion for the ballets and tells us that this passion came not from his reading of the notated scripts but from his loving memory of the ballets as they had been danced onstage. He used his memories on British dancers of the 1930s and 1940s, a number of whom are still alive – and a proportion of whom have healthy memories.

My paper raises more questions than answers. I have not spoken to all those who worked with Sergueyev, I have just gleaned a few memories from a few of those who did, and I have looked at a number – not all – of the photographs of his stagings. There is more work to be done, and I hope that some scholar or scholars will soon undertake it. These dancers are now in their seventies or eighties, and too much of their knowledge has already been lost.

Some of the fruits of this kind of research, when it is more fully undertaken, will not be practically useful onstage. We will come across, in fact, some bizarre details – details where we will think 'Oh, that's why Ninette [or Fred, or Margot] changed that!'

Nonetheless, we must investigate, because it will bring us closer to the essence of 'Petipa'. Far too often today we assume that what we have watched onstage, for one or five decades, is the original, whereas it is in several cases a deliberate departure from Sergueyev's text. And when new producers make the adjustments that they may well rightly feel should be made, they are often not revising – as they may think – the original, but are revising revisions, or revisions of revisions of revisions. Every generation must make its revisions, for sure, but I propose that we help the revisers to have a clearer idea of the old texts before they decide on the nature of their adjustments.

Let me give you three examples of lost details from Sergueyev stagings, at least two of which we are most unlikely to want to see onstage today:

1. According to Julia Farron, in the first few performances of the 'Vision Scene' of his 1939 production of *The Sleeping Princess*, there was a moment when four nymphs used to run off into the wings and bring on an artificial sea-shell which contained an old-fashioned toehold into which Margot Fonteyn, as Princess Aurora, had to place her foot and then balance in *arabesque*. The toehold was at a ludicrous angle, obliging Fonteyn to turn her leg in, and the whole incident lasted so short a time that it was more fuss than it was worth. Very possibly this is authentic Petipa from the 1890 original, but I do not much want to see it restored to the stage today. However, I do want it recorded; I do not want modern producers thinking that what occurs onstage at that moment today, and has occurred for decades, must be the original.

2. We have photographs of what used to happen at the end of the adagio for Odile and Siegfried in the ballroom act of *Swan Lake*. Both of them were in profile to the audience; it seems that Siegfried would kneel, holding both his arms out wide, and that Odile, holding both his hands,

Margot Fonteyn and Robert Helpmann in Act III of *Le Lac des Cygnes*, Sadler's
Wells Ballet, 1937. Photograph by Gordon Anthony. Plate 22, in *Margot Fonteyn
C.B.E.* by Gordon Anthony, Phoenix House, 1950, p. 55

would address him in an *arabesque* on pointe. (Photograph of Alicia
Markova and Robert Helpmann in Dame Alicia Markova, *Markova Remembers*, Hamish Hamilton, 1986, p. 52.) This, though it no longer
occurs, does not strike us as odd; it reminds us of certain Balanchine
ballets. But then, it seems, Odile would let go of his hands and, still

'The most interesting single photography in dance history.' The apotheosis finale of Act III of the Vic-Wells production of *The Sleeping Princess*, 1939. Designs by Nadia Benois. June Brae as Lilac Fairy, top left; Margot Fonteyn, Robert Helpmann, and Jack Greenwood, centre, as Princess Aurora, Prince Désiré, and Carabosse. Plate 63 of *The Sleeping Princess*, camera studies by Gordon Anthony, text by Nadia Benois, Arnold Haskell, and Constant Lambert, Routledge, 1940.

facing him, would clutch his raised knee while her raised leg moved into a higher *penchée*. This is, to our eyes, odd, although the Vic-Wells went on doing it until the 1940s. (1937 Gordon Anthony photograph of Margot Fonteyn and Robert Helpmann in Act III of *Le Lac des Cygnes*: see Plate V of *Margot Fonteyn*, camera studies by Gordon Anthony, with an appreciation by Eveleigh Leith, Gordon Anthony, 1941; and plate 22, p. 55 of *Margot Fonteyn C.B.E.* by Gordon Anthony, Phoenix House, 1950. See also Chance photograph of Fonteyn and Helpmann in P. W. Manchester, *Vic-Wells: A Ballet Progress*, Gollancz, 1942.)

3. Gordon Anthony's book of photographs of the 1939 production of *The Sleeping Princess* includes what I call the most interesting single photograph in dance history, although it has received almost no critical attention. (Plate 63 of The Sleeping Princess, camera studies by Gordon Anthony, text by Nadia Benois, Arnold Haskell, and Constant Lambert, Routledge 1940). We can see from other photographs that, despite the

limited stage conditions at Sadler's Wells, Sergueyev insisted that a new backdrop be used for the apotheosis of the ballet, in which respect almost no subsequent producer has followed his example. (His designer, Nadia Benois, had seen several different productions of the ballet at the Maryinsky and may also have been drawing on her memories of them.) In several ways, this draws us back to the original intentions of both Vzevolozhsky, who composed the ballet's scenario, and Petipa, who in turn plotted so detailed a minutage for Tchaikovsky (Wiley, 1985: 188, 333, 359, 370). The 1939 backdrop shows us Apollo in his chariot, and we know that Vzevolozhsky and Petipa wanted Apollo to appear at this point (although they, curiously, asked for 'Apollo in the costume of Louis XIV' (Wiley 1985:359). It reminds us of the classical tradition; and it reminds us, among other things, that Aurora's name means 'Dawn' – dawn to the bright sun. (Apollo was the god of sunlight, of art, of healing.) The photograph also shows us Carabosse standing near the married couple. This too is in accord with Petipa's intentions; Aurora's parents were not going to make the same mistake by forgetting to invite Carabosse twice, although in this photograph she looks as if she is still on the boil.

But the most extraordinary part of this photograph is the position of the Lilac Fairy: at the top of a staircase, with three attendants on successive steps gesturing up towards her and a fourth behind. She is gesturing, not to her attendants, not to the happy couple, but to Apollo in the sky. We have no evidence that this is what Petipa required. Julia Farron recalls that, in 1939, the Lilac Fairy started off with eight attendants in the Prologue and, because so many of them were needed elsewhere in the small Vic-Wells company, gradually lost most of them as the ballet progressed; which may explain why here there are only four. However, that does not explain the remarkable feature of this tableau, which is that it reminds us of the apotheosis at the end of Balanchine's *Apollo* (1928). Possibly this staircase comes not from the 1890 Petipa original but from a later Maryinsky staging, which Balanchine would have known: in which case both Balanchine and Sergueyev were inspired by the same feature. Equally possibly, in 1939, Sergueyev, or Ninette de Valois, or Frederick Ashton, said, 'We can't use the Lilac Fairy in the way Petipa intended, so, since Apollo is on the backdrop and since she only has three attendants left, let's use her and them to refer to the ending of Balanchine's *Apollo* [which had not been seen in London since 1929].' Whatever the answer, I find the idea and meanings of this photograph both marvellous and dramatic, and if the Lilac Fairy's ascent up the staircase had any of the glory of Apollo in Balanchine's ballet, well, what a thrill! We are unlikely ever to see this onstage – but I confess I would like to.

My theme is not Sergueyev alone. When you keep watching the old ballets today, it is startling to see that, in almost every big or famous moment, there is more than one version of the choreography. We need now to develop a tradition of historical textual analysis. For example, Pamela May recently recalled that one passage of Aurora's choreography in the coda of the 'Vision Scene' in *The Sleeping Beauty* was changed, between 1948 and 1952, by Frederick Ashton (Macaulay, 1997a). She, Fonteyn and other Auroras had been taught by Sergueyev to do a series of beaten jumps there; Ashton changed this to a series of turns. This occurred so long ago (without ever being credited to Ashton) that it has been incorporated into numerous Western versions as being by 'Petipa'. Again, this does not mean that we should rush out and reconstruct the Petipa original here. But I do propose that we try recording better who actually did compose each bit of our current Holy Writ.

Here I address just six examples of textual variation in current performance practice. Each one brings up different matters for analysis: matters of provenance, yes, but also matters of interpretation. They are all well-known passages. Sometimes the divergence is small, but it makes all the difference in the world.

The diagonal series of jumps in *The Sleeping Beauty*, in which Aurora makes her final entrance of Act I. All Auroras here do a crescendo series of *ronds de jambe sautés*. But that is all the Russians do, whereas Royal Auroras do a more explosive *jeté/assemblé* variant of the jump, the legs suddenly opening further in the air after the *ronds de jambe*.

A further problem is that Roland John Wiley says in *Tchaikovsky's Ballets* that the original Stepanov notation requires here 'a flurry of turns' (Wiley, 1985: 176). *Turns?* Turns exist in no version of the choreography. (My own suspicion is that Wiley here has misread the notation for '*ronds de jambe*' to mean '*pirouettes*', but I have not checked the notation.)

According to Pamela May and Julia Farron, Sergueyev in 1939 required *ronds de jambe sautés* with the extra *jeté/assemblé* emphasis, even though Fonteyn, the first-cast Aurora of that production, had no jump to speak of. My dance experience and cynicism lead me to suspect that the simpler Bolshoi and Kirov version was fixed upon, generations ago, by an ageing or weak Aurora. As Mahler said to the Vienna Philharmonic Orchestra, 'What you people call tradition is merely slovenliness' (Porter, 1979: 192-3). I have seen a weak Royal Aurora go for the same simpler jumps too, but fortunately that has not, to date, become a local tradition.

I should add that both May and Farron say that modern Auroras at the Royal Ballet 'don't quite get that diagonal right any more', although I – who have no dance training – have not yet ascertained precisely how they feel it should go, or used to go.

The *arabesques* with which, in Act II of *Giselle*, the corps de ballet of wilis hop across the stage. The corps is divided here into two halves. The left and right groups move, hopping in *arabesque*, towards each other, through each other's ranks, and over to the opposite side of the stage; then they cross back again. Until the mid-1980s, the Royal Ballet wilis always did these hops with their heads down, addressing the floor. The Kirov and Bolshoi companies, however, have for decades made a great effect by hopping with their heads up and their backs erect. Nobody who has watched either the Kirov or Bolshoi corps de ballet at its best would wish it to dance any differently; the posture of those Russian backs is thrilling, preserved so firmly in the *arabesques*, and it changes the entire dynamics of the hop excitingly.

The old Royal or Sadler's Wells way is far less exciting (although it too used to win waves of applause on American tours). The backs leant forwards and the heads were angled down (almost out of sight), concentrating on the floor. However, when Peter Wright, in his 1986 *Giselle* production for the Royal Ballet (one of his innumerable restagings of this ballet), changed this step and made the British wilis hop in the Russian way, I at once knew, with a pang, what I missed (apart from the obvious fact that the British wilis did not have Russian backs and could not bring to the step the same exciting control as the Russians). By addressing the floor, the old *arabesques* made you attend to the central drama of Act II of *Giselle*, in which spirits arise out of a burial ground, to which they will soon return. Giselle herself will presently ascend from that ground, and the wilis' hops prepare the terrain and the drama.

The opening gesture, in Act III of *Raymonda*, of the ballerina's great czardas variation in which she claps her hands to 'cue' the conductor. The music here starts slowly, with one series of three rolled chords, which is repeated; and each series is 'cued' by this handclap. Then

Raymonda, who has risen with the last chord onto pointe, starts to drift backwards in *bourrées* on pointe while the solo piano (a sound so unusual in ballet) starts its gorgeous, exotic, johnny-one-note lines.

Royal Ballet Raymondas, as coached by the late Rudolf Nureyev, audibly clap their hands in those beginning gestures – not too crudely, mind, but with a firm percussive effect that should be audible in Row Q of the amphitheatre – whereas Kirov and Bolshoi Raymondas do the clap silently, brushing their fingers together without real sound. The *bourrées* are different, too: the Russians do them spaciously, generously, but the Royal begin them with a quality of resistance, performing *bourrées* on the spot at first and seeming to be pulled backwards from behind through the spine and rear arm.

Now, the handclap is a terrific moment for pedants, and much ink has already been been spilt about it. The Soviets, who are capable of such fabulous snobbery, have said that to 'sound' the handclap is vulgar. Well, those of us who have seen the authority and refinement of Irina Kolpakova or Ludmila Semenyaka here would probably not wish them to have dance it differently by an iota.

However, it is not just a matter for Russians versus ignorant Westerners. Alexandra Danilova and George Balanchine 'sounded' the handclap in their various stagings of *Raymonda* material in New York. I believe also that the ballerinas of Petipa's day, who so often danced folk dances onstage, would here have kept the 'folk' quality of a handclap in Petipa's ultimate classical variation on czardas material. Once, when I wrote at some length and with some pedantry about this in *The Dancing Times* (Macaulay, 1984), my colleague Clement Crisp rang me to say that he had been to ask Alicia Markova about the matter. Markova had told him that the audible handclap was correct, that *Raymonda* belonged to a genre that she had been educated to call 'character-classical', and that she remembered not only Danilova but also Nemchinova here. Well, this takes us somewhat nearer the horse's mouth, does it not? And to me, who am fond of the audible handclap, it was gratifying news. However, Clement, who has long proclaimed the superiority of the inaudible Soviet method, was not satisfied. When Yuri Grigorovich brought his Bolshoi Ballet staging of *Raymonda* to Covent Garden, Clement asked Grigorovich about the matter. Grigorovich said that he had learnt it from Yekaterina Geltzer, who danced it in Petipa's day. With this, the matter comes yet nearer the horse's mouth. I confess that I have my doubts about Grigorovich's reliability. But perhaps, having established that both versions of the handclap seem to have impressive Russian pedigrees, we should leave the matter of provenance there.

Yet I cannot leave the handclap there, because I am less concerned with authenticity than with feeling. As I have said, I do not want the Kirov or Bolshoi to change its manner, but the reason why I also love the Royal way of doing it – and why I resist the Russians when they call the audible handclap vulgar – is because it satisfies me, and because it lodges meanings in my mind. What meanings do I mean? That handclap, especially when sounded, is the most overt example in the nineteenth-century repertory, perhaps in the entire ballet repertory, of a ballerina giving the cue to her conductor. It is as if she is announcing 'Hey, music maestro!' But then she *bourrées* backwards; and when she *bourrées* with resistance, as at the Royal, she gives us the directly opposite feeling. It is this opposition that I love. The handclap said 'I am mistress of my music'; the *bourrées* say 'I am my music's slave'. These two contrasting meanings sum up a ballerina's relationship with her music, both active and passive, and they bring a ballerina's relationship with her music closer to the surface than anywhere else in the old repertory.

The most intimate passage of the great adagio of the first lakeside scene in *Swan Lake*, choreographed by Ivanov in what I have argued is Petipa's style (Macaulay, 1997b). Throughout this adagio, Odette has been withdrawing from Siegfried and has been caught again or reassured by him in one way or another. Here, however, when she has withdrawn from him towards 'Rothbart's corner', he, forlorn, has chosen not to follow her. This time *she* turns, sees him standing there, and makes the decision to rejoin him. She arrives suddenly before him in a 'swan' *arabesque*, standing on pointe, her arms raised. Kirov and Bolshoi Odettes stand with Siegfried's arms on their waists. They fold down one arm, and then the other; and then they stretch away from Siegfried, down into *penchée*. That continues the steady lyricism of this adagio, and it shows us Odette again withdrawing from Siegfried even when in contact with him. With the Royal Ballet, however, it is Siegfried who folds down one of Odette's arms and then the other; each time, her head and neck crane back towards him; and then he, encircling her waist by holding her folded arms crossed with his, rocks her gently, in time with the music.

This moment has, in the Royal version, been called 'the most beautiful moment in all ballet', so I think it deserves a little pedantry. What is striking about the Royal version, after all, is that it seems awfully British;

indeed, awfully 'Fred'. The straining for maximum physical contact, the reassuring embrace, the Garbo-like arch of the neck, the sweet rocking in his arms... do these not seem suspiciously Ashtonian? So should we enquire whether it is simply a British variant on the original?

One source to consult is in the Rambert Archive (a copy is in the New York Public Library Dance Collection), and I confess that I have not consulted it for some 16 years. It is the 1930 film of Alicia Markova dancing the adagio with the young Ashton as Siegfried. Markova had been taught this adagio only a few years before by Kschessinskaya, who had been taught it by Ivanov (Dolin, 1973: 119–20). Now, the film raises several other problems. Along with many other historical questions that this film raises, it is obviously cramped by being danced in a small studio for a fixed camera, and Markova's *penchées* and 'swan' *ports de bras* are so removed from any performance practice of recent decades that they seem absurd. But memory tells me that Markova is 'rocked' by Ashton without making much of it.

There are other sources. Pamela May has recalled Danilova being 'rocked' there, and how wonderful it was. Moreover, = in 1991 I was able to interview Danilova about this and other moments. She told me that she believed the 'rocking' was 'correct' and that she could remember it being danced that way at the Maryinsky by Elena Lukom. Now, Lukom was the ballerina who, according to Margot Fonteyn, Sergueyev most revered, so this loops us back to the Sergueyev/Royal tradition (Fonteyn, 1975: 59). (Fonteyn, however, is wrong in describing Lukom as belonging to the generation before Pavlova; she was in fact from a later generation.) It is at any rate possible that the current Russian way of dancing this passage is in fact a relatively recent revision and that the Royal way may be 'authentic'. Certainly its origins are Russian.

Again, however, authenticity matters less than meaning. What I have loved in the Royal version – at any rate, with some ballerinas – is the fact that its intimacy matches the music. For this is the moment when the solo violin and solo cello come together most intimately, and the choreography, in catching this aspect of the music, gives us a dramatic image of closeness which is crucial to the ballet. This proximity is what Odette has craved as well as feared (it occurs twice, and each time it is she who eventually moves forth from his embrace) and, alas for Odette, it will never be matched by anything again in her choreography. It is the ideal which she and Siegfried hope in vain to recapture.

Earlier in Act I of *The Sleeping Beauty*; the *piquée arabesque* with which Aurora opens her first extended variation. The music here has three beats in the bar, marked by slow pizzicati ('plink', 'plunk', 'plonk'). Bolshoi Auroras (in my experience) use the first 'plink' beat as a preparation, the second 'plunk' beat for the *arabesque* itself, and the third 'plonk' beat for stepping out of the *arabesque*. The Kirov also use the first 'plink' beat for the same preparation, but are slightly more vague in the timing of the *piquée arabesque* itself and of stepping out of it. The *arabesque* is the physically momentous part of the dance phrase, and Russian Auroras emphasise its quality of forward gesture, sometimes making it more of an upward gesture.

However, over the pizzicato accompaniment, the music has a melody. It is a simple, slow, iambic melody on the solo violin ('ti-*tum*..., ti-*tum*...') and the violin begins the long 'tum' note on each of the first beats of the bar, over the pizzicato 'plink'. The Royal Ballet has Aurora arrive in her *arabesque* on that *first* beat of the bar, and she sustains the *arabesque* there. Her dance, in short, matches not the accompanying pizzicati but the solo violin and its melody.

We have here two different schools of musical response. It is possible that the Russian style of dance musicality – using the downbeat for a preparation and following the music often by the distance of a beat (or more) – goes back to Petipa's day and/or to the guest Italian ballerinas who lit up the Russian stages in Petipa's day (and on whom the ballerina roles in *The Sleeping Beauty*, *Swan Lake*, *Raymonda* and other ballets were created). It is also possible that the British style of musical response is relatively modern, and that de Valois, Ashton and Constant Lambert developed it in the 1930s and 1940s. We know that de Valois found Sergueyev musically wayward, even bizarre (de Valois, 1959: 106). We know that de Valois and Ashton agreed that Spessivtseva, the first-cast Aurora of the Diaghilev production they had both watched in 1921, was unmusical – although this fact alone was enough to put de Valois off Spessivtseva, whereas Ashton used to say to de Valois that 'All your British girls are "musical", and none of them is Spessivtseva!' Pamela May simply says, about her teachers in the 1930s, that 'None of the Russians were musical'. However, the fact that de Valois did greatly admire Trefilova (the second-cast Aurora of Diaghilev's production) may lead us to suppose that Trefilova danced with something at least akin to de Valois's taste in musicality. Who knows? The Fonteyn, 'Royal', way of

Princess Aurora in *penchée arabesque,* Act I of *The Sleeping Princess*: Margot Fonteyn in the 1939 Vic-Wells Ballet production. Plate 18 of Gordon Anthony, *The Sleeping Princess*, op. cit.

timing this *arabesque* may have been based on someone's memories of Trefilova here. And of Trefilova, more anon.

The matter grows more complicated when we ask further about the step, and when we look at photographs. For Pamela May insists that Sergueyev required Aurora here to step into *piquée arabesque* and then, while still on pointe, to move into . And this *penchée* is what is recorded in a Gordon Anthony photograph. (Plate 18 of Gordon Anthony, *The Sleeping Princess*, op. cit.) May recalls that the *penchée* got smudged out before 1946. Possibly it did not greatly suit Fonteyn, whereas May – who says 'I loved *penchée*' – found it becoming.

However, I think the matter is more complicated yet. Another 1939 photograph shows Fonteyn, in the studio, doing at this point not *penchée* but extreme *allongée arabesque* here – an *arabesque* in which the raised leg is the highest part of the body (which qualifies the step as *penchée* according to some definitions, though not mine), while the body leans as far forward (rather than down, as in a true *penchée*) as possible, the arm gesturing straight ahead in space. (Gordon Anthony 1939 studio photograph of Margot Fonteyn in Arnold Haskell's *Balletomane's Album*, A. & C. Black, 1939), p. 66 (top right). It seems that Fonteyn, from 1939 on,

Princess Aurora in *allongée arabesque* in Act I of *The Sleeping Princess*: Margot Fonteyn in the 1939 Vic-Wells Ballet production. Gordon Anthony 1939 studio photograph, Arnold Heskell's *Balletomane's Album*.

experimented with more than one version of this step, and that, sooner or later, she plumped definitively for the *allongée* rather than *penchée* emphasis (and a less drastic *allongée* too; from 1946 on, she and other Royal Auroras performed a more conventional first *arabesque*). Remember that Fonteyn took advice on Aurora's choreography not only from

Sergueyev but also, unlike May, from other Maryinsky veterans: Preobrajhenskaya, Karsavina and Volkova. Certainly there is one account that Trefilova danced an extreme *allongée* here ('in the variation she stressed the *arabesque allongée* at the beginning and she stretched and stretched forward and then came out of it into *attitude posé*, with less emphasis on the *chassé* and *glissade* which came in between'). And Fonteyn may have been, on the advice of others, trying to recapture Trefilova's much admired classical style (*A Conversation with Mary Skeaping*, 1977–78: 19).

Still, *penchée* was a more congenial emphasis for May than for Fonteyn, and today it is a congenial quality for most ballerinas. Might the old *penchée* be offered to the Bussells and Guillems as an option? I wonder.

However, the height of the leg in the *arabesque* is, I believe, less important than the *arabesque*'s duration and its musicality. I do not cry out to see Darcey Bussell doing an extreme *penchée* here – but I did feel alarm when I saw Gelsey Kirkland plucking the *arabesque* briskly as if its duration was of no consequence, and sentimentally placing all the emphasis on the gesture of sweet regard that follows.

Most important of all is that the *arabesque* should be secure. Whether you prepare emphatically for it as do the Russians, or arrive in it as if out of the blue as did Fonteyn and colleagues, you have to arrive and be on your balance at once. Robert Greskovic wrote tellingly in the 1980s of Auroras with the Sadler's Wells Royal Ballet who spent most of the duration of the *arabesque* adjusting their weight and line, making the step meaningless (Greskovic, 1986: 64-66).

The *piquée arabesque* with which Giselle opens her Act I variation. (Who choreographed this variation, with its famous *ballonné* hops on pointe, is another problem; but not one I intend to address here.) Kirov and Bolshoi ballerinas here do a more or less conventional first *arabesque*, whereas Royal Ballet Giselles do an *arabesque* with arms *en couronne*, which is like no other *arabesque* in extant nineteenth-century ballet.

What makes this tricky to research is that it is not simply a matter of the Russians saying 'tomayto' while the British say 'tomahto'. Royal Giselles have done *arabesque en couronne* since 1937, as photographs of Fonteyn show. (Gordon Anthony 1937 studio photograph of Fonteyn, plate XVI of Anthony; reproduced on p. 45 of Money, 1973). Now, in textual matters, the Sadler's Wells dancers were taught that there was one correct version of everything, from which they were given no leeway;

you did what the steps that you were told were traditional, and it was largely your business to bring them to life, to find their meaning (Fonteyn, 1975: 96). This task of interpretation was what the young Fonteyn, in particular, undertook, with signal effect on the Western performance history of the nineteenth-century classics. In the case of this *arabesque*, Fonteyn always did it the one way for more than 30 years, and so one is inclined to assume that she was copying the precedent of Alicia Markova, who had been, in 1934, the company's only previous, and definitive, Giselle. And yet a 1937 photograph of Markova, now dancing Giselle with the Markova-Dolin Ballet, shows that she did not do the *arabesque en couronne*, but a more conventional first *arabesque*, much as practised by the Soviet companies. (Photograph of Alicia Markova in Markova, 1960, plate 11.)

What does this tell us? Possibly, Fonteyn was the first to perform the *arabesque* with arms *en couronne*. If so, why did she do it the new way? Equally possibly, Fonteyn was copying the *arabesque* that Markova had done at Sadler's Wells in 1934 (in general, that was how the young Fonteyn worked on all the old ballets, with no textual departure from Markova's precedent) – which would mean that Markova herself revised the *arabesque* when she began dancing in other productions. This is possible. In *Giselle and I*, Markova says that during her time with the Markova-Dolin Ballet, Bronislava Nijinska 'helped me a good deal with the role of Giselle', encouraging Markova to adjust and extend certain moments. 'She spoke of the need for breadth and extension of move-ment, the out-flowing gesture that goes right through to the finger-tips and on into infinity!' (Markova, 1960: 54). Perhaps Markova revised the *arabesque* at this point, and perhaps Nijinska had remembered certain Russian Giselles taking this option.

I cannot solve this problem of provenance here, but I do think the music gives us a clue to justify the Fonteyn approach. The music here plays an iambic melody; but, whereas the Tchaikovsky iambic melody for Aurora's first-act violin variation is legato, Adam's melody, although for full orchestra, has a staccato emphasis: 'ker-*chunk*' (pause), 'ker-*chank*' (pause), and so on. The conventional *arabesque* opens out into space with a spatial amplitude that would suit legato music, but the unusual *en couronne arabesque* has a finite quality that catches the quality of staccato suspense in Adam's music.

I have given these six examples, partly because it is very interesting to research the performance history behind them, but also, more valuably, because if we analyse the meaning of each version we may illuminate the style and meaning of the choreography. I do not mean always to favour the Royal versus the Russians. There are moments, for example, such as in the conclusion of the adagio of the 'Bluebird' *pas de deux* in *The Sleeping Beauty* where I believe the music tells you that the Royal text is wrong or, rather, unstylish.

Authenticity – if and where we can determine it – is an important issue, but it is not the most important one. The Royal Ballet productions of *The Sleeping Beauty* and *The Nutcracker* include, or have included in the past, several features where they choose to honour Tchaikovsky's original score rather than the abridged and/or rearranged version which Petipa and/or Ivanov used. And – partly because people of taste, such as Ashton, showed how to make Tchaikovsky's original work – these features seem to me preferable to the Petipa text. For example, in the 'Vision Scene' of *The Sleeping Beauty*, Bolshoi Auroras dance what is more or less Petipa's original choreography, to music which Tchaikovsky actually composed for the Gold Fairy in Act III. The Royal Ballet at that passage dances the music composed by Tchaikovsky for Aurora, as choreographed by Ashton. Here I prefer musical authenticity to choreographic authenticity; but I do not know that I would, were it not for Ashton. One must be flexible in these cases.

Another example of the inauthentic version being preferable is the very famous series of balances (*équilibres*) in *attitude* (arms *en couronne*) that Princess Aurora performs in Act I of *The Sleeping Beauty*. These were developed by Margot Fonteyn, and they become so standard, so musically and poetically satisfying when well delivered, that even the Kirov has recently started to adopt her version (see Money, 1975). Quite right, too.

I also propose that we should consider seriously the idea of textual options in these ballets. Ninette de Valois may have insisted that there was only one correct text in the classics, but Sergueyev did not. Nor did those before him. The Stepanov notation for *Swan Lake* has two versions of the main dances for Odette; the 1895 Legnani one (which included Benno for the adagio) and the 1901 Kschessinskaya one (which set the adagio for Odette and Siegfried alone). It is not quite clear whether the later version was choreographed or sanctioned by Ivanov, who died in 1901, or by Petipa, or by whom (Wiley, 1985: 263–4 and 1997: 180).

Markova had learnt the latter version as a girl from Kschessinskaya. In 1934, Sergueyev taught her the Legnani version of the adagio (the Royal and other companies preserved Benno until the early 1960s), but offered her a choice of options elsewhere. He also offered her options in the choreography of *Giselle* (Markova, 1986: 45–6). The Soviet Russians also preserved the practice of offering options to ballerinas, as we know from the experiences of Beryl Grey and Nadia Nerina as guest ballerinas with the Bolshoi and Kirov Ballets, although some of their options seem to have been relatively recent (Grey, 1958: 15; Nerina).

It should, however, be obvious that some options are less stylish and expressive than others, and it should also be obvious that too much leeway over options can create thoroughly unstylish practice. I remember one season at the Royal (c. 1984) when, in Act III of *The Sleeping Beauty*, the several leading *danseurs* performed as many as six different versions of some of the Prince's choreography in the coda to the *grand pas de deux*, some of which were particularly cheap arrangements of standard bravura steps with no choreographic interest.

In ballet we need, therefore, a new discipline of textual criticism – even of what I may term choreographic palaeography. We are in a situation akin to that faced by scholars of Latin and Greek texts. In Tom Stoppard's new play *The Invention of Love*, the aged A.E. Housman speaks about this: 'By taking out a comma and putting it back in a different place, sense is made out of nonsense in a poem that has been read continuously since it was first misprinted four hundred years ago. A small victory over ignorance and error. A scrap of knowledge to add to our stock. What does this remind you of? Science, of course. Textual criticism is a science whose subject is literature, as botany is the science of flowers and zoology of animals and geology of rocks... Literature, however, being the work of the human mind with all its frailty and aberration, and of human fingers which make mistakes, the science of textual criticism must aim for degrees of likelihood, and the only authority it might answer to is an author who has been dead for hundreds or thousands of years. But it is a science none the less, not a sacred mystery. Reason and common sense, a congenial intimacy with the author, a comprehensive familiarity with the language, a knowledge of ancient script for those fallible fingers, concentration, integrity, mother wit and repression of self-will – these are a good start for the textual critic...' (Stoppard, 1997: 38–9). For 'literature', in our case, read 'choreography'.

We need open minds about this. It is shocking to find how often both

Russian and British dance professionals and enthusiasts assume that their local version is not simply right but also 'original'. This year, I heard a ballet mistress of English National Ballet, a former Royal Ballet dancer, say on the radio that she thought the best version of *Swan Lake* was 'the original'. She explained that she meant by this 'the old Royal production, with Sir Fred's fourth act.' Did she think that Sir Fred's fourth act was in the original? or even that all the rest of the old Royal production was 'the original'? Even Clive Barnes, who really should know better, has referred to the old Royal version as 'the original'. This kind of provincialism is the last thing that is needed now.

We live in a dance world where Russian and Western dance people have unprecedented access to each other and to each other's traditions. There is much to be learnt, about the past, and about the options available to the future. In the 1920s, Feodor Lopukhov used to say to the Maryinsky/Kirov dancers: 'Forward to Petipa!' Now that all the great ballet choreographers are dead, the past is the only way forward. Forward to Petipa; forward to Balanchine; forward to Ashton.

References

A Conversation with Mary Skeaping, interview with Peter Anastos, *Ballet Review*, Vol. 6 No. 1 (1977–78)

Anthony, G. (1941), *Margot Fonteyn*, camera studies by Gordon Anthony, with an appreciation by Eveleigh Leith, London: Gordon Anthony

Anthony, G. (1945), *Ballerina – Further Studies of Margot Fonteyn*, introduction by Eveleigh Leith, London: Home & Van Thal

Anthony, G. (1950), *Margot Fonteyn C.B.E.*, London: Phoenix House

Anthony, G. (1940), *The Sleeping Princess*, camera studies by Gordon Anthony, text by Nadia Benois, Arnold Haskell, and Constant Lambert, London: Routledge [although the book was not actually published until 1942].

Dolin, A. (1973), *Markova – Her Life And Art*, London: White Lion Publishers

Fonteyn, M. (1975), *Autobiography*, London: W.H.Allen

Greskovic, R. (1986), '*The Sleeping Beauty*, the British, and Ballet', *New York Ballet Review*, Winter

Grey, B. (1958), *Red Curtain Up*, London: Secker & Warburg

Haskell, A. (1939), *Balletomane's Album*, London: A. & C. Black

Macaulay, A. (1984), 'Clap Yo' Hands – Raymonda at the Century's End', *Dancing Times*, November

Macaulay, A. (1997a), 'Pamela May', *Dancing Times*, May

Macaulay, A. (1997b), 'An Amiable Apparatchik', *Times Literary Supplement*, December, pp. 16–17

Manchester, P.W. (1942), *Vic-Wells: A Ballet Progress*, London: Gollancz

Markova, A. (1986), *Markova Remembers*, London: Hamish Hamilton

Markova, A. (1960), *Giselle and I*, London: Barrie & Rockliff

Money, K. (2nd edn, 1975), *The Art of Margot Fonteyn*, London: Dance Books

Money, K. (1973), *Fonteyn: – the Making of a Legend*, London: Collins

Nerina, N. (n.p.d.), *Ballerina*, London: Weidenfeld & Nicolson

Porter, A. (1979), *Music of Three Seasons: 1974–77*, London: Chatto & Windus

Stoppard, T. (1997), *The Invention of Love*, London: Faber

de Valois, N. (1977), *Step by Step*, London: W.H. Allen

de Valois, N. (1959), *Come Dance With Me: A Memoir, 1898–1956*, London: Hamish Hamilton

Wiley, R.J. (1985), *Tchaikovsky's Ballets*, United Kingdom: Clarendon

Wiley, R.J. (1997), *The Life and Ballets of Lev Ivanov*, United Kingdom: Clarendon

Identity and the Open Work[1]

Sarah Rubidge

I write as one who is grappling with the issues raised by the 'open work' both artistically and theoretically. As an artist I am creating works which have a fluid form. As a theorist I am trying to understand what implications this practice has for extant theories of identity in dance.

As this paper was written to be read at a conference entitled 'Preservation Politics', I was asked to focus my paper on reconstruction. My topic being the 'open' work, my first thought was: In what sense can one talk of 'preserving' or 'reconstructing' an open work, if at all? And if it does make sense (and I am not altogether convinced that it does) in what sense, if any, might the open works which originated in, say, the 1960s and 1970s be preservable for future generations?

The notion of *preserving* an open dance work is problematic. The major identifying feature of the open work in the performing arts is the fluidity which characterises the form and appearance of its instantiations[2] in performance. Now whilst it could be argued that, to some extent, *every* work of the performing arts is an open work, the minor variations within a (more or less) stable overarching form which occur in the performance history of a work are not my concern in this paper. The open works with which I am concerned are those which are intended by the originating artist to exhibit frequently radical changes in form from performance to performance. They are those in which variations in each performance may be so great that it becomes difficult for audience members to recognise multiple performances of an open work as performances of the same work.

It is perhaps here that we encounter our first question: is a work's *identity* tied to our ability to recognise its instantiations? Indeed, if two performances are so different that audience members are not able to recognise them as performances of one and the same work, that is, as artefacts which flowed from a common origin, is it coherent to talk of such works *as* works? Or should we be arguing that another term needs to be found for such artefacts?[3]

Our underlying concept of 'the work' obviously comes into play at this point. What *are* the pivotal properties of 'workhood' in the performing arts? Conventional wisdom holds that works, in order to be *works*, have to meet certain criteria. *It* is produced by an author, and made to be attended to by a spectator, listener or reader. *It* must endure in some identifiable way. *It* exhibits certain consistent structural and/or physical features which enable us to recognise it from occurrence to occurrence. These last two criteria tend to be founded on an ontological position which favours an ontology of substance,[4] under which rubric a work, even of the performing arts, is a relatively stable artefact.

In the performing arts in general and in dance in particular, standard arguments have focused on the question as to whether a specified performance is a performance of the work it purports to be, or a performance of a different work (the relationship of the token performance to the work-type). The arguments tend to cluster around the degree from which a performance can deviate from a notated score (or an original performance or production) and still be considered to be a performance of *that* work (Goodman, 1976; Armelagos and Sirridge, 1978; Dils, 1992; Giffin, 1992; Ingarden, 1986; Thom, 1993). Normally in dance, the author of the work (or an authorised surrogate, frequently a performer who was in the first production of the work in question) has the final say as to whether a particular revival counts as an instance of the work it purports to be. In this way what is seen as the authorial 'integrity' (and in consequence the identity) of the work is protected.

Whether the two (authorial integrity and a work's identity) are so closely allied is at the heart of my current concerns. Works, thus conceived, are implicitly ahistorical in as much as their histories, both physical and conceptual, do not impact upon their individuating criteria. The identity of the work is intimately connected to its originating impulse and its original form.

Post-structuralists, and increasingly philosophers from other traditions,[5] unhappy with the criteria for workhood outlined above and the reliance on authorial intention as a determining factor for a work's identity (both of which tend to lead to a condition of closure), abandoned the designation 'work', and replaced it with the notion of the 'text'. The 'text' is subject to change in terms of its meaning each and every time it is interpreted, even if its outer form does not change.[6] The 'reader' or interpreter can access the text through many entrances, and mobilise many codes whilst exploring the possibilities that the text presents. The reader thus becomes an active participant, reconstituting the text at each reading. The author does not have final say, as far as the meaning of the text in reader, audience or performance interpretation is concerned. Indeed Roland Barthes famously proclaimed the death of the author and, along with the post-structuralists, privileged the 'reader' over the originating author as the 'author' of the text (Barthes, 1977b: 142-8).

Post-structuralist thinkers clearly adhere to an ontology of flux or variance. There is no original work to which subsequent instantiations, or indeed interpretations, must *necessarily* conform. This is a clear contrast to an ontology of substance which relies on just such conformities.

In general I accept the terminology of the post-structuralists and the rationale underlying it unhesitatingly. I am however unwilling to relinquish the notion of the author altogether, and thus the notion of the 'work'. However underdetermined the terms of that authorship[7] might be, I would contend that the author is not 'absent' from the work, if 'authorship' means that an author, or group of authors (Barthes' 'scriptors' (Barthes, 1977b: 145)) originated its initial ideas and the framework within which the play of reading takes place. However much the original ideas might be modified and extended by their 'readers' and interpreters, during a reading there is, or was, something which was made available to be modified and extended. This something was authored, was an intentional 'object', an object of someone's thought.[8] Further, it is that 'something' which is generally the source of further readings, not the newly constituted text which appears with each reading.

Such a claim is no longer particularly contentious philosophically (see Margolis, 1995) or artistically. Many contemporary artists deliberately create works for which they claim authorship, which allow for, indeed demand, such modifications and extensions. That is, they author 'texts' not works. Inspite of appearances this is not a contradictory assertion. Indeed in view of both the mode of reading practice outlined above and contemporary theories of interpretation, I would suggest that the notion of the work against which Barthes was arguing in his seminal works (Barthes, 1977a and 1977b) has been modified to such an extent that, for all practical purposes, 'work' and 'text' may now be considered to be almost synonymous.

But how do I arrive at that position? As noted earlier, theoretical discussions concerning the individuation of the work have taken place under the constraints of a metaphysical theory which adheres to an ontology of substance (or invariance). (They also bear the vestiges of the

Romantic definition of art and the artist, namely that the art work is a unique expression from a unique mind.) I would suggest that this ontology is rapidly being replaced by an ontology of flux (or variance) not only among the post-structuralists (although they may have been responsible for the changes in the conceptual framework which have taken place) but also among philosophers from the analytic tradition. Concomitantly a great many artists from all disciplines have embraced an ontology of flux and abandoned the Romantic understanding of art and the artist during the last forty years, indicating that this conceptual framework has been developing on all fronts.

However, in dance, even whilst accepting that a dance work is necessarily in the process of becoming (Armelagos and Sirridge, 1978: 130) and thus is closer to the concept of a 'text', we still seem, both as artists and as viewers, to seek to individuate[9] works, *all* works, through the strategies of an ontology of invariance (or substance) rather than those of an ontology of flux. When individuating dance works, we rely on the identification of essential (which may be merely consistent) perceptible properties, that is, features which are observable in the presentational form across several performances. The result is that whilst acknowledging it is not possible for a dance work to be instantiated through *identical* performances (and therefore is a 'becoming-object' (Benjamin, 1994: 17ff.)) we demand that certain necessary features, which identify the work, must carry across presentations if the latter are to be considered instantiations of it. Such strategies lead us to nail our colours to the mast of an ontology of substance. This mode of operation, whilst it may be appropriate for works with a relatively stable presentational form, does not lend itself easily to radically open works.

It may be that if we are to make sense of the notion of identifying open works, or perhaps we should say recognising radically dissimilar performances as being of the same work, we need to recast our enquiry.

It is obviously necessary to individuate a work, that is, to find the regularities which enable us, at the very minimum, to refer to it as a predicable entity, to describe it. However this only allows us to individuate it, to locate its numerical identity, not to locate its identity *as* a particular work, to identify its 'nature'.[10] Even those who hold to an ontology of flux must individuate the work, or text, at this minimal level if they are to be in a position to make reference to it.[11]

The way in which we seek out or identify the regularities through which we are able to refer to some entity *as* that entity, however, betrays the underlying ontological position which informs our understanding of a phenomenon. The regularities we tend to seek in dance are frequently held to be properties such as movement materials, choreutic properties, eukinetic properties, costumes, music. This belies adherence to an ontology of substance. However it may be that in some contexts, with some works, we should be seeking regularities which are not so immediately obvious. That is, there may be some feature, or property, which identifies a work but is not perceptually evident in its instantiations.

For instance, an open work may merely constitute a set of, perhaps underdetermined, elements and/or operating structures and may only be individuatable (that is, its instantiations recognisable) through prior knowledge of these features, in as much as they are not immediately apparent to those who do not know the work. Let me give you an example. A particular work may require that its performers enter a space, sense the physical structure of this space as it is constructed by their presence and/or action at any one moment, and move in accordance with that understanding of the spatial configurations of the environment and their immediate psychological responses to it. (This imaginary work is not far removed from Stockhausen's group of works *Aus den seiben Tagen* (1968), the immediate successor to *Kurzwellen* (1968). These works made use of chance sound events and the players' responses to them as a means of forming the work in performance.) Instantiations of the work will change from presentation to presentation, and from venue to venue. It would be difficult to identify the work through reference to the surface characteristics of its individual instantiations. The 'work' requires a particular mode of attention from the performers to particular structural parameters of the performance space if *it* is to be realised. It is here, in this indeterminate performative 'space' that the 'work', both as artefact and as process, lies. In such an instance a title, coupled with the attribution of a certain author to a work, may be acceptable as minimum, but sufficient, individuating criteria. However such criteria (title and author) are sufficient only to allow us to individuate a work for referential purposes, they are not sufficient to locate its identity *as* a work, or to help us to understand what is 'going on' in the work. Nor do they help us to recognise an instantiation of such a work. Indeed it may be that the very point of the work is that its instantiations are difficult to recognise. The latter is therefore part of the work's 'nature', of its identity.

Neither of the two recognitional strategies I have outlined (that is, using either concrete features or operating instructions as identifying characteristics of a work) is *necessarily wrong*, but it may be that in some contexts the use of one or the other of these strategies is inappropriate. Indeed I would suggest that whatever our ontological position, in different contexts (for instance, different types of work) we may need to seek different kinds of regularities if we are both to individuate and identify a work.

Let me unpack this a little. In individuating a work one is merely making it possible to recognise and refer to the work (give it 'number'), not to make any claims about its 'nature'. However it is this very 'nature' which is frequently used as an identifying criterion in dance – find the essential, the invariant, 'nature' of the work and you have found the 'work'. It is frequently claimed that deviations from that 'nature', effected by changes in the substance (rather than the detail) of the perceptual form as determined by the originating author, render a performance invalid as an instantiation of the work. (This is the argument implicitly cited in relation to both Tudor's *Dark Elegies* (1937) and Limón's *The Moor's Pavane* by Giffin (1992) and Armelagos and Sirridge (1978) respectively.)

It is precisely this position that the post-structuralists, and more recently philosophers such as Joseph Margolis and Andrew Benjamin, are disputing. They suggest that the 'nature' of a work constitutes little more than its salient regularities.[12] The salience of the regularities, and consequently the 'nature' of the work, however, are not inherent in the work, but are ascribed by human beings. When the salience of the regularities changes, for whatever reason, the 'nature' of the work changes. There is no doubt that during the course of their histories, what are taken to be salient features of art works may change over time (admittedly over a very long time). However under the rubric of an ontology of flux these changes do not damage the identity of the work, for they are part of what that work is. This contrasts directly with an ontology of substance.

In the open work it is this notion of change that has been taken up and articulated by the artist. Indeed change at a tangible level is the very purpose of the work. An open work is the framework for a set of possibilities, or potentialities, not a set of predetermined, prearranged elements. The open work is necessarily in flux. It has a 'career' (Margolis, 1995: 137), a history, rather than an essential nature.

I would suggest that the identity and form of the open work is, more than any other kind of work, constantly deferred, demonstrating what Andrew Benjamin (Benjamin, 1994: 24) calls an 'ontology of becoming'.

Benjamin argues that the ontological status, the 'nature' if you like, of all art works, even those of the plastic arts, is such that it changes over time, even when the outer form remains relatively stable. The work of art is a 'becoming-object'. He notes that 'what is captured immediately by the formulation of the becoming object is the linkage, or perhaps more accurately the incorporation of the object into a process, one which concerns coming to presence' (Benjamin, 1994: 22). *Any* work then is subject to its own history and that of the world in which it is presented.

If this is so for any work it is even more so for the open work. An integral, even essential, part of the identity, the 'nature', of the open work *is* that flux, *is* the shift in form, *is* the work's 'becoming'. The 'work' of the work lies equally in its conception and in individual constructions of its elements into a form, the latter executed either by the spectator or by the re-presenter of the work. But I would maintain that this does not mean that 'anything goes'. Rather it means that the individual composition of elements, the latter provided by the author, sets certain minimal constraints. Spectator or presenter can formulate both an idea of one of a multitude of potentialities inherent in the 'work' and a temporary form for it from those elements.

However various and unpredicted the forms which can constitute an instantiation of an individual work may be, it is the elements that the originating author created which are shaped by the reader. They may be concrete images, structures, any number of things. There will be no single 'right' way of putting them together, although there may be some ways which, at an aesthetic level, are said to work better than others (although what constitutes 'better', and who determines it, may change over time). Both presenter and spectator thus engage in a dialogue with the work and in doing so contribute to its 'nature', that is, to its 'career'.

Open works, I would suggest, are a deliberate challenge to the ontology of invariance. As a result, for many open 'works', methods of identifying a group of performances as instantiations of **x** or **y** work which rest on the identification of perceptible samenesses in performances of the work are inappropriate. Other methods of identifying the work which accommodate the variety of the forms these works take and which are relevant to the work in question, must be brought into play.

In the light of this preamble let me re-phrase the question with which I opened this paper. If the 'nature' of the open work is its career, is it possible to preserve an open work through reconstruction? If we were to reconstruct Yvonne Rainer's *Terrain* (first performance 1963), through reference to performances of *Terrain* which took place in the early 1960s, would we be preserving the work, or merely presenting a reconstruction of a performance (or imagined performance) of the work as constructed at that time? And if we were to do so what status would that reconstruction have?

I would suggest that it would have no status at all with regard to the work's identity. The only way in which *Terrain* and its identity, could be preserved in the 1990s would be through its re-presentation using 1990s performers and following the instructions left by the originating author, with no recourse to original performers, to photographs, films or any other traces, for it is in its very fluidity of manifest form that the identity of the work lies, not in its perceptible samenesses. With *Terrain* and other works Rainer was consciously operating in the context of an ontology of flux.

I am arguing therefore that radically 'open' works have no 'original' author-determined performance or instantiation against which all other performances can be compared (although there will have been, of course, author-determined performances). The very point of such an open work is that each performance is merely one performance amongst many variant performances generated from the same set of instructions. This is its salient identifying feature. The 'work' is the idea, the active engagement of the dancers one with another and with the material and any other factors which might come into play (props, site, transient digital images and so on). It is not embodied in any given manifest form. The conception which lies beneath the procedures which enable an instantiation of the work to be generated is the 'work' of the work. The author's versions in performance cannot be privileged with regard to the authenticity of the shape of the tangible form each performance takes if the, frequently underdetermined, instructions are followed. Indeed *Terrain* and other works by Yvonne Rainer were deliberate attempts to challenge the very concept of the 'work' as it was generally perceived at the time, and thus implicitly set up a challenge to the very notion of reconstruction.

My claim is then that recognition of perceptible regularities does not necessarily enable us to identify an open work, because if the author's instructions are followed but the outcome differs from the original, that outcome would still be an instantiation of the work even though the 'world' the performance presents may be radically at variance with that envisaged by the artist. The author of the open work is not the author of the Romantic era, the genius with a unique message to communicate to its audience, with an invariant world to present. Rather the author of the open work provides the framework for a series of possible worlds within and across which the 'reader' can play and tangibly affect the form, the 'world', the career, and thus the nature and identity of the work in process. The open work is therefore far more than its surface features. Indeed it is only through the 'work' of the work that we can identify it.

So, with regard to my question at the beginning of my paper as to whether a reconstruction of an early performance of an open work would be a reconstruction of the work, my answer has to be that it would not. Indeed, I would argue, it would not be advisable to reconstruct a performance of an open work several years after its genesis as the reconstructed performance would, through this reference back to the origins of the works, implicitly or explicitly become a benchmark for correctness. It would thus interrupt the career of the work by setting its parameters within very particular, arbitrarily chosen bounds. Such an endeavour would be at variance with the 'nature', the identity, of the work and thus not an instantiation of it. The open work has no 'original', nor has it an ideal performance. It has instead clear originating ideas from which performances are generated. It is in these ideas, not in the external forms, that the identity of the open work lies.

Notes

1. An 'open' work is a work the form and/or movement content of which alters from performance to performance. The author of the work provides the raw elements and/or instructions from which any performance of the work is constructed. Much of Yvonne Rainer's work exemplifies the open work in dance. She notes, 'I... seem to be about variety, changes and multiplicity... a spectrum, of possibilities in terms of spatial density... and perhaps most important of all, duration and sequence' (Rainer, 1974: 151). Pieces made using task-based instructions, the detail of the performance being left in the hands of the performer, would be open works as would works which have the movement content pre-determined, but the order in which the movement phrases are performed differs from production to production, or performance to performance.

2. The term 'instantiation' refers to occasions in which the work (which may 'exist' only as a written score, script, or video recording) is made visible or audible. An instantiation, for instance of a performance work would be a performance or production of the work.

3. Earle Brown suggested that some of his open form works should be called

'musical activities', not works at all, as they did not fulfil certain central criteria of workhood. He argued that 'a work must have an identifiable [musical] content which can then be formed. (Brown, 1966: 61).

4. Ontology is that branch of philosophy which relates to the 'being', or essential nature, of phenomena. The term 'ontology of substance' (also known as 'ontology of invariance') refers to an ontological position which argues that phenomena have an essential, fixed nature.

5. For instance Joseph Margolis, Andrew Benjamin, Arthur Danto.

6. Arthur Danto argues that with each new interpretation the structure of the work changes and that each viewing is a new work (Danto, 1981: 125). Barthe's notion of text might be a more appropriate (see Barthes, 1977a).

7. The concept of 'author' against which the post-structuralists were arguing was overdetermined, holding that authorship endows an author with a *rightful* control over the form, expressive surface, and content of the work produced. An underdetermined idea of authorship merely allows that the author originated the source from which texts flow.

8. In short, an intentional, and thus interpretable, object.

9. That is, to distinguish *this* work from *that* work.

10. On this very difficult notion of the 'nature' of a work, Margolis argues that whilst interpreted texts (objects, whatever) may have certain stable properties, they need not have fixed natures. That is, 'The formal fixities of discourse, of reference and predication, have nothing to do with deciding what the intrinsic nature of [a] text may or must be' (Margolis, 1995: 35).

11. The very reason that problems of identity are a traditional topic of philosophical thought is that things do change, and if we are to talk of something changing we have to be able to say what that something is. However in doing so we may not be describing the unchanging *essential* features of that something, merely referring to features which, at that time, enable us to recognise it. In some cases those features may change over time as they do, for example, with people. Continuity is frequently offered as a criterion of identity to accommodate such phenomena.

12. These may be concrete regularities (movement, structure, etc.) or less visible regularities, for example, interpretative regularities.

References

Armelagos, A. and Sirridge, M. (1978), 'The Identity Crisis in Dance', *Journal of Aesthetics and Art Criticism* Vol. 37 No. 2, pp. 129-40

Barthes, R. (1977a), 'From Work to Text', in *Image-Music-Text*, ed. S. Heath, London: Fontana/Collins, pp. 155-64

Barthes, R. (1977b), 'The Death of the Author', in *Image-Music-Text*, ed. S. Heath, London: Fontana/Collins, pp. 142-8

Benjamin, A. (1994), *Object.Painting*, London: Academy Editions

Brown, E. (1966), 'On Form', *Darmstadter Beitrage zur Neuen Musik* No. 10, pp. 57-69

Danto, A. (1981), *The Transfiguration of the Commonplace*, Cambridge, Mass. and London: Harvard University Press

Dils, A. (1992), 'What Constitutes a Dance?: Investigating the Constitutive Properties of Antony Tudor's *Dark Elegies*', *Dance Research Journal* Vol. 24 No. 2, pp. 17-18

Giffin, J. (1992), 'A Dance Director's Investigation into Selected Constitutive Properties of Antony Tudor's *Dark Elegies*', *Dance Research Journal* Vol. 24 No. 2, pp. 19-24

Goodman, N. (2nd edn, 1976), *Languages of Art*, Indianapolis/Cambridge: Hackett Publishing Company Ltd

Ingarden, R. (1986), *The Work of Music and the Problem of Its Identity*, transl. Adam Czerniawski, ed. E. J. G. Harrell, London: Macmillan

Margolis, J. (1995), *Historied Thought, Constructed World: A Conceptual Primer for the Turn of the Millennium*, Berkeley and Los Angeles: University of California Press

Rainer, Y. (1974), *Work 1961-1973*, Halifax and New York: Novia Scotia College of Art and Design and The New York University Press

Thom, P. (1993), *For an Audience: A Philosophy of the Performing Arts*, Philadelphia: Temple University Press

Revisiting History in Postmodernism
Resurrecting Giselle... again... and again!

Vida Midgelow

Giselle rises and falls, rises again... falls again. Bursting from her grave she gasps for air... air to resuscitate her, the air of life. Gesture, collapse, gesture, collapse... attempting to find a new language with which to speak before she disappears into history... disappears into myth... disappears into thinnest air.

Postmodernism has reinstalled history as significant. This paper seeks to set the reworkings of the classic ballets that have taken place in recent years into this postmodern context. The words that start this paper are a description of the opening images of my own revisiting of the ballet *Giselle* (Coralli and Perrot, 1841). This dance is ironically entitled *The Original Sylph* (1997). I will argue that the desire to revisit a classic, such as *Giselle*, and the attempts by postmodern reworkers, such as myself, to transgress the power and authority of such classics places these dances in political flux.

In this world of multiplicity the past and the present come together in a dizzying medley; Coralli, Ek, Lansley, Dean, Wright, Tchernychova – a list of creators and of re-creators of the ballet Giselle. Images oscillate and fragment before me as the past is revisited, recycled, re-envisaged and reformed; Giselle as vampire, Giselle as ethereal being, Giselle as sexual woman, Giselle as drag queen, Giselle as not Giselle. A constellation of styles and approaches collide... parody, spoof, psychological, Romantic... forming contradictory messages and radical juxtapositions in 'knowing' re-creations. Or to take another view – the past becomes commodified and we wallow in pseudo- historical depth.

The 'fascination with the past' in postmodern dance has been high-lighted by Valerie Briginshaw as she briefly identified some of the modes by which posmodern dance has incorporated history (1991:18). The use of classical techniques in the work of artists such as Michael Clark and Karole Armitage is one such mode. *Drastic Classicism* (1981) and *The Watteau Duets* (1984) by Armitage present movements from the ballet canon with a raw energy in a punk context. Sally Banes has suggested that Armitage 'deconstructed ballet' and whilst her work assaults the senses it is also 'consciously interwoven with art world and dance world achievements' (Banes, 1994a: 298).

A fascination with the past is also evident as thematic content and Briginshaw points to examples by Yolande Snaith. *Step in Time Girls* (1988) and *Germs* (1989) both recall women's past lives via historical references in the costumes. Snaith suggests that 'women's clothing is tied up with the body and the different ideals for the human body have changed so much, look at paintings to see the absurd outfits women wore to fit in with the ideals of the time' (cited in Adair, 1992: 225).

The allusion to past events in a manner that both reclaims and re-states the past can also be seen in much of Ian Spink's work. *Two Numbers* created by Spink in 1977 juxtaposes sections of material from *Coppélia* (1870) and references to the horrors of the suppression of the Paris Commune, an event which occurred in the same year as the ballet's premiere (Jordan, 1992: 186). The propinquity of the two elements serves to contextualise the ballet in a horrifically telling manner, making a harsh statement about the gap between the romantic ideas of the ballet and reality.

Dances such as *The Hard Nut* (1991) by Mark Morris, a remaking of *The Nutcracker* (1892), and *Aurora* (1994) by Meryl Tankard, a decon-structive version of *The Sleeping Beauty* (1890), overtly and self-con-sciously rework the dances of the past. *The Hard Nut*, set in a retro-70s past, presents a pop culture of television, oversized toys and mutant offspring. The dance has an ironic tone but is both critical and nostalgic for the ballet at its source. In *Aurora*, Tankard presents images that are disrupted and discontinuous. Playfully making use of an eclectic range of styles, the dance is formed as a gleeful hotchpotch, the choice of per-formance styles cutting across boundaries and happily mixing tradition-ally disparate elements. *Aurora* is an uncompromisingly contemporary work that comments on both the present and the past.

Reworkings revisit our dancing heritage. Through this revisiting, the choreographers of such works adopt, embrace and question this heritage. Ballet has been the prime focus for such reworkings, the genre sometimes being revisited to re-present the form as despised, sometimes to celebrate it as magical, sometimes to frame the ballet as socio-politically laden. Whatever the mode of the reworking, these works draw attention to history as an issue. Historical contexts are reinstalled as significant, whilst also problematising the entire notion of historical knowledge, making the viewer aware of the nature of the historical referent.

Hayden White (1978) has shown us that the past, which becomes history, manifests itself to us in traces and our perceptions of it are shaped by artifacts in the form of photographs, paintings, etchings and sculptings and through stories; aural, written and danced. Drawing from the personal, social, visual, aural and the kinetic, hybrid tracings of the past are formed.

Opening the archives of history, of Giselle's story and my story – finding records of the past, revealing traces of possibilities...

A programme from the 'Sadler's Wells Royal Ballet'; dated 12-17 June 1978. Peter Wright's production of 'Giselle' (after Petipa after Coralli and Perrot). Contents reveal biographies, synopsis, statements of policy and of vision, advertisements and calls for financial support. All that is left following an evening of viewing dance... I know I was present... I have the programme... but my memory of this specific evening of dance has gone... disappeared... vanished... evaporated into thinnest air

Choreographic log book – evidencing ideas from workshops, from improvisations, stages of planning and notations of results... a fragmented text which is already disappearing as the memory fades and the pencil marks rub off.

An item of clothing – full of colour and texture – a list of names telling of previous wearers... elastic from my wearing... I do not have time to hook up the dress in the performance – the dress reminds me of driving around North London trying to find English National Ballet's costume department in torrents of rain.

A shoe – in the wrong box!

Ballet shoes... covered in soil from my latest performance of 'The Original Sylph'. Childhood Tutu showing signs of neglect... sweat shirt along with black splatter marks – following too careless a use of shoe dye... and lastly a video tape... a tool for the recording and playing of past events.

These disparate leavings, all with a dancing story embedded within, suggesting connections and memories, telling of absences and of gaps as the layers of my history rub off on one another and I construct an account on my identity.

These 'primitive' textual artifacts which are relatively unprocessed historical records are organised into 'invented' or 'imagined' narratives in traditional histories. All interpretations of the past are as much invented (the contexts) as found (the facts), argues White (1973, 1978). Histories, because of this fictive element, cannot be literally 'factual' or completely 'found' or absolutely 'true'. This 'inventing' is, however, generally hidden as the 'non-primitive' (the narrative) obscures the 'primitive' (the found): the construction of the narrative is thereby displaced rather than overtly exposed. Traditional histories in the manner of Carr and Elton are, states Keith Jenkins:

> too certaintist, too mystifying, just too committed to the pretence that they can engage in a 'real' dialogue with 'reality' of a (somehow) non-historiographically-constituted past as history, to be reflexive enough guides to the question of what is history today. (Jenkins, 1995: 10)

History becomes histories and questions in postmodernism. It asks: whose history gets told? For what purpose and in whose name? 'Postmodernism is about histories not told, retold, untold. History as it never was. Histories forgotten, hidden, invisible, considered unimportant, changed, eradicated' (Marshall, 1992: 4). Thereby, rather than coming towards the end of history or a rejection of history as suggested by some commentators, history is proliferating. We now have multiple histories which are inclusive of herstories and your stories. History has become overtly narrativised as the facts of the past become known to us as constructed accounts. So rather than forming a grand narrative, postmodernism constructs a montage of narratives to form our history.

Postmodernism, as stated earlier, reinstalls historical contexts as significant and also problematises the entire notion of historical knowledge. As Eco writes, 'The postmodern reply to the modern consists of recognising that the past, since it cannot really be destroyed, because its destruction leads to silence, must be revisited: but with irony, not innocently' (1983/4: 67).

Linda Hutcheon presents a parallel view when she states that 'for artists, the postmodern is said to involve a rummaging through the image

reserves of the past in such a way as to show the history of the representation their parody calls to our attention' (1989: 93). In postmodernism,
history and the historically mythicised are revisited and opened up to
questions. Hutcheon suggests that a parodic reprise of the past is one of
the key ways in which artists revisit history.

Postmodern parody is described by Hutcheon as 'ironic "trans-
contextualisation" and inversion... repetition with difference' (1985: 32).
Given that postmodern dance reworkings are inevitably discursive of
other texts and involve 'repetition' and 'difference' to differing extents,
Hutcheon's definition of parody might usefully be applied here. A parody
references the desired source and, via 'trans-contextualisation', offers the
possibility of transgression, of critique and of difference.

Frederic Jameson (1991: 1-30) argues however that postmodern quotation keeps us imprisoned in the past and that pastiche prevents us from
confronting our present. In Jameson's gloomy view, postmodernism is in
a 'cynical embrace with commodity capitalism'. 'Aesthetic production has
become,' argues Jameson, 'integrated into commodity production generally' (1991:65). The postmodern pastiche replicates or reproduces, thereby
reinforcing the logic of late capitalism. This view is not without substance, for within parody there is a certain ambivalence between that
which is conservatively repetitive and thereby operating as a homogenis-
ing and hierarchising force and that which is denormatising, promoting
revolutionary difference.

For as Hutcheon suggests, 'one of the lessons of the doubleness of
postmodernism is that you cannot step outside that which you contest,
you are always implicated in the value, you *choose* to challenge' (1988:
223). The sources which are quoted or subverted in reworkings carry
their own values. Given that these values may not be the ones I wish to
endorse, how am I to avoid being co-opted by the source, which in a
reworking, is explicitly used?

The solution to this problem may be found in the form or ethos of the
reworking. The reworking may be innocently reverential, ridiculing, di-
dactic, ironic, accepting or inverting. In that reworkings both recall and
deconstruct, recycle and create, it is possible to invoke things we have
not seen before. The potential of a reworking is therefore two-fold. Firstly
the revisited text can be displayed in a new way, allowing the past to be
seen in a different light. Secondly, the created text has the potential of
any cultural production to communicate meanings and give rise to different ways of looking. Whilst that which is reworked is not completely

divorced from its original aura, it is placed in surprising new contexts and combinations. Each sign becomes another whilst not altogether losing its particular history and integrity; the juxtaposition of different discourses manipulating old signs and incorporating them with a new logic. As Hutcheon argues in *The Politics of Postmodernism*:

> [Parody] does not wrest past art from its original historical context and reassemble it into some sort of presentist spectacle. Instead, through a double process of installing and ironising, parody signals how present representations came from past ones and what ideological consequences derive from both continuity and difference. (Hutcheon, 1989: 93)

However, the difficulties of being truly transgressive within parody remain and the politically motivated artist today might well be urged to follow Hal Foster's suggestion. He encourages artists not to re-present given representations and generic forms but to investigate the processes and apparatus which control those representations. A critical role for the postmodern artist is developed, a role that incorporates the positioning of the subject within dominant cultural discourses and offering strategies for counter-hegemonic resistance. Thus the artist exposes the processes of cultural control without trying to transcend hegemonic discourse (Foster, 1985: 143–53).

It becomes possible through such a procedure to draw a distinction between making representations that reflect hegemonic ideology and representing the hegemonic representations of that ideology. In this way the 'mythicised past', which is duplicated and viewed as natural, can be presented as specific and contextualised. The viewers' attention being called to the processes of naturalisation and thereby, the past is de-mythicised. The desire to draw on the past remains, but the impossibility of the desire truly to transgress is acknowledged, and a mode which is resistant is suggested.

In all this postmodern babble I am reminded of a statement by Eco on the postmodern attitude, and it is this – alongside Giselle's kinetic 'statements' – that I now parody.

(The text and gestures that follow are an extract from my 'The Original Sylph' 1997 and were presented at the conference in a performative mode)

'I love you madly'

Circle wrist at the ear open out forearm, cut fist down to waist and clench in left hand, pull hands apart…

'a woman who loves a very cultivated man knows she cannot say to him "I love you madly"

Removed, abstracted and manipulated: the circle of the wrist, the stroke up the body, the clench at the chest, gestures full of meaning becoming de-mythicised.

'because she knows that he knows (and that he knows that she knows) that these words have already been written by Barbara Cartland.'

Two hands rotate, wrist in contact with wrist: Two hands, a finger and a thumb, pluck: Two fingers resting together stroke up the body from groin to over head: Two hands clasp, open, clasp.

'Still, there is a solution to this problem. She can say "As Barbara Cartland would have put it, 'I love you madly'." At this point, having avoided false innocence, having clearly said that it is no longer possible to speak innocently, she will nevertheless have said what she wanted to say: that she loves him, but that she loves in an age of lost innocence'

The pattern accumulates… and in its own accumulation, its own self-referentiality, its own positioning to the spoken words, false innocence is avoided and double coding achieved.

(after Eco (1984: 67–8) and the *Giselle* of Coralli and Perrot (1841))

I now turn to a consideration of some other potentially 'resistant' re-workings of *Giselle*. In recalling and inverting the Western canon, post-modern reworkings are not, I contest, attempting to preserve or to con-demn (although this could be said to be a feature of some of these works) but are presenting history as problematic. In this also lies the questioning and simultaneous reinforcement of the canon itself. The use of 'classic' texts reinstates the presence of that which is authoritative in our culture, but the manner of the use serves to highlight (if not managing to under-mine) the nature of that which is canonical. 'Resistant' reworkings:

> embrace questions about dance history, the 'genre' divisions within
> dance (for example, ballet, modern, and folk dance),… the relation
> of dance to other art forms, the relation of 'high' art to folk and

mass culture, and, as well, larger social questions about gender roles, ethnic identity, and moral/political education.
(Banes, 1994b: 282–3)

Mats Ek's *Giselle* (1982) strips the work of its Romantic trappings and emphasises sexuality and the repression of women. Giselle in the second act finds herself not in the land of the living dead but in what appears to be an asylum with Myrtha as head nurse. This setting reminds us that over half the patients in mental hospitals are women and questions the nature of madness. Through this 'trans-contextualisation' Ek presents a new role for Giselle as a woman, although this representation of woman as 'mad' and unable to control her emotions might also be said to re-inforce negative images of women. The work is not without other diffi-culties. In its total reworking of the choreography it tends towards the presentation of a new 'truth' rather than opening the work to the reader's response and the potential of multiple visions.

Les Ballets Trockadero de Monte Carlo's all-male version of *Giselle* is also problematic. The Trockaderos aim to present 'classical ballet in parody and en travesti' (programme notes, 1997: 6). The 'parody', how-ever, is rather one-dimensional in nature taking the form of imitation and exaggeration to achieve a comic effect. The men, short, stocky, slender and petite, dance *en pointe*, wear Romantic tutus and heavy make-up. In this version the Wilis are vampirical spirits and Giselle, danced by 'Margeaux Mundeyn', is self-assured. Whilst the gender subversion does make the viewer aware of the highly specific and gendered vocabulary of Romantic ballet, in the end the Trockaderos' desire to perform the skills of a ballerina better than a ballerina simply reinforces the image of the ballerina as an ideal. This reworking is ultimately supportive of hegemonic ideology, reflecting rather than questioning or revealing its source.

A more resistant vision is found in *I, Giselle* (1981), by Jackie Lansley and Fergus Early. This dance takes the established narrative and exam-ines its politics, ideology and sexual roles. Huxley writes that in '*I, Giselle* Albrecht is trapped by the Romantic role accorded him, in a version where Giselle discovers his subterfuge in Act One, and he is punished for his deception rather than his noble love' (Huxley, 1988: 168). The dance makes direct use of the Romantic ballet's movement vocabulary, but this is placed alongside other styles and performed in a self-effacing (rather than presentist) manner. The reinterpretation disrupts the values embedded in *Giselle* and in the Romantic style. As Lansley and Early state in their programme notes, they wished to 'reclaim some of [ballet's] positive elements and skills, particularly its theatrical quality and use these in new contexts' (cited in Huxley, 1988: 167). 'These new contexts,' I posit, are the site of resistance through which we come to know the narrative, characters and style of *Giselle* differently.

So where am I left in all this as I tip-toe through histories, plod through theories and turn within a multiplicity of references? I am not a historian dancing with dead bodies or hoping to solidify the bodies of the past, but a choreographer who seeks a dialogic relationship between past and present bodies, examining their role in the production of meanings. I imagine a revisiting of history in which the dances of the past are reframed, my personal past is acknowledged and my own dancing past is interspersed.

In recycling and critiquing the past and the present, I am interested in inventing new stories rather than documenting those of the past, creating a multi-layered/multi-voiced text, punctured by allusions and subtexts. Anthologised, each element becomes a coded fragment of culture, a piece of a puzzle that may never be resolved since its various parts shift places and meanings. In the creation of this dance I acknowledge the nature of the task being undertaken, via the signalling of the use and abuse of exterior texts. I aim, through this parodically resistant reworking, to offer a view of the world in which we can know the dances of the past, but that we can know them differently. And so I begin.

Images, fragments, traces, whispers..

A gesture which hints at the already known; the crumpling of a tutu... a sign of distaste; teetering steps, a precarious balance... the response to a particular pink ribboned shoe.

'Buffeted by too much history'... she shuffles from buttock to buttock, arms flail, gesturing in 'port de bras' ... circle, arabesque, crossed, fifth, open fifth.

In this age of lost innocence she proclaims; As Barbara Cartland would have put it...,

Images, fragments, traces, whispers...

Her body falling, arching, twisting... 'Poor body'

Cut and pasted kinetic resonances are juxtaposed; one body part to another, one

moment to the next, the past to present and the present to the past.

Knees collapse, heels raised ... 'because she knows that he knows' (and he knows

that she knows.)'

Images, fragments, traces, whispers...

Tentative, speculative actions... her hand marks a pathway overhead, the fore and mid fingers held together ..a root it has taken before, an action that is recognisable. Insubstantial nebulous tendrils draw her ...a grave, a tutu, a daisy, a gun, a pair of shoes .. vestigial relics of the near and more distant past.

Plucking Daisies,

Masticating Daisies.

References

Adair, C. (1992), *Women and Dance: Sylphs and Sirens*, London: Macmillan

Banes, S. (1994a), 'Classical Brinkmanship: Karole Armitage and Michael Clark', in Banes, S., *Writing Dancing in the Age of Postmodernism*, Hanover: Wesleyan University Press, pp. 297-301

Banes, S. (1994b), 'Happily Ever After? The Postmodern Fairytale and the New Dance', in Banes, S. *Writing Dancing in the Age of Postmodernism*, Hanover: Wesleyan University Press, pp. 280-290

Briginshaw, V. (1991), 'Postmodern Theory and its Relation to Dance', in *Postmodernism and Dance*, discussion papers, West Sussex Institute of Higher Education, pp. 10-22

Eco, U. (1983/4), *Postscript to the Name of the Rose*, translated Weaver, W., New York: Harcourt Brace Jovanovich

Foster, Hal (1985), 'For a Concept of the Political in Contemporary Art' in *Recodings: Art, Spectacle, Cultural Politics*, Port Townsend: Bay Press, pp. 143-53

Hutcheon, L. (1989), *The Politics of Postmodernism*, London: Routledge

Hutcheon, L. (1988), *A Poetics of Postmodernism: History, Theory, Fiction*, London: Routledge

Hutcheon, L. (1985), *A Theory of Parody: The Teachings of Twentieth Century Art Forms*, London: Methuen

Huxley, M. (1988), 'Approaches to new dance: analysis of two works', in *Dance Analysis: Theory and Practice*, ed. Adshead, J., London: Dance Books, pp. 161-80

Jameson, F. (1991) 'Postmodernism, or the cultural logic of late capitalism', in Docherty, T. (1993) ed. *Postmodernism: A reader*, Hertfordshire: Harvester Wheatsheaf

Jenkins, K. (1995), *On 'What is History?': from Carr and Elton to Rorty and White*, London: Routledge

Jordan, S. (1992), 'lan Spink', in *Striding Out: Aspects of Contemporary and New Dance in Britain*, London: Dance Books, pp. 182–207

Les Ballets Trockadero de Monte Carlo, (1997), Programme, Sadler's Wells at the Peacock Theatre, London, 15–28 September

Marshall, B. (1992), *Teaching the Postmodern*, London: Routledge

White, H. (1978), *Tropics of Discourse; Essays in Cultural Criticism*, Baltimore: The John Hopkins University Press

White, H. (1973), *Metahistory*, Baltimore: John Hopkins University Press

Postmodern Play with Historic Narratives in the Reconstruction of Lea Anderson's *Flesh and Blood* (1989)

Valerie A. Briginshaw

The reconstruction of dances inevitably involves history; dance history. It is a kind of history in the making as well as involving historical research. Reconstruction involves the choreography and performance of history in its attempt to re-present the past in the form of dances, dance texts or historic narratives. Reconstruction can be compared to doing or writing history. Concepts of what it means to do or write history in this postmodern era which proclaims the end of such things as history, have changed radically. I will illustrate some of these changes in practice through an examination of the reconstruction of Lea Anderson's *Flesh and Blood*.

Flesh and Blood was created by Lea Anderson in 1989 for her all-female company of seven dancers, The Cholmondeleys. It was a 50-minute piece that was performed 38 times in 16 British venues and 5 in Belgium, France and Switzerland, between November 1989 and November 1991. A 15-minute video of some sections of the piece directed by Margaret Williams, which included an interview with Anderson, was made in 1990 as part of the Arts Council's 'Taped!' series. When *Flesh and Blood* was recently adopted as a set work for study on the 'A' level dance public examination syllabus, it was suggested to Anderson that she reconstruct it for live performance. It has not been performed live since 1991. In February and March 1997, *Flesh and Blood* was reconstructed with a cast that included only two of the original performers, Gaynor Coward and Emma Gladstone, although the rehearsal director, Alexandra Reynolds, had also performed in it in 1989. In March and April it toured to 14 venues including five nights of virtually sold-out performances at the Place Theatre, London.

When considering the ways in which concepts of history have changed recently, it is important to recognise that historic narratives are *interpretations* of the past. The whole of the past consists of interpretations. So history or historic narratives are interpretations of interpretations. In this sense the past is not 'real': there is no such thing as 'reality', only interpretations of the 'real'. This is because any concept we have of the past or the real is mediated through other people and their language, whether it be verbal, pictorial or choreographic. In this sense there is no distinction between the real and the imaginary in that imagination is an inevitable part of interpretation and language.

Flesh and Blood is a historic narrative in several senses. As a narrative or interpretation it consists of interpretations of interpretations involving imagination. In one sense it is a historic narrative of the body or bodies. Its title belies that as do the various historic narratives that inform it: Dreyer's film of *The Passion of St Joan* (1928), Giotto and Della Francesca paintings, the *Oxford Book of Saints*, religious communities of women, Escher illustrations and Rodin sculptures.

If reconstruction is seen as writing or doing history as it re-presents the past, then in the reconstruction process of *Flesh and Blood*, the original 1989 version of the work is only one of many interpretations and historic narratives, just as the various sources for the work, such as the Dreyer film and the Della Francesca paintings, are other historic narratives and interpretations of interpretations. In fact, the way in which Lea Anderson openly acknowledges and discusses these sources with her performers in the making and reconstructing of the work in workshops and subsequently when discussing the work publicly in interview on video and in print, underlines the fact that the work, *Flesh and Blood*, is, in one sense, a collection of interpretations or narratives. Anderson herself also recognises the tension or blurring between the real and the imaginary in the subject matter of the work, which is why she titled it as she did. She explains at the end of the video, 'The title, *Flesh and Blood*, is really a title to try and balance out the show and to give an idea of what it's really about. It's really about reality and physicality, although the sources that we've taken into the show are ones that are more spiritual or emotional or esoteric kinds of ideas, essentially they only exist because they are in people, and people are real; flesh and blood.' The key here is that Anderson recognises that her sources only exist because they are in people, historic people such as St Joan, Della Francesca, Rodin and so on, and contemporary people such as her dancers.

It is through people that ideas and images are imagined and interpreted as they are passed from person to person through the language of historic narratives such as dances and works of art. This is why attempting to reconstruct an authentic original dance text to be as it was, is in some senses a pointless exercise, because reconstruction, just as the original choreography and performance, involves people, their imaginations, interpretations and memories and is therefore a fictional rather than a wholly scientific enterprise.

The role of memory in this process is crucial. As Nicola King has stated when writing about autobiography, 'what is being reconstructed is... the memory of the event not the event "as it really was"'(King, 1996: 53). In dance this often involves a kinaesthetic, movement or body memory. In the reconstruction of *Flesh and Blood* body memories were often key sources of the original choreography because a score did not exist (Anderson said she would have loved to be able to reconstruct from notation but they could not afford a notator) and the only video of the original stage version available was, in parts, very poor. Emma Gladstone said of the role of body memory in the reconstruction process, 'we would learn stuff and your body starts to take over, so you then start to dance stuff before you've learnt it again, because your body remembers' (Gladstone, 1997). She admitted that different people remember things differently, acknowledging the role played by interpretation and memory itself over time in altering things. She said, 'we made different stories' and 'I made up my own logic if there's a gap'. She also spoke of her role as a dancer from the original version, aiding the five new dancers to learn the material in reconstruction. She spoke also of how she would try to give them images to work with that she remembered Anderson employing originally. She said, 'it made me realise how much imagination is needed to make it work' (Gladstone, 1997). However, one of the new dancers for the 1997 version, Anna Pons Carera, commented that despite references to the original made by Anderson and the other dancers, she remembers 'just being there and trying to find it there in the studio with the new people, not going back so much'. (Pons Carera, 1997). Gaynor Coward, the other dancer who had performed in the original version, commented how teaching excerpts from *Flesh and Blood* in workshops and adapting them accordingly had affected her body memory. She stated that 'I'd completely adapted some of those sections depending who I was teaching...and this body was now remembering something quite different or I'd maybe slotted a few different ideas together'(Coward, 1997).

All of these examples of the complex workings and interactions of bodily, psychic and social memories of several different participants in the reconstruction process underline the textual and fictional nature of memory. As King states, 'memories are constructed in part out of fantasy, and "retranscribed" and "retranslated" over time, incorporating new material and ideas' (King, 1996: 61) and 'memory:.. is a text to be deciphered, not a lost reality to be discovered... an awareness of the past involves not only the discovery of "what really happened", but also an awareness of how and why we may have reshaped it in the light of our changing knowledge and interests' (ibid.: 62). Again the interaction or blurring of the real and the imaginary, or fact and fiction, in memories (which are also texts, stories, historic narratives) plays a crucial role. As will be discussed later when *Flesh and Blood*'s status as an 'A' level set work is examined, in the writing of history, in this case dance history, there is often a temptation to fix these texts or narratives and transform fiction into fact, fantasy and imagination into reality; a temptation to search for and locate the 'correct version' or interpretation of a work. As Ramsay Burt has stated, 'there is a tension between the memory of dance practice and what happens when this is put into discourse as dance history' (Burt, 1997: 2).

The fictional nature of these historic narratives, such as memory, gives them literary or poetic potential. Hence the use of the term narrative; a literary device which recognises that the business of history or reconstruction is about telling stories. It can therefore employ all the literary devices, tropes and conventions that go with the business of telling stories, and in this sense the narrativity involved can be seen as an 'enabling assumption', as Hayden White has suggested (quoted in Soja, 1996: 174).

One of the ways in which history or reconstruction seen as narrative is enabling, is evident in Ankersmit's statement that 'in historical narrative the relationship between language and reality is constantly destabilized – historical narrative is the birthplace of new meaning' (Ankersmit, 1994: 40). Following this, the relationship between the reconstruction and the original is also constantly destabilised through the reconstruction process, which in turn generates new meanings. In the reconstruction of *Flesh and Blood*, many more historic narratives than the sources already mentioned came into play, which produced new interpretations. These included *Flesh and Blood*'s choreography. Certain sections were dropped, others reworked, and there are some new elements. Its performance acted as another narrative; only two members of the original 1989 cast remained in the 1997 version. Its accompaniment was another; the music has been reorchestrated. The piece also has new lighting and slightly different costumes. All of these historic narratives and interpretations interact with each other in a complex manner in live performances and in the video version of the work, so that the relationship between these and the 'reality' of the original is constantly destabilised.

The role of language in the reconstruction process, and this might be a choreographic or performance language, together with its narrative, fictional, imaginative and interpretive characteristics, is central to the understanding of exactly what happens when a dance is reconstructed. This theory of history and reconstruction is based on the premise that language operates as a system of differences. Seeing one thing as different from another generates meaning. As Bann states, 'To perform, in the sense of reading and interpreting historical representations, implies a capacity for specific discriminations and distinctions'. (Bann in Ankersmit and Kellner, 1995: 197). He writes of conceiving the 'task of representing history as one of establishing perceptible differences' (ibid: 210). In other words it is important to see that there is no one fixed history or narrative but rather that there are many histories. This was evident in *Flesh and Blood* from the outset, before it was ever reconstructed. When the video version was made there was no attempt to recreate the stage version, but rather to create another piece with new meanings. This is typical of Anderson, she has filmed and videoed several of her dances and all have been radically different from the stage version. There is never an attempt to tell only one story, always several, and usually the filmed versions of her works are retitled as well, further emphasising this. For example, *Birthday* (1992) becomes *Perfect Moment* (1992) and *Immaculate Conception* (1992) becomes *Jesus Baby Heater* (1992).

The differences between the stage and video versions of *Flesh and Blood* are quite marked. The video version is about 15 minutes long whereas the stage version is 50 minutes long. Only five of the nine main sections of the stage version appear in the video and all of these are shortened. Three are placed in different environments: outdoors, in a church in front of the altar and in the crypt. Coward, one of the two dancers who has danced in all versions of the piece, said of the video version, 'it is much more fragmented... because of the space and the way it's got different settings gives it a very different feeling' (Coward, 1997). Throughout the piece the camera also presents very specific and quite different views of the choreography than are possible when watching the stage version in a theatre. Close-ups and overhead shots are frequently used, as are video techniques such as blurring and slowing down the image. This opens the piece up to possibilities of a host of new meanings

underlining the differences and distinctions, and precluding any assumption that only one narrative exists. As Ankersmit states, 'historical insight… is only born in the space *between* rival narrative interpretations'
(Ankersmit, 1994: 41). In this sense the video version and, I will argue,
the recent reconstruction, allow the different pasts, histories and voices
in the work to find expression. Anderson's choreography and her reconstruction of it are in this sense, as Ankersmit says of historiography,
'attempts to bring about the dissolution of what seems known and
unproblematic' (Ankersmit, 1994: 42).

The recognition that history gives way to many histories accords with
Lyotard's view of history. He criticises conceptions of the *unity* of the
past, and rather sees the past as broken up into a number of disparate
fragments – 'petits recits' (little stories) instead of 'un grand recit' (one
grand story or narrative or a metanarrative) (Lyotard, 1979: 60).
Anderson's source material from *Flesh and Blood*, ranging as it does from
Renaissance paintings to a 1928 film of the story of Joan of Arc to Escher
illustrations, also seems to accord with the view of history as made up of
many fragmentary and disparate stories. Indeed I would argue that her
choreography is almost always episodic. This is certainly the case in *Flesh
and Blood*, which consists of nine or ten clearly-named sections of material grouped into three acts (see Table 1 – N.B. the names of the sections
in *Flesh and Blood* such as 'insects', 'Joan' and 'knees' are not for public
use, they are the terms used by Anderson and the dancers to identify
different sections).

It is also possible to see in Table 1 the main choreographic changes
that were made. The quartet was lost from the first version and the first
duet moved from the beginning of Act I to the beginning of Act III. The
'insects' section of Act I was extended with more repeats in it and the
'pre-knees' section introducing the final 'knees' section of the dance was
changed considerably. Most of the decisions about these changes were
made when Anderson watched the original video with Steve Blake, the
music composer. Then she realised how good some of the work was and
relished having the opportunity to rework elements in the process of
reconstruction. Anderson and Blake often agreed on sections that worked
and could be extended, and others that needed editing. Also, when
Anderson watched the dancers performing in rehearsal she made changes
to accommodate the new cast, the different personalities and bodies of
the dancers. For example, a completely new duet (the '50s duet') was

made for two new dancers in Act III to replace the previous one which had been for Anderson and Sonia Bucci.

Even where the choreography was not changed, the new cast made a difference. Coward noted the effect of a change of partner on one duet. She stated, 'With "Duets" it's very different to work with Anna [Pons Carera]. With Marissa [Zanotti] she's quite tiny and really light, with Anna it's much more equal which was nice cos I think that's what it should have been about constantly giving and taking, of who's in control or not, how equal it is, it had a different feeling with "Duets" last time, I felt a little bit more in control most of the time, I felt slightly stronger just because of the size' (Coward, 1997). Anderson recognised that, being outside the dance this time round, she was able to cast it according to dancers' abilities rather than pragmatically, for example, because a par- ticular dancer happened to be offstage in the right place for an entrance. Coward commented on an overall difference in the performance and look of the piece that may have arisen becauseof this. Speaking of the current version she said, 'I think things got much bigger physically this time... there were certain things we definitely did smaller before. "Duets" we did smaller. It was much more contained first time around. I think that's something that is about now. Then it was really working completely on the detail, the detail's still there, but it's now about reading it as well, about being more aware' (Coward, 1997).

These changes illustrate the episodic nature of Anderson's choreo- graphy. Importantly they are also evidence of the many historic narra- tives that have come into play in the reconstruction process. These his- toric narratives do not merely exist in each performance and interpreta- tion of the work, they also come into play each time the work is per- formed and interpreted. They confirm that the dance text is not just one history or story but many. This is further emphasised when other changes that have taken place in the reconstruction process are examined.

A new lighting designer, Simon Corder, produced a completely differ- ent design involving many more special effects created by the use of colour and dry ice. When Corder discussed his ideas of using smoke with Anderson, she was very enthusiastic. She said that 'the idea of an ephem- eral something and incense and ghosts and ectoplasm, and to light it and make something intangible, solid there above the dancers, I like that idea'. She was very pleased with the result, and thought it 'an extraordi- nary addition' (Anderson, 1997). As Gladstone said of the lighting, 'it helps to create a world. It was very menacing at the beginning... it also helps to train your eye and close off the rest of the stage, like when you're in a trance, in a closed-in world.' She also proclaimed it 'the strongest change of all the elements...the most adventurous and the bravest change from what we'd had before' (Gladstone, 1997).

Another change was in the reorchestration of the music. Again, this was declared an improvement by Gladstone, who said, 'It had a lot more depth and layers to it than the original music... there was a wider range in both instruments and musicians... they had a wider range of sounds that they were working with which... lead to a much richer and more textured sound which... overall was a vast improvement' (Gladstone, 1997). Coward described a specific example of a change in the music which affected her performance which illustrated the play of one narrative with or on another. She stated that 'there's this soaring sax, it didn't always happen quite at the same time as it did last time, ... I remember something feeling really luscious and getting carried away with it, and this time I was sort of, not struggling, but you have to fight maybe that bit harder to retain maybe what was there... the difference betweeen the instrumentation gave it a different feeling, a much different feeling. It was more pushy first time round, a bit more staccato and a bit more insecty and this time for me it didn't have that.' She also commented that she thought the musicians sped up a bit during performances this time round and that 'things like that make a difference' (Coward, 1997).

The design and material of the costumes also changed. Of the fabric Anderson said, 'The glitter comes off much quicker... they [the dresses] were completely black by Derby, the last performance of the tour, so the audience got a different thing' and also the material was 'stiffer and stretchy in one direction and not so stretchy in the other direction, it was very different' (Anderson, 1997).

All of these changes, together with the choreographic changes outlined and demonstrated, are further evidence of the many interpretations of interpretations and historic narratives at play in the work. These together with the episodic nature of Anderson's choreography mitigate against the possibility of reading her work as one grand narrative with a clear beginning, middle and end. As Ankersmit says, 'narrative interpretations are not necessarily of a sequential nature' and 'historical time [as a linear or chronological concept] is a relatively recent and highly artificial invention of Western civilisation. It is a cultural... notion' (Ankersmit, 1994: 33).

In a postmodern sense Hayden White suggests it is more useful to see history in terms of 'lived time' which is 'filled with multiplicities, many different planes of social time, as well as with hidden experiences, undecipherable codings, unexplainable events.' (Soja, 1996: 174–5). The subject-matter of *Flesh and Blood*, as well as its episodic structure, is redolent with such multiplicities. The range of source material from many different pasts or times that has inspired and informed the choreography of *Flesh and Blood* allows different planes of social time to be present in the work. These are evident in the costumes, which are both historic and contemporary in style and cloth. Also within the choreography there is a juxtaposition of quite Grahamesque, expressionistic, large whole-body modern dance movements with the minutiae of fingers pointing and eyes looking heavenward in a menacing, medieval and mysterious manner (within Dreyer's intimate film-acting style). The ways in which this pseudo-religious community of women relate to each other make *Flesh and Blood* resonate with hidden experiences, undecipherable codings and unexplainable events.

Of all the differences that exist in history and language and between interpretations and historic narratives, the most obvious in the reconstruction process is that between past and present. As Foucault has recognised, 'history... is always written from the perspective of the present' (Lechte, 1994: 111) and he uses the term 'genealogy' to describe this process of 'history written in the light of current concerns' (ibid.: 112). This is particularly pertinent when *Flesh and Blood* is considered, because the main reason for its current reconstruction has been a present concern, the fact that it is a current set work on the 'A' level Dance syllabus. The past historic narrative of *Flesh and Blood* has been played with and reconstructed with this in mind. The reconstruction process has also been mediated through many other current concerns and present perspectives. These include those of the dancers who perform the 1997 version, in conjunction with the memories of Anderson, the two dancers from both casts (Coward and Gladstone) and the rehearsal director (who was also a dancer in the 1989 version).

The present concerns of the status of *Flesh and Blood* as an 'A' level set work and the need to sell the work to venues certainly affected the reconstruction process and the resultant work. Anderson was at one stage keen to reconstruct *Flesh and Blood* for her all-male company the Featherstonehaughs. She persisted with this notion for about four weeks until her administrative director and her tours and projects manager finally persuaded her against it. They said that they had mentioned it to a number of venues who were going to book it, but who indicated that if it were to change to an all-male cast they would no longer buy it. Consequently Anderson was persuaded by the market to revert to an all-female version of *Flesh and Blood* for reconstruction purposes.

The status of *Flesh and Blood* as an 'A' level set work and an object of study has meant that its reconstruction has been surrounded by other historic narratives such as study aids in the form of resource packs, workshops (over 500 have been given in the last 2 to 3 years), post-performance talks and published interviews with Anderson about the work. This status has fixed it in recent British dance history as part of the national heritage, giving it a particular 'aura' (Benjamin, 1973). As a result, *Flesh and Blood* is in danger of becoming a grand narrative with one history, recognised as a 'correct interpretation' fixed for study. This was evident at some of the post-performance talks where teachers commented on the problems for them of studying a work that they found hard to pin down, because they had just seen a version nearly four times as long as the video version they were familiar with, and different in several significant respects. Anderson also tells of an instance when one of the Featherstonehaughs teaching a workshop rang her and asked, 'Do we tell somebody their interpretation of it is "wrong"?' and Anderson said, 'Well, if they're doing an 'A' level I think we'd better tell them that it's "wrong".' She admitted that this contravenes their normal practice, where such statements that tend to close a work down would not be made.

Flesh and Blood was no doubt chosen as an 'A' level set work at least partly because of its public availability through its existence on video. The video for most teachers and pupils has become the major object of study. Consequently the *Flesh and Blood* workshops for schools and colleges concentrated almost entirely on those sections of the dance that were on the video and could be referred to in the workshops. However Anderson partly got her way in terms of the involvement of her all-male company in the enterprise, because during the tour of *Flesh and Blood* earlier this year, she had members of the Feathersonehaughs go out and teach the workshops whilst the Cholmondeleys were performing. School and college students got to learn the video sections of *Flesh and Blood* from male dancers. Gladstone, who had taught the Featherstonehaughs the material for the workshops, comments on the differences in the men's performance. She states, 'The fluidity wasn't always there in the same way... they had a different softness and subtleness... something...

changed when guys did it, partly because... their quality of attack... was quite different... they have a different kind of connection that still was gentle... and soft,... it was definitely a male thing... it lost that particular lusciousness... the softness changed from a sensuality to a gentleness' (Gladstone, 1997). She agreed that new meanings were the result. Coward commented that 'it was interesting seeing men do what I think is very much a women's piece and to different extents, different men got a sense of the style'. She also said of their performance, 'the lusciousness wasn't always there, it would be a bit sort of snapped into some things, rather than a real pull of tension in the body' (Coward, 1997).

The status of *Flesh and Blood* as an object of study has meant that its reconstruction has been very much bound up with present concerns and it has underlined the fact that 'no past era can be seen purely on its own terms' (Lechte, 1994: 111). The original version of *Flesh and Blood* needs to be continually re-evaluated in the light of recent or intervening developments. For example, Anderson has made other works since *Flesh and Blood*, notably *Jesus Baby Heater* (1992) and *Joan* (1994), that have used similar sources of inspiration. *Jesus Baby Heater* drew on narratives of Renaissance paintings and *Joan*, Anderson's televised solo, was a response to the mythological nature of the narratives surrounding Joan of Arc. Anderson admitted that in the reconstruction process she realised that she had taken different strands of the original *Flesh and Blood* such as 'an approach to movement, or an actual vocabulary, or a structuring or a way of thinking about things', into other subsequent works. She developed them, sometimes losing the original motivation and taking them somewhere else. Whilst reconstructing, she says, 'I had all that in me and I'd do something and I'd think, no that's like the last section in *Precious* (1993) which has very different rules, and I hadn't realised how different it was until I put in something inappropriate, then I realised how I had to go back a long way and think of those things that inspired it originally and not a language that I've developed later' (Anderson, 1997). Anderson's repertoire then, and her status as an artist, are further historic narratives that come into play when the reconstruction of *Flesh and Blood* is considered.

Anderson's role as reconstructor in the reconstruction process is central. She is effectively writing history but, as an artist and choreographer, her creative and interpretive role is publicly acknowledged and accepted. Unlike regular historians, and perhaps those reconstructors who are not the original choreographer, her emotional involvement with her subject does not need to be declared or revealed, it is part of what it means to choreograph.

When she changed role, from inside the piece as a performer as well as choreographer, to outside as reconstructor, she gained, in a very obvious sense, more distance from the piece. She could possibly be more objective. This is the ideal role of the traditional historian that 'he "efface himself" and offer a "reenactment of the past" from which he himself is as absent as possible' (Ankersmit, 1994: 195). But the postmodernist would argue that this distance is impossible and inappropriate, that 'separating subjectivity from objectivity (thus creating the possibility of objectivity) is an arbitrary, if not violent, act. It not only obliterates the narrator in the process but determines the situation of the reader' (Orr in Ankersmit and Kellner, 1995: 90).

Has this distancing happened with Anderson's withdrawal from performance in the reconstruction of *Flesh and Blood*? I do not think so, because, although Anderson was outside this time, she was still inside in many senses. In rehearsal she would often perform and demonstrate moves to show the dancers how she felt in her body that it should be performed. She continually returned to her notebooks and sources to help herself and her dancers to get inside the emotions and experience of the work again.

One of the main differences between Anderson as reconstructor and a historian or a reconstructor who has not been involved in the original creation of the work, is that she was part of that history that she is re-creating. Objectivity inevitably dissolves into subjectivity in the process because of the particular experience Anderson has of the original. In this sense she unifies past and present through her own experience which, to use Ankersmit's term, is 'nostalgic' (1994: 201). The value of nostalgia in this process, according to Ankersmit, is that 'what we experience... in nostalgia is not "the past itself" but the *difference* or *distance* between the present and the past' (ibid: 201). This distance or difference is not the kind that makes the past more remote and objective, rather it allows for relationships between past and present to surface. The past is seen through the eyes of the present, which is forever changing and, in the process, continually affecting interpretations and narratives of the past. In this sense 'nostalgia... extends the range of potential historical experience' (ibid: 206).

The importance of the role of people in historical experience is crucial. All experience can be said to be historical since it is always in the process of instantly becoming part of our pasts. Ankersmit states that for Aristotle, 'experience and knowledge are the interaction between us and the world and not an abstraction from it' (ibid: 42) and for Hegel, 'experience is our means for "appropriating" the world and for making it part of ourselves and our identity' (ibid: 210). Ankersmit takes this notion further, adding that for him 'the object of historical experience… is the experience of what used to be part of ourselves but has become strange, alien, or defamiliarized' (ibid: 210). This defamiliarisation opens up possibilities of new meanings which traditional, scientific objectification tends to close down. Anderson's reconstruction of *Flesh and Blood* does precisely this. There are plenty of examples of the potential for new meanings in the changes that have been made to the work.

This postmodernist approach to history, seeing the end of history as we know it, in the sense of an objective, scientific discipline which has as its aim to uncover and rediscover the facts of the past, has much to offer dance reconstruction. Instead of closing down possibilities of dance texts, by recognising the complex interactions of lots of little stories, histories and historic narratives which are fictional, possibilities for new meanings and texts are continually opened up. As Ankersmit states, 'we ought to see the postmodernist notion of the historical simulacrum as a challenge to *clarify* the nature of historical representation rather than as too facile an injunction to *abandon* the concept of representation for the writing of history altogether' (Ankersmit, ibid: 192).

References

Anderson, L. (1997), Interview with the author, June 1997

Ankersmit, F. (1994), *History and Tropology*, Los Angeles: University of California Press

Ankersmit, F. and Kellner, H. (eds) (1995), *A New Philosophy of History*, London: Reaktion Books Ltd, chapter 4, Orr, L. 'Intimate Images: Subjectivity and History – Stael, Michelet and Tocqueville' pp. 89-107, chapter 9, Bann, S. 'History as Competence and Performance: Notes in the Ironic Museum' pp.195-211

Benjamin, W. (1955, transl. 1968, Fontana ed. 1973) *Illuminations*, Glasgow: Fontana

Briginshaw, V.A. (1995), 'Lea Anderson talks to Valerie Briginshaw about *Flesh and Blood*', *Dance Matters*, No. 13, pp. 4–5

Burt, R. (1997), 'Laban in Yorkshire: interrogating the grand narratives of dance scholarship', Society of Dance History Scholars 20th Conference Proceedings, Barnard College, New York, June, 1997, pp.1-8

Coward, G. (1997), Interview with the author, September 1997

Gladstone, E. (1997), Interview with the author, August 1997

King, N. (1996–97), 'Autobiography as Cultural Memory: Three Case Studies', *New Formations* No. 30, pp. 50–62

Lechte, J. (1994), *Fifty Key Contemporary Thinkers*, London: Routledge

Lyotard, J-F. (1984), *The Postmodern Condition*, Manchester: Manchester University Press

Pons Carera, A. (1997), Interview with the author, September 1997

Soja, E.W. (1996), *Thirdspace*, Oxford: Blackwell

Table 1 Sections in Flesh and Blood

1989 STAGE VERSION	1990 VIDEO VERSION	1997 STAGE VERSION
Act 1		Act 1
Duet(in Duets at beginning of Act 3 in 97 version)	Duet	Stand in smoke
Quartet		
Insects	Insects(shorter)	Insects(slightly shorter)
Joan & rocks	Joan & rocks(shorter)	Joan & rocks
Veils		Veils
Act 2		Act 2
Slow insects		Slow insects
Trio & duet		Trio & duet
Waltzing		Waltzing
Act 3		Act 3
Duets(2 in unison)	Duets(shorter)	Duets(2 in unison + duet from beginning of '89 version)
50s duet(Anderson & Bucci)		50s duet(Pons Carrera & Leung – completely different)
Pre-knees		Pre-knees(very different)
Knees	Knees(shorter)	Knees

Deborah MacMillan interviewed by Christopher Cook and Monica Mason's demonstration of the solo for the Chosen One from MacMillan's *The Rite of Spring* (1962)

Scribe: Henrietta Bannerman

As custodian of the legacy of Sir Kenneth MacMillan's works, Deborah MacMillan tries to ensure that his ballets are revived or restaged under the best possible conditions. This involves ensuring that companies who ask to stage the works have the necessary skills and resources to do them. For example, even though several companies requested permission to perform *Mayerling* (1978), only the Royal Swedish Ballet had been given approval and they are the first company, outside the Royal Ballet, to stage this MacMillan work. The procedure followed in planning revivals begins with the establishment of contractual agreement that allows suffi-cient stage time for the realisation of the ballet's decor, costumes and lighting. Deborah MacMillan takes full responsibility for dealing with any arguments or misunderstandings that may crop up. For example, the casting of the overseas productions of MacMillan's ballets is carried out by Monica Parker, however, it is Deborah MacMillan who settles any dispute over the choice of dancers for particular roles. In the case of the Royal Ballet decisions about casting are made in consultation with Anthony Dowell and Monica Mason, but here again, if difficulties arise, it is Deborah MacMillan who acts in the interests of MacMillan's estate.

Deborah MacMillan views her relationship with the Royal Ballet as 'a very special one' although she specifies that any revivals undertaken by the company must adhere to the notation of the ballet in question. Notation was very important to Kenneth MacMillan and he always made sure that his ballets were recorded, as accurately as possible, in the Benesh system of notation. She referred to her 'enormous faith' in Anthony Dowell and Monica Mason and expressed the view that revivals can only be as authentic as any live performance can ever be and that the element of interpretation brings about change at all times. When his ballets were being revived during his lifetime, MacMillan had always involved dancers who had been close to the various roles in them.

In the case of some revivals of MacMillan's works after his death Deborah MacMillan had to make some difficult decisions. When Dowell wanted to restage *Anastasia* (1971), there was detailed discussion in order to comply with MacMillan's intentions to revise the work. The destruction of some of the costumes meant that the ballet had to be redesigned and she chose Bob Crowley, MacMillan's collaborator on the Rogers and Hammerstein musical, *Carousel* (1945). MacMillan was working on this production at the time of his death and admired Crowley's skill in creating imaginative, non-naturalistic sets. She had also sanctioned a considerable cut in Act I of *Anastasia* and, following MacMillan's view about the excessive amount of dancing here, which, he thought, held up the story-line, she felt the ballet should be cut for dramatic reasons. In agreement with the conductor Barry Wordsworth and with advice from Monica Mason, revisions were made that had proved to be beneficial when the ballet was restaged.

The element of design is important to Deborah MacMillan, 'creating a different look for a work can make it live again'. She also remarked how detrimental it can be if a ballet is not 'beautifully lit'. On the other hand, due to the rising costs of production and the lack of resources that some companies face, she was not adverse to there being an alternative set for some works. For example, at the time of his death MacMillan was involved in a different production of *Manon* (1974) which used flying sets as opposed to the full, composite setting. The alternative set makes the ballet easier to tour. Deborah MacMillan also considers that revisions in the design of a dance can be a solution to some of its choreographic problems. She cited the example of the revival of *The Invitation* (1960), a work that MacMillan himself had been loathe to restage. When Anthony Dowell had decided that, as a seminal MacMillan ballet, it should be revived, the designer Nicholas Georgiadis, had proposed a change in the use of colour for the cock-fighting scene. Deborah MacMillan felt that this helped to compensate for the adjustments to the choreography that MacMillan had intended to make although he never had the chance to do so.

Discussing the role of the video in the passing-on of MacMillan's legacy, Deborah MacMillan expressed the view that there is a difference between a film made for archive purposes where the video is often a straight recording of a work and 'good, commercial videos.' These are influenced more by the eye of the director and may often show a close-up of a dancer's face rather than revealing the stage picture of what is going on in the ballet as a whole. Of equal importance in the preservation of MacMillan's work is the contribution of dancers, such as Lynn Seymour, who created roles in MacMillan's ballets and are able to coach young performers. Deborah MacMillan pointed out, however, that interpretations must change if a ballet is to live on for new audiences.

Although Deborah MacMillan had not already done so, she agreed that it would be useful if she kept records of the processes she followed in the staging of MacMillan's works. This would enable her to chart subtle points of production which arose on a daily basis. For example, certain adjustments to the lighting had cropped up in Sweden after the official rehearsals of *Mayerling* had been completed and information such as this would be useful for future revivals of the work.

Deborah MacMillan does not assume an authoritarian approach to the guardianship of MacMillan's legacy because she had often seen him change movements for new dancers taking over roles. She is committed, therefore, to following his flexible policy and stressed again that, in order for works to live on, new dancers coming to a ballet for the first time must be allowed to find their own interpretations. She emphasised the need to note differences between performances rather than to make value judgements about the merits of one over another.

Mason created the role of the Chosen One before she turned 21, danced it frequently over the years and hated not being able to dance every performance of it. But as she got older and had to teach her role to younger dancers, she loved the role even more. She was very surprised when MacMillan announced that the dancer Simon Rice was to perform the role of the Chosen One. Her reaction of 'devastation' made her realise that she was not as 'incredibly flexible' as she thought herself to be. But, she went on, when teaching the role to Simon Rice, 'I discovered that the miracle of the choreography was that it was not at all feminine.'

According to Mason, MacMillan's choice of the Australian artist Sidney Nolan as designer for the ballet was an appropriate one since his paintings were 'close to the earth'. The costume for the Chosen One was created on her body and there were no designs for it. She was 'pulled' into an orange body-stocking onto which Nolan and his wife pinned hands cut from newspaper. They then sprayed more orange paint onto the body-stocking and when the newspaper hands were peeled away, the lighter colour orange hand-prints were left.

The solo occurs at the end of the second movement of the ballet and begins when one of the three elders pushes the Chosen One forwards. She or he has been on stage throughout the whole 20 minutes of the preceding dance before having to perform the exacting solo. Following Deborah Bull's performance of that solo, Mason related how MacMillan had made the choreography over a period of eight or nine days in 45-minute rehearsals and that the movements had 'tumbled' out. She had experienced complete satisfaction as a dancer in having the choreography tailor-made for her. When she had started teaching the role, she had often been surprised that what to her had been fairly natural was for other dancers 'awkward' and she had been asked, at times, how she had ever managed to do certain movements.

The two dancers taking part in the demonstration, Deborah Bull and Ricardo Cervera, had both worked with Kenneth MacMillan. Bull, whose dancing MacMillan admired, had danced the Chosen One during his lifetime and was very familiar with the role. Cervera had worked with MacMillan at the Royal Ballet School but had had only three short rehearsals with Mason on the solo for the Chosen One.

Mason showed how she taught the solo using Cervera. Gregory Gage and Angelina Spurrier, two Roehampton students, also took part in the demonstration and marked the movements being taught to Cervera. Mason demonstrated a position where the arms are inverted from the shoulders with the lower arm hanging at right angles from the elbow joint. This 'hanging from a clothes-line' was a shape that MacMillan 'loved' and it appears frequently in *Song of the Earth* (1965). A *sissonne* forwards with the bent back leg being drawn in fast was referred to as the 'rabbit' jump. The jumping movement is accompanied by an inwards circling of the bent left arm with the hand held against the shoulder. In order to get Cervera to produce more urgency in the jump, Mason gave him the image of a 'pursued rabbit'. She stressed the need for some of the violent arm and leg movements in the solo to be flung outwards from the body and to look as though they happened inevitably, organically. They should not be controlled or placed. When coaching another jump in the solo, Mason related how it had been altered when Rice took over the role, although she could not remember whether MacMillan himself had changed it for Rice. Here, both bent legs are flung out behind as the body arches backwards. Mason felt that it was easier for men to jump with both legs in the same position whereas women tend to have one leg slightly in front of the other.

Although the solo is 'choc-a-bloc with choreography', it is important that the moments of stillness are registered. As the dancer tires these moments of stillness tend to be preceded by the slowing-down of gestures. This, however, is wrong, as the effect of the stillness should be a sudden arrest from fast, often frantic movement. The turning movements in the solo, too, should seem impromptu and no preparation for them should be visible.

The demonstration concluded with Mason teaching Cervera, joined by Bull and the Roehampton students, a section of material for the Chosen One that was entirely new to everyone apart from Bull. Mason remarked that, without consulting the Benesh notation, she could not remember the precise ordering of the complex Russian folk-style foot-patterning in this section and whether it started with toe or heel movements.

During the questions session Mason was asked what kind of dance she had watched or been involved in doing when *The Rite of Spring* was made. She had loved doing the Twist and had been aware of MacMillan watching her at a party so she 'twisted harder.' She also referred to her childhood experiences of growing up in South Africa and how MacMillan's choreography had awoken memories of the red soil of South Africa's farmland and of the song and dance performances of the Zulu people. 'I remember,' she said, 'some movements in the ballet felt as though my feet were on the earth, pounding on the soil.'

There was a suggestion that Nijinsky's *Le Sacre du printemps* and MacMillan's *Rite of Spring* would make an interesting reconstruction programme. Mason felt that it would be more appropriate to recover the new solo for the Chosen Maiden that MacMillan had made for her to perform in the film *Nijinsky* (1979). MacMillan, following drawings and photographs of Nijinsky's movements, had created the choreography for this film in which he had also made an interesting version of Nijinsky's *Jeux* (1923). Here he had responded, amongst other sources, to the influence of Nijinska.

Several of the questions that came from the audience concerned the subject of notation. It was established, for example, that MacMillan had looked on this as a tool which helped him in his creativity. He had often asked the notator Monica Parker to remind him of particular movements that he had set at different points throughout the choreographic process. Mason commented on how useful certain notators were in their observations on the way that choreographers worked and how they could supply additional information which the dancers, who had learned the movement, had not absorbed. She remarked, however, that notation could not supply all the answers when it came to interpreting various finer points of style or the way in which certain movements should be danced. Dance, as an art-form, observed Mason, is a matter of collaboration and requires the skills and expertise of people from different disciplines if it is to be produced or reproduced satisfactorily.

One member of the audience commented that the solo from *The Rite of Spring* was very unusual choreography in the repertory of the Royal Ballet and, as it looked unlike any other MacMillan work, wondered how the dancers reacted to performing it.

Bull remarked that, as a dancer from a younger generation, she was more accustomed to 'not having to look attractive all the time' and that she felt quite comfortable with, for example, the angular, accentuated hip movements. She also felt that some of these movements might have been harder for Mason and the Royal Ballet dancers of an earlier era to come to terms with, although Mason commented that the dancers had found the choreography a 'wonderful release'. A member of the audience who had been in the Royal Ballet Company commented that dancers had found *The Rite of Spring* 'really challenging' and that it was a ballet, like *Les Noces* (1923) and Ashton's *La Fille mal gardée* (1960), in which the dancers felt involved and part of an organic group.

Mason described the power of the live music and the experience of being on stage when it was played. However problems had arisen when conductors varied the tempi. Even though the dancers had been forced, at times, to accommodate musical interpretations that were too slow or too fast for comfort, she still felt that it was preferable to dance the work to live music rather than to have the stability of a recorded score.

Matthew Bourne interviewed by David Leonard

Scribe: Henrietta Bannerman

Matthew Bourne, Artistic Director of Adventures in Motion Pictures (AMP), maintained that, from early in his career, he had enjoyed working with 'real dance scores.' His first opportunity to do this had come in 1993 with Opera North's commission for a new version of Tchaikovsky's *The Nut-cracker*[1]. Bourne observed that he had never been interested in historical reconstructions of the classics but that he loved 'working with ideas.' On the other hand he welcomed a situation where there was existing music and a structure that were already familiar to audiences but that would allow him to create his own ideas. He explained that the reason he made new versions of the classics stemmed from the 'great music' that was written for them and from his interest in narrative. When using scores like those for *The Nutcracker* or *Swan Lake*[2], the audience may be expecting to see a certain kind of dance or ballet with which they are familiar but Bourne likes to surprise his audiences and make them react in a different way. He remarked that 'if you see the classics too many times, you cease to see the movement and you stop listening to the music.' In Bourne' s versions, you can hear the music differently. This is particularly true with his setting of Act IV of *Swan Lake* where the male swans swarm aggressively over the Prince's bed drawing attention to the turmoil in Tchaikovsky's score.

When asked if he was saying something about the original work or making a completely different statement of his own, Bourne replied that it was inevitable that he was making a comment on the original work although he never imposed anything on it. His intention is to break the mould, to bring ballet into the next century and to stop it becoming old fashioned. Bourne observed, however, that one of the reasons that people come to the theatre is to be entertained and that he stresses that element in his productions. Cook commented that other choreographers such as Mats Ek and Maguy Marin were taking a similar approach in their work and Bourne remarked that he admired Ek's *Giselle*[3] and *Swan Lake*[4] particularly from the point of view of the narrative aspect and the movement style. However, he considers that his work presents a more literal narrative and that his dancers work in a similar way to actors. They research their roles and create histories for their characters. He described Lynn Seymour's process in the development of her role as the mother in *Cinderella*[5] and how, during the rehearsal period, she acted out the story of her own life in order to flesh out her approach to the role. In relation to the reconstruction of works, Bourne observed how difficult it would be for future performers to achieve such depth of interpretation unless they also went through a similar process in the recreation of roles. He remarked, however, that roles had been taken on satisfactorily by new performers in his productions and that the success of changes in casting may be due to the fact that Bourne himself is there to supervise and guide the dancers and help them build their own interpretations.

On the subject of preserving his dances, Bourne commented that he had tried to develop a sense of the history of his company but that the demand was always for new productions. Although he would like to have two or more works in a repertory, the fact that the company is now a commercial one with no Arts Council subsidy, means that they have to concentrate on the box office takings of the current production in order to stay in business. On the other hand, Bourne explained that he constantly changes the choreography of his works, remarking that 'whilst the choreographer is still contributing to and still working on something, it will change. When *The Nutcracker* is revived in 1998, Bourne expects that he will 'probably re-choreograph it.' When it comes to the possibility of reviving earlier pieces, Bourne considers that AMP has created a broader theatre audience for whom the earlier dances would no longer work and that he and the company 'want to do new things and move on.' He explained that, for the first time, another company would be performing one of his dances since an American cast was about to take the production of *Swan Lake*. Bourne remarked that it would be interesting to see how a new cast would tackle the dance and to find out what would work and what would not. The process of keeping dances alive during long runs is demanding and depends quite heavily on the presence of Bourne himself. Even when a dance it performed on a daily basis, it is necessary for the choreographer to keep a sharp eye on the dancers as the choreography 'softens, filters away, the detail goes and the edges get rounded off'. Sometimes the mind goes and the body takes over and Bourne has to prod the dancers and remind them of his intention: why they were performing a movement in a certain way and on what basis that movement had been created.

Notes

1. AMP's production of *The Nutcracker*, commissioned by Opera North, was originally presented as part of the Tchaikovsky centenary celebrations during the 1992 Edinburgh Festival. It appeared in a double-bill with Tchaikovsky's short opera *Iolanta*.
2. The first production of Bourne's *Swan Lake* took place at the Sadler's Wells Theatre, London in November, 1995.
3. The Swedish dancer and choreographer Mats Ek, reinterpreted *Giselle* (Perrot-Coralli 1841) in 1982.
4. Mats Ek reinterpreted *Swan Lake* (Petipa 1877) in 1987.
5. The first production of Matthew Bourne's *Cinderella* took place on September 26th 1997 at the Piccadilly Theatre, London.

Biographies

Tim Albery

Tim Albery directs both opera and theatre. Most recent theatre productions include Schiller's Wallenstein for the RSC and Martin Crimp's *Attempts on Her Life* at the Royal Court. Recent opera productions include *Das Rheingold* for Scottish Opera, *Beatrice and Benedict* in Santa Fé and *The Merry Widow* at the Metropolitan Opera, New York.

Kenneth Archer

Kenneth Archer is an English art historian and scenic consultant who together with Millicent Hodson is known internationally for the reconstruction and creation of ballets with decors by Roerich, Baksh, Léger and others. He received his MA and Ph.D in art history and theatrical design from Antioch College and Essex University. In 1992 they were both recipients of the Nijinsky Medal from Poland. Archer's book Nicholas Roerich was published by Penkstone in 1999.

Matthew Bourne

Matthew Bourne has been Artistic Director and Choreographer with Adventures in Moving Pictures for over ten years and was one of the founder members. He trained at the Laban Centre and was awarded a BA Hons in Dance/Theatre. His many works include *Swan Lake* (1995), for which he won several awards including the Olivier Award for Best New Dance Production. His production of *Cinderella* is currently running in the West End and future plans include *Swan Lake* on Broadway in 1998 and a revival of *Nutcracker* (1998).

Michele Braban

Michele Braban is a Fellow of the Benesh Institute and currently Rehearsal Director and Personal Assistant to Christopher Bruce at Rambert Dance Company. She trained at the Victorian College of the Arts in Melbourne, Australia, completing her studies at the Benesh Institute, London. From 1982 she worked as choreologist then répétiteur with Ballet Rambert. Later, with London Festival Ballet, she was primarily responsible for the choreography of Christopher Bruce whose works she has taught internationally. From 1989, at the Benesh Institute, responsibilities included librarianship, teaching, examining and publications. She has worked freelance for the Royal Ballet and returned to Rambert in 1994.

Valerie Briginshaw

Valerie Briginshaw is a Reader in Dance at University College Chichester, where she teaches undergraduate courses in Dance, Related Arts and Women's Studies, leads a Masters degree in Collaborative Arts and supervises M.Phil/Ph.D research. Her publications include chapters on postmodern dance and politics in *Analysing Performance* (Manchester University Press, 1996) on the use of city settings for dance in *Dance in the City* (Macmillan, 1997) and *City Visions*,

(Longman, 2000). She has just completed a book entitled *Dance, Space and Subjectivity* to be published by Macmillan in 2001.

Ramsay Burt
Ramsay Burt is Senior Research Fellow at De Montfort University, Leicester. He is author of *The Male Dancer* (1995) and *Alien Bodies* (1998).

Moira Goff
Moira Goff is an independent dance historian who has published many articles on court and theatre dance in London and Paris during the late seventeenth and early eighteenth centuries, and has reconstructed and performed many of the dances which survive in Beauchamp-Feuillet notation. She has recently completed her doctoral thesis on the English dancer-actress Hester Santlow. She works as a curator for the British Library.

Millicent Hodson
Millicent Hodson is an American choreographer and dance historian who, with Kenneth Archer, is known internationally for the reconstruction and creation of ballets with choreography by Nijinsky, Balanchine and Börlin. She was awarded her MA and Ph.D in arts of spectacle from the University of California, Berkeley. They have exhibited project sketches in New York, Paris and Montreal and she has had several solo shows of dance drawings in London. From 1988-1990 she was Radcliffe Research Fellow in Dance, University of Surrey and in 1980-81 had choreographic grants from the National Endowment for the Arts, USA. She has published two reconstruction scores with her drawings: *Nijinsky's Crime Against Grace - Le Sacre de printemps* and *Nijinsky's Bloomsbury Ballet - Jeux*, Pendragon, 1996 and 2001.

Ann Hutchinson Guest
Her study of dance notation systems of the past have given her unique access to the dance heritage handed down in notated form. As a result of her research, the *Cachucha*, the dance made so famous by Fanny Elssler, a leading ballerina of the Romantic Period, was revived in 1967 and has been danced by present day ballerinas in London, Vienna, Milan, and New York. Through her research the *Pas de six* from *La Vivandière* was revived in 1976 from another old notation and subsequently performed by the Joffrey Ballet as well as the Sadler's Wells Royal Ballet. Her most recent breakthrough, working together with Claudia Jeschke, has been the deciphering in 1987 of Vaslav Nijinksy's system of dance notation and the transcription of the score which he wrote of his ballet *L'Après-midi d'un faune*, thus making available to dancers and audiences the original ballet as Nijinsky conceived it, in contrast to the much changed memory-based versions.

Madeleine Inglehearn
She studied ballet in Bradford, Yorkshire, and later early dance with Wendy Hilton in London, since when she has devoted herself to research into European social and theatrical dance from the fifteenth to the eighteenth centuries, and is director of The Companie of Dansers. She is Professor of Early Dance at the Guildhall School of Music and Drama, London, and from 1994 to 1996 was principal lecturer and course adviser on dance history for the Turku School of Art

and Communication, Finland. She is chairman of the European Association of Dance Historians.

Alessandra Iyer

Alessandra Iyer has a Ph.D in Art and Archaeology awarded by the School of Oriental and African Studies, London. Her recent book *Prambanan: sculpture and dance in ancient Java* (Bangkok: White Lotus, 1998) is a study of dance iconography in ancient Java and India. She is now Senior Lecturer in Dance at the University of Surrey Roehampton.

Angela Kane

Angela Kane is Senior Lecturer in Dance at the University of Surrey. Her research interests and publications span nineteenth to twenty-first century theatre dance and her doctoral thesis was on the work of the American choreographer, Paul Taylor. She has published many articles on Taylor's work and other choreographers in *Dance Research*, *Dance Theatre Journal* and *Dancing Times*, and has contributed several entries to *Fifty Contemporary Choreographers* (Routledge) and *International Encyclopedia of Dance* (Oxford University Press).

Clare Lidbury

Clare Lidbury is a teacher exploring the theories developed by Kurt Jooss and Sigurd Leeder. She now lectures at the University of Birmingham. Her doctoral research focused on the work of Kurt Jooss and specifically on *The Green Table.*

Phyllida Lloyd

Phyllida Lloyd was born in Bristol in 1957. She graduated from Birmingham University with a degree in English and Drama in 1979. She has directed extensively in regional theatre at Worcester, Ipswich, Cheltenham, Manchester and Bristol. Her productions include, *The Comedy of Errors*, *A Streetcar named Desire*, (Bristol Old Vic), *The Winters Tale, The School for Scandal* (Manchester Royal Exchange). London theatre includes: *Six Degrees of Separation* and *Hysteria* (Royal Court and West End transfer), *The Threepenny Opera* (Donmar Warehouse), *Dona Rosita* (Almeida), *Pericles, What the Butler Saw, The Way of the World* and *The Prime of Miss Jean Brodie* (Royal National Theatre). Her opera productions include, *L'Etoile, La Boheme, Medea, Carmen* and *Gloriana* (Royal Opera House and Opera North), *Macbeth* (Opera National de Paris). *Dialogue of the Carmelites* (English National Opera and Welsh National Opera), *The Handmaid's Tale* (The Royal Danish Opera), *Verdi Requiem* (English National Opera).

Alastair Macaulay

Alastair Macaulay is chief theatre critic of *The Financial Times* (for which he also reviews dance and music) and chief examiner in dance history to the Imperial Society of Teachers of Dancing. In 1983, he was founding editor of Dance Theatre Journal and in 1988 and 1992 he served as guest dance critic to *The New Yorker*. His short biography of Margot Fonteyn, the first since her own Autobiography, will be published by Sutton Books in 1998. He is currently at work on a book looking at Merce Cunningham's choreography for Farrar Strauss Giroux publishers (US).

Deborah MacMillan

Born in Boonah Queensland and educated in Sydney, Deborah MacMillan won a scholarship to the National Art School where she studied painting and sculpture. She settled in London in 1970 where she met and married the choreographer Kenneth MacMillan. She returned to full-time painting in 1984, exhibits regularly in London and has work in private collections in the UK and abroad. At present, as well as painting, she is a member of the Arts Council of England, Chairman of the Dance Panel, and takes care of her late husband's work.

Lesley Main

Lesley Main is Principal Lecturer in Dance and Chair of the Dance department at Middlesex University, where she teaches Humphrey-based Technique, Repertoire and Performance. She is one of the leading exponents of Humphrey's work in Europe and has worked extensively with Ernestine Stodelle in the USA, the Netherlands and in the UK. In 1995 she established the Doris Humphrey Foundation, produced 'The Dance Tradition of Doris Humphrey – A Centennial Celebration' and directed a new production of *Passacaglia* for the series of performance events. In 1997 she performed Humphrey's solo work, *The Call/Breath of Fire* at The Place Theatre, London. She is undertaking a Ph.D at Roehampton Institute London, and, in 2000, set up the Humphrey Video Project. Works currently under development are *Water Study*, *The Shakers*, and *With My Red Fires*.

Carol A. Martin

Carol A. Martin is Senior Lecturer in Dance History and Aesthetics at the Royal Academy of Dance where she is also responsible for the development of distance learning programmes. Having gained both an undergraduate and postgraduate degree at the University of Surrey, she is currently undertaking a Ph.D in British ballet history drawing on postmodern perspectives and methodologies.

Monica Mason

Born in Johannesburg, she came to England aged 14 and trained with Nesta Brooking and at The Royal Ballet School. She joined the Company in 1958 and was made a Soloist in 1963 and Principal in 1968. She created the Chosen Maiden in *The Rite of Spring*. She also created roles in *Manon, Elite Syncopations, The Four Seasons, Rituals,* and *Isadora*. She danced in the first performances by The Royal Ballet of *In the Night, Dances at a Gathering, Adagio, Hammerklavier, Liebeslieder Walzer,* and *Dark Elegies*. Her repertory included roles in *Swan Lake, The Sleeping Beauty, Giselle, The Firebird, Enigma Variations, La Bayadère, Cinderella, Mayerling, Romeo and Juliet*. She was appointed Principal Répétiteur, 1984, Assistant to the Director, 1988, and is now Assistant Director of The Royal Ballet. In July 1996, under the auspices of Roehampton Institute London, she was awarded an Honorary Doctorate by the University of Surrey.

Susan McGuire

Susan McGuire possesses diverse experience of teaching and performing in the disciplines of both classical ballet and modern dance. Wholly involved with classical ballet at the beginning of her career, from 1958-71 she danced with the Ballet Guild of Cleveland, also teaching Ford Foundation Scholarship students placed with the Guild. After having seen both the Jose Limon and Martha Graham dance companies, she relocated to New York to study at the Alvin Ailey American Dance Center. She joined the Martha Graham Dance Company a year later, dancing as a soloist until 1976. From 1973-76, she taught Graham technique in the Graham School and throughout the USA and Europe. In 1977 Ms McGuire joined the Paul Taylor Dance Company, where she remained until 1989. She performed in 33 Taylor dances, taking principle roles in 23. In 1989 she was appointed one of Paul Taylor's rehearsal directors, before choosing to pursue a career in Europe and teaching for a year in Berlin. In 1991 she was appointed to succeed Jane Dudley as Artistic Head of London Contemporary Dance School. Ms McGuire continues to teach technique and repertory as a guest at the Paul Taylor School, as well as reconstructing Taylor works for companies in the United States and Europe.

Nadine Meisner

Nadine Meisner is a writer on dance who has contributed to many newspapers and magazines. She was deputy editor of the monthly magazine *Dance & Dancers*. She now writes for *The Independent*.

Vida Midgelow

Vida Midgelow is a dance scholar, choreographer and performer. Currently she is Visiting Assistant Professor in dance history and philosophy at Florida State University. Having completed her MA in Dance Studies at the University of Surrey in 1994, she is currently undertaking Ph.D research. Her research area in postmodern dance and the reworking of classis is both choreographic and written. Vida is also the Artistic Director of Foreign Bodies Dance Theatre, company in residence at University College Northampton.

Giannandrea Poesio

Giannandrea Poesio was born in Italy. After a brief performing career he moved to England in 1990. He is a lecturer and the Director of the MA in Dance Studies at the University of Surrey, the dance critic for *The Spectator* and the author of various essays and papers on nineteenth-century ballet.

Nancy Reynolds

After dancing for five years with the New York City Ballet, Nancy Reynolds began a new career as a writer and editor. Her books include *Repertory in Review* and several projects with New York City Ballet co-founder Lincoln Kirstein. She was research director for the catalogue raisonné of Balanchine's works and the two-part public television documentary *Balanchine* and was an editor of the six-volume *International Encyclopedia of Dance*. She is currently Director of Research for The George Balanchine Foundation and is writing a history of dance in the twentieth century.

Sarah Rubidge

During her career Sarah Rubidge has straddled the worlds of the theatre dance profession and the academic institution. She gained an M.Phil from the University of Surrey while working with Rambert Dance Company and, more recently, a Ph.D from the Laban Centre, London, while developing her career as a digital dance artist. She headed the MA in Dance Studies at the Laban Centre from 1992-96 and is currently AHRB Research Fellow in the Creative and Performing Arts at University College, Chichester.

Lesley-Anne Sayers

After a first degree in drama, Lesley-Anne Sayers undertook postgraduate studies in dance at the Laban Center London, and has written regularly on dance since 1984. Her Ph.D research (Bristol University 1999) into Diaghilev's production of *Le Pas d'acier* (1927) produced a model reconstruction of Georgy Yakulov's set designs for the ballet, recently exhibited at the Palais du Centenaire in Brussels. Based in the school of Fine Arts at Cheltenham & Gloucester College of Higher Education, she is currently pursuing post-doctoral research in dance and art history.

Marian Smith

Marian Smith is Chair of Music History at the University of Oregon School of Music and author of *Ballet and Opera in the Age of Giselle*. Her articles on ballet and opera have appeared in scholarly journals, including *Dance Chronicle* and the *Cambridge Opera Journal*.

Helen Thomas

Helen Thomas is Reader in Sociology and Head of the Sociology Department at Goldsmiths College, University of London. She has published numerous articles on dance and presented papers on her work in Europe, North America and Japan. She is editor of *Dance, Gender and Culture* (1993) and *Dance in the City* (1997), and is author of *Dance, Modernity and Culture* (1995). She has also conducted two large-scale surveys for British Equity, the actors' union. Currently she is comleting a book *The Body, Dance and Cultural Theory* and is conducting an AHRB-funded study, *Dancing into the Third Age*.

Ann Thompson

Ann Thompson is Professor of Englishat King's College, London. She is one of the General Editors of the Arden Shakespeare series and is co-editing *Hamlet* for that series. She has previously edited *The Taming of the Shrew* and has published extensively on Shakespeare, concentrating recently on editing and on feminist criticism.

Muriel Topaz

Muriel Topaz is the author of *Pillar of Fire: The Life of Antony Tudor* to be published shortly by Scarecrow Press. Her other books include *A Guide to Performing Arts Programs* (with Carole Everett) and *Elementary Labanotation*. Topaz has served as senior editor for *Dance Magazine* and executive editor for Gordon and Breach dance publications. She has been active as a notator and has restaged and directed many dances from score among them works of Antony Tudor, Anna Sokolow and Doris Humphrey. Formerly she was Director of the Dance Division of the Juilliard School and Executive Director of the Dance Notation Bureau. Topaz was a 1998 Fellow of the John Solomon Guggenheim Foundation.

Ann Whitley

Ann Whitley is a Fellow of the Benesh Institute. She began her career as a dancer and later studied Benesh Notation. She was Rambert Dance Company's first choreologist and director of its touring educational unit. Since 1977 she has specialised in opera productions, notating and restaging choreography for dancers, singers and actors. She has worked internationally for many choreographers and companies and in dance administration and teaching. She wrote *Look Before You Leap: an advice and rights guide for choreographers* published in 1995 by Dance UK.

Mariette Redel

Mariette Redel was born at Leiden in Holland. She was trained at the Conservatory in The Hague, then joined the Rotterdam Scapino Ballet. In 1993, she went to the Zürich Ballet, where she has danced many solo roles. Particularly memorable for us were her performances in *Gras* by Mats Ek and *Visions Fugitives* by Hans Von Manen. Mariette is a visual artist as well as dancer. She has designed costumes for ballet and has exhibited her collages and dance figurines.

Kinsun Chan

Kinsun Chan was born in Vancouver, Canada and was trained at the Pennsylvania Academy of Ballet. He was a finalist in the Varna Competition and danced with the Cincinnati Ballet. In 1993, he joined the Zürich Ballet and has become a distinguished soloist. Featured in ballets by Heinz Spoerli, Hans Von Manen and Bernd Bienert, Kinsun created a remarkable Abderakman in Bienert's *Raymonda*. Also a painter, he has exhibited most recently at Zürich's Eselstein Gallery.

Luiz Bongiovani Martins

Luiz Bongiovani Martins was born in São Paulo, Brazil, where he trained in ballet, modern dance and in the indigenous acrobatic martial art form, Capoeira. Between 1989 and 1994 he performed there in the company of the choreographer, Johan Kresnik, then joined the Zürich Ballet, where he created many roles in ballets by Bernd Bienert. His performance in Ed Wubbe's *White Streams* was unforgettable. Since the 1996-97 season Luiz has been with Rotterdam Scapino Ballet.